Juvenile Offenders:

From Big Wheels to the Big House

Edited by Rosemary Jenkins

A Meredith *Etc* Book

JUVENILE OFFENDERS:
From Big Wheels to the Big House

edited materials with contributions by Rosemary Jenkins

Copyright © August 2018 Rosemary Jenkins

Foreword by Congresswoman Barbara Lee

Introduction by Rosemary Jenkins

Overview by Anthony Andrew Ferguson

Cover design art by A. Wilson

Published by **Meredith** *Etc* in softcover & hardback.

Keywords: Juvenile offenders, California prison system, poetry, essays, prison writings and art, Juvenile Justice

First Printing, 408 pages, 6"x 9"
Hardback Edition Printed by IngramSpark
ISBN: 978-0-9993226-4-2
Trade Paperback Edition Printed by CreateSpace
ISBN: 978-0-9993226-5-9

Visit the author page online:
https://meredithetc.com/juvenile-offenders/
Twitter/Facebook: meredithetc

First Edition

JUVENILE OFFENDERS:
From Big Wheels to the Big House

Edited by Rosemary Jenkins

CONTRIBUTORS:

Eric Ardoin
    Sheryl C.
James B. Elrod
    Anthony Andrew Ferguson
Louie Gomez
    Steve Grant
Juan Moreno Haines
    Karen Heil
Johnny Martinez
    Raymond Martinez
Ronald Patterson
    Eved Romero
Hector (Sleepy) Romero
    Esteban Tabarez, Jr.
Joey Vasquez
    Mark Vigil
Keith L. White
    A. Wilson

Meredith *Etc*
1052 Maria Court
Jackson, MS 39204-5151
www.meredithetc.com
Twitter/Facebook: Meredithetc

TABLE OF CONTENTS

*It is easier to build strong children
than to repair broken men!*

Frederick Douglass, 1855

ADVANCE PRAISE FOR *JUVENILE OFFENDERS: FROM BIG WHEELS TO THE BIG HOUSE*

This book is a powerful tool in countless ways. It gives a voice to those who have been silenced. It offers important insights into crime, punishment, and circumstance. It provides an opportunity for empathy and understanding – for the offenders and the victims.

• Congresswoman Barbara Lee, CA

Most valuable in this book are the searingly honest reflections by prisoners on the damage they inflicted on their victims and the victims' families, the sense of shame and regret, the determination to live a better life, and the hope of redemption. Louie Gomez' powerful essay, "In My Victim's Shoes," is stunning.

• Jeanne Bishop, Assistant Cook County Public Defender/Author, *Change of Heart: Justice, Mercy and Making Peace with My Sister's Killer*

This book not only serves as a source of enlightenment on our justice policies, it also offers important insights into how to rectify many of the problems inherent in the system. *Juvenile Offenders* is well-worth the read!

• Dr. Brian Grossman, PhD,
California Prison Psychologist

DEDICATION

I dedicate this book to all the men (and women) who started out at the extremes of life and have suffered in their own way for it.

I dedicate this book to all those who can learn from their mistakes and can thus avoid repeating them. Their mistakes are not meant to be emulated, but their personal transformation and strength to change ought to be.

Most of all, I dedicate this book to all victims whose abuse can never be undone. Their lives have been forever changed in ways that we likely can never imagine because of the actions of misguided, often thoughtless, selfish, and ego-centric perpetrators and for those who have died at their hands, there are no take-backs.

Yet, we must also understand that they ask not forgiveness for the deeds they have committed. It is through their genuine remorse and contrition and their ardent desire to do something different and productive with their lives that we can all benefit. We can learn from their stories and regrets and from their fervent desire to leave a positive mark on the communities to which most of them will eventually return.

And it is through their life stories that we too can grow. We must dedicate our own lives to creating a society in which the seeds for such behavior can never flourish ignoring those truths can only victimize us.

A special Thank You to Mule Creek State Prison, Salinas Valley State Prison, San Quentin State Prison, High Desert State Prison, Corcoran State Prison, Richard J. Donovan Correctional Facility, California State Prison, Los Angeles County Prison, and Arizona State Prison (Perryville) for allowing me to correspond with their inmates for this very inspiring project.

FOREWORD
by Congresswoman Barbara Lee

Our criminal justice system has worked to the detriment of many – especially minority youth sentenced to inordinately long terms, often for relatively minor crimes.

For mistakes made early in their lives, our young people too often serve life-long punishments, limited by the record they carry with them. With these reduced opportunities come added burdens – barriers to housing, employment, education and community engagement. Congress has a role to play in rectifying these injustices, through legislation like "Ban-The-Box." But the criminal justice reform movement – and the young people who have served – also require greater understanding from our community at large.

This book is a powerful tool in countless ways. It gives a voice to those who have been silenced. It offers important insights into crime, punishment, and circumstance. It provides an opportunity for empathy and understanding – for the offenders and the victims.

Juvenile Offenders: from Big Wheels to the Big House concludes with amazing poems, vignettes, and drawings by many current and former inmates. Readers can see prisoners from a new point of view and come to recognize our common humanity. The demonstrated talent on display in this book suggests the many possibilities that the formerly incarcerated have to offer. Clearly, the participants in this book are eager to contribute to our society. They served their time. They deserve a second chance.

EXCERPTS FROM THE WRITINGS OF INMATES

Ronald Patterson:

"Our bodies grow old/as we dance/on the threshold of Supreme Oneness--/battered and bruised/taking a tally of our losses/and wondering how much more we will lose.//Understanding that what we carry/is too heavy for the average, simple man.//So, thus-thus,/ we look close and see/the Power that is instilled/in our empty hands."

Anthony Andrew Ferguson:

"Much has been written . . . on the subject of Juvenile Justice. [So many lament] about the sometimes absurdly excessive and disproportionate sentences meted out in our nation's courtrooms. . . .[M]any of us are here because we are the result of the 'Tough on Crime' Juvenile Justice Policies. . . and are not serving sentences that are equal to our crimes."

Esteban Tabarez, Jr.:

" I had been a good" kid, a role model, a straight-A student, attended church regularly, was a picture-perfect son, community leaders, and outstanding citizen, and yet I [committed a horrendous crime]. How did this happen?"

James B. Elrod:

"Writing down [the story of my crime] . . .is devastating for me. Facing the ugly fact that I was so cowardly, sick and uncaring, and knowing the pain and shame I continue to experience is *nothing compared to the unspeakable damage I caused to* [my victim] *and her family.* I robbed [them] of a lifetime of of memories and experiences. . . . I did that!"

Juan Moreno Haines (managing editor of the *San Quentin News at the time of this printing*):

" *San Quentin News* is the only prisoner-operated newspaper in the California prison system. Its reporters have a unique access to, and knowledge of, the workings of the state prison system that set them apart from any other journalists in the field. The newspaper focuses on providing an accurate view of prison life to its readers and on the analysis of criminal justice policy."

Louie Gomez: *(writing about what he thinks his victim was thinking):*

". . .Oh, God! Don't let me die. It hurts so bad. I've never felt this much pain before. Please God, help me. . . .It can't end like this. This isn't fair." *To my victim's family*: In 1982, I was a sixteen year old, no good street punk. I had no respect for myself, and thus, I had no respect for other people. yet, more than three decades later, I am nothing like the troubled kid, or hoodlum, that I was then."

Mark E. Vigil:

"From that night [of my release], my life changed. [During the transitional phase], my path to freedom took root. Every day at 'The Ranch,' they allowed me. . . the things I required in order to establish myself in society and be treated once again like a human being."

INTRODUCTION

by Rosemary Jenkins

The purpose of this book is to serve as a jumping off point for discussion during self-help groups among prison inmates and staff facilitators regarding experiences, often comparable, shared by these inmates themselves. This volume is also meant for use in post-incarceration transitional groups to reinforce insights gained during their prison life. Furthermore, this manuscript can be utilized in justice classes offered at high school, college, and graduate levels . . . and beyond, and by anyone else who is interested in learning more about his subject. This book has been critically reviewed by a number of experts, representing a broad number of fields, whose own individual contributions have been and continue to be invaluable.

The book is in four parts:

The first part includes articles exclusively written by inmates, all of whom entered the system as juveniles. The columns share their insights into their early life situations that created or produced the circumstances that led them to criminal activity. These articles take us to an understanding of the crimes themselves and the evolution these prisoners have undergone over a period of time to become individuals that deserve a section chance.

The second part includes articles, written by Rosemary Jenkins, that provide important discussion on a variety of justice-related issues: how early childhood experiences can lead to criminal activity, how the current justice system has served and disserved those affected by it, how legislation is being promoted to recognize how juveniles, tried as adults, need to be re-evaluated and, in most cases, have their terms in prison reduced.

Part three includes articles by a variety of experts on the legal system, particularly as their expertise pertains to juvenile-offender issues. This section also shares at least one first-hand account by a survivor who was a victim of the kind of abuser one might or should find behind bars.

The fourth part contains drawings, vignettes, and poems by a number of inmates--offering a different view of who these people really are. Their work clearly demonstrates that they are human beings who have shown growth over the years and whose artistic endeavors reflect that development.

The goal of *Juvenile Offenders: from Big Wheels to the Big House* is to contribute to our overall understanding of prison and justice issues and the reasons why so many of our young people find themselves within the system and the roadblocks that hamper their re-entry into society as valuable contributors. It is our job as part of the greater society to appreciate the magnitude of these matters and commit to reforming the justice system into a system that is truly just.

Juvenile Offenders: From Big Wheels to the Big House

OVERVIEW

by Anthony Andrew Ferguson

When Mark Vigil [a fellow inmate] approached me about his idea for this project, I honestly didn't know what to expect. Our facility had been abuzz with talk about the newly-enacted *Senate Bill 260*—the Youth Offender Parole Bill. Every one of us (people, while still mere children, who had found themselves within the clutches of the system) was aglow with a new- found hope and motivation that the system had tried so hard over so many years (and had, at times, succeeded) to beat out of us.

Mark told me that he had a vision of assembling a collection of writings from guys who were on the receiving end of excessively long sentences before even becoming old enough to vote, smoke, or drink legally. Mark's idea would capture a microcosm of the general pain, ignorance, and misguidance that accumulates in combination with individual experience and (unfortunately) too often culminates in the tragic circumstances that merit this book.

He told me how he had been trying (with a little luck) to get the project off the ground for some time. At first, I thought the idea was ..well, just a good idea to bounce around, like, "Wouldn't it be cool if." But the more I thought about it and the more juvenile offenders I encountered (who had done the work to change their lives and were eager to tell their stories), the more the feasibility of such a project began to take shape.

At the time, I pitched the idea to my friend Rosemary Jenkins, a Los Angeles-based educator, blogger, activist, poet (the list goes on), who agreed to talk to her publishers at *LA Progressive* about printing the prison-written articles as an on-line series. The publishers agreed, and thus, "The Juvenile Offender Series" was born.

Much has been written over the past few decades on the subject of Juvenile Justice Psychologists, criminologists, journalists, sociologists, activists, and politicians have all lamented in one way or another about the sometimes absurdly excessive and disproportionate sentences meted out in our nation's courtrooms. The truth is that many of us are here because we are the result of the "Tough on Crime" Juvenile Justice Policies of the 1980's and 1990's and are not serving sentences that are equal to our crimes

On the other hand, these experts have also expressed their very genuine and reasonable concerns about how to handle the sentences for adolescents who do commit serious crimes. Thus, arriving at a just and fair balance between the two types of offenders is a genuine conundrum that clearly must be resolved.

While having good intentions (and, in many cases, suggesting judicious solutions to the problem), many of these professionals speak only from an academic perspective. Unfortunately, for the most part, they have looked chiefly to secondary research data (and rarely to primary sources) to draw conclusions regarding issues they have not experienced first-hand

It is for these reasons and others that we, who offer our personal accounts in this book and who often serve as the subjects for their assumptions, felt compelled to speak for ourselves and reveal candid truths about which even the many well-intended professionals have no inkling

Truth be told, it is a unique experience to be 14, 15, 16, or 17 years old and be handed a long- term or life sentence. Indeed for many of us, at the time we committed our crimes, the concept of reaping long-term, harsh consequences for our impulses was, for the most part, foreign to us. It had never occurred to those with stories reflected in this book that anything would come of those early behaviors or of the ill-conceived exploits that emerged from them

From the little Texas boy whose childhood abuse from a family member spurred a drug habit that ultimately led to murder to the Mexican kid whose only view of what his life could or should be was found in the "Barrio Stars" he saw whenever he looked out of his window to so many other painful stories comes the inspiration for this book which is ultimately a reflection of the painful hindsight with which these men recount their lives. These stories illustrate the context for "big wheels to prison bars."

Whether environment, experience, instruction, genetics, a lack of a fully-developed critically thinking brain, or all of these are to blame for the particular set of circumstances that led to the acts that drastically changed so many lives is almost irrelevant, even though such considerations are at the heart of Juvenile Justice Reform.

At issue here—at least in part--is the physical, mental, and spiritual toll that the consequences of our crimes have taken on us. Many reading this might say that such consequences are well- deserved and do not merit anyone's pity or sympathy. On the other hand, is the way we currently treat offenders, particularly juveniles, something that will produce the kind of results that incarceration has ideally been intended? These very human inmates, who have frequently been the ongoing objects of in-prison mental and physical brutality, are people who are likely to become hardened criminals and re-offenders and not people who have been rehabilitated and waiting for a second chance to be useful outside the confines of prison walls.

If we do not help these once-young people resolve their issues, what will happen to them and to us once they are eventually released? The kind of rehabilitation that we envision will not have been achieved and recidivism will be the eventual result—often from new crimes that are even worse than the original. If these inmates are not treated as human beings capable of reform, what can be expected of them when they are re-introduced into society?

The fact is that, regardless of our offenses, we have all paid for our crimes through the irretrievable loss of precious time. Aside from the cumulative effect of the 1000 daily indignities that accompany prison life, we have live every day with the knowledge that parents have lost their children because of us; that children have lost their parents; that communities were made less safe, and that subsequent generations have been given the false impression that antisocial behavior is the norm—and the knowledge and guilt that we can never undo what we have done but also with the awareness that there may still be time after prison to try to make up for our wrongdoings.

It is within this context that our stories can be told, enlightening to you and self-affirming to us.

Every person travels a different road in life. The beaten paths by the authors of these stories began in different times, places, and ways. Each of us took an unfortunate and reprehensible (but hopefully not unforgiveable) detour that brought us to this unbearable pit-stop! For me it is a pit-stop because it is not our journey's final destination. To accept otherwise would be to accept defeat and that would imply that no hope exists for us—a thought just too unacceptable. But we do have hope—hope and confidence.

We have the hope that our experiences will serve as cautionary tales for today's youth who, for whatever reason, seem to be headed for that same dreaded pit-stop where we have found ourselves, attempting for years and years to find a way out.

We are confident in our cause and in our sincerity. I think I can speak for every offender who contributed to this project when I say that imparting our sincere words to this work is the very least we can do to prove that point.

Finally, this is a collection of articles from incarcerated men who were arrested as juveniles, yet were tried and sentenced as adults. In light of recent legislation in California (*SB 260/261*), some of them will be given a second chance through the possibility of early parole.

In the meantime, it is their desire to share their stories with the public and with each other and so we have this Juvenile Offenders Series and other articles. Their stories reflect their own individual experiences--of people who have had to "grow up" in prison because of their crimes.

The stories in this series are real and personal. They also illuminate long overlooked questions regarding our legal system: How did these souls get there and what really happens to them once we've locked them up and thrown away the key? What are the effects of long-term incarceration on these adolescents?

MARTIN LUTHER KING JR.

CHAPTER ONE

From Big Wheels to Life Behind Bars

--From the Mouths of "Accidental" Prisoners

"It [prison] has gotten 'worse' over the years. At times, trying to be 'an adult' or carrying yourself as an intelligent/mature person is like walking a tight rope without a net, so one struggles to maintain his balance at all times, but sometimes violent winds blow your way."

"Something simple or small takes on a different weight in prison. Prison politics is a big determiner."

Ronald Patterson

PRÉCIS TO CHAPTER ONE

Something both terrible and wonderful was behind the inception of this book. *Terrible* was the crime committed. *Wonderful* was the birth of an idea—to write only one article, the concept and reception of which was so well-received that what started small soon proliferated (before we recognized what was happening) into a multitude of columns The totality eventually became a manuscript which took a very serendipitous journey before the idea of publication was conceived and later became a reality. A book—this book—certainly had not been our intention when this project began.

Going back to the beginning, I knew one of the authors because we shared membership on a community action board. He was one of the youngest yet most committed participants who had so many exciting ideas for quality-of-life improvements in our neighborhoods and beyond that I took special note of him and his potential.

Unfortunately, his path took a tragic wrong turn before he could fulfill those goals.

Being Latino, gay, and bi-polar posed issues throughout his young life with which he was continuously conflicted. His was a life in a dysfunctional family where drugs and alcohol, physical and mental abuse, parental infidelity, feelings of isolation and rejection abounded.

After he committed the crime for which he was convicted, I stayed by his side, trying to help in any way I could. His lawyer was a high-priced hack who clearly intended not to offer an affirmative defense and would not even investigate the circumstance of the crime to which his defendant had immediately admitted guilt even though there were numerous circumstantial issues.

I attended each of his hearings and then began to write to him. Once he was convicted and sentenced, I corresponded with him in prison. Over time, one of his "cellies" asked if he also could write to me. I agreed and we have been writing ever since.

I recognized that this "new" young man was close to being brilliant. He was self-educated and read everything he could lay his hands on, including histories and science, and a breadth of literature. I was so impressed by his writing style that I asked my publishers from *Los Angeles Progressive* if they would print one his of essays. They agreed and what was once one article led to more and, ultimately, included the musings of a number of inmates at several California prisons.

What follows is an amalgam of writings that are true and heartfelt and written from the soul of each author. It is the hope of all of us involved in this project that not only these prisoner-written articles but all that follows be a springboard for discussion not only for prison therapy groups but for post-incarceration prison groups, justice classes, for library readers, and for the general public which has increasingly demonstrated its interest in all the issues tangential to our current justice system.

By reading the contents of this book, we can experience vicariously at least some of the experiences described and hopefully become more enlightened about what leads a once-innocent person to crime and prison, what transpires within the walls, and what happens to many of these once-incarcerated human beings (we never lose our humanity) subsequent to their release.

At the very least, you will recognize the common thread that binds all these offenders and, hopefully, feel compelled to support and demand the kind of changes in our prison system and in our society that can mitigate and alleviate so many of the factors that lead to the circumstances described within these pages.

Juvenile Offenders: From Big Wheels to the Big House

Introduction by Mark E. Vigil

STEVE'S STORY by Steve Grant

There is a common thread that binds the lives and tragic stories of most men who are incarcerated. Their assertions of innocence echo through a labyrinth of prison corridors and the endless spiral of time. Such claims are compounded by their collective struggles for justice which invariably fall upon deaf or unsympathetic ears—ears that are unwilling to take heed of the facts that could ultimately separate truth from fiction.

The indifference can become a living nightmare that offers no way out of these places—human aviaries for jailed birds that cannot fly on clipped wings. These are victims in their own right because they have been wrongly convicted for a crime they never committed.

When I consider the ramifications of wrongful imprisonment, weighed against the bitter and ugly realities of prison life, it must be a truly miserable, frustrating, and soul-crushing experience. These are people who are being forced to endure being locked inside a box the size of a walk-in closet for the remainder of their lives for crimes for which they are not guilty.

These very circumstances are what occurred in the case of *Steve Grant*. I have taken the liberty of helping him piece his story together for the sake of demonstrating just how cruel a wrongful conviction can be. . . .

Steve's Story in Steve's Words
I am an innocent man!
By Steve Grant

I am an innocent man!

I would rather be a homeless man than to live where I am now, incarcerated for life in prison for a crime I could never consider inflicting on any human being for any reason at any time. I repeat and cannot stress enough, *I am an innocent man*!

photo by Stuart Miles

This nightmare began back in 1981 when I was a much younger man. I was arrested for the murder of a man who was a deacon in a church—a man of God. He was 67 years old when he lost his life in a brutal robbery that went bad.

His name was William Edwards—a name that will live with me for as long as I live--a name that has haunted me ever since the days when I was first arrested for his death.

Mr. Edwards was burned alive for money he did not have by a callous and petty gang of young men who encountered the victim one night as he was walking back to his car which had run out of gas. It seems that before he was able to make it back to his car, he was confronted by this gang of thugs and pushed around until the gas can Mr. Edwards was carrying was taken from him and used to set him aflame.

Though I was never there that night, I can only imagine what it must have felt like to experience that sort of excruciating pain and suffering.

Had I been present, maybe then I could have somehow helped Mr. Edwards because I could not have stood by to let anyone be attacked that way. I am not that sort of man, yet the circumstances around his death are what have ever since shadowed and condemned my life. It was that night when my life came to a sudden stop!

Thirty-five years later, I am still reliving the horrors done to Mr. Edwards when his life was tragically and senselessly taken and when I was robbed of my own freedom as a result of his death.

Yes, it is said that all prisoners claim their innocence but there really are some—too many—whose claims ring true, and mine is one of them. I understand the suspicion that accompanies such claims, but mine is indisputably one of the exceptions. I have maintained my story from the very beginning, despite the lies and false testimony people have used against me.

I am an innocent man!

Each time I go before the Parole Board, I express the same truths. I had nothing to do with Mr. Edward's death, but my protestations are never enough. The commissioners do not want to hear the truth. They always want to paint me in the dimmest light they can, and they can do this in good conscience and without guilt because I am not convincing. The fact is, I am not an educated nor an eloquent man who might otherwise be able to end this hell if I could only explain just how I got caught up in a situation that cast doubt on my innocence.

They don't want to hear the truth!

It seems there exists no currency in the truth. There is only the court record and that record states that I am guilty of this heinous crime. So why *should* they believe me?!

The people who were arrested and also charged for this crime were Crip gang members. I was 23 years old and they were 16 and 17 year-old boys at the time.

I was *never* with a street gang. I was neither affiliated with those young men nor did I share their ways of beating and abusing people in and around the neighborhood. We had absolutely nothing in common. In fact, they were from the same gang with whom I had long-standing problems--they had bullied, harassed, and eventually killed my sister in an unrelated earlier crime.

Perhaps there was a plea bargain for a lesser sentence. Perhaps, they implicated me out of some kind of revenge over my sisters' murder which they had committed—in order to get me out of the way. I don't know to this day what sentences they received, but I cannot help but believe, to this day, that somehow my own freedom and innocence were swapped over some nefarious compact.

So, initially, I was arrested but let go days later for lack of evidence. Strangely to me, when I got out, I recall people asking me all sorts of questions about my involvement in this crime, but (naïvely) I didn't give it much thought because I didn't have anything to do with the crime. I figured things would come out in the wash.

Justice would somehow prevail!

When I was re-arrested, I thought the cops had made another mistake, but this time they turned up the heat and threatened me with hard time. When that failed, they proceeded to beat me up in order to obtain a confession, but even that could not get me to change my story.

So I clung to the truth!

They say, The truth shall set you free, but in my case that has proven not to be the case. Instead, my freedom was taken and I have been subjected to a life where beatings, muggings, and death are commonplace.

The guards and the inmates are all alike. They use and abuse each other and make our world a living hell. As for me, I spent nearly 3 years fighting this case from the Los Angeles County Jail until I was finally convicted and sent to Folsom Prison.

Once there and over time, I saw many men die—some at their own hands! What I witnessed was like shock-and-awe—experiences that always sent chills down my spine and continue to give me nightmares.

In the early '80s, Folsom Prison was experiencing a series of race wars between the Blacks and Mexicans that were fueled by hatred, anger, and the need for blood-letting. For those who could not stomach that level of brutality, suicide became a way out. And there I was, in a system that went and stuck me right in the middle of this battlefield of lunatics and mad men!

I have asked myself repeatedly, Why should I take my own life when I was and am an innocent man?!

Over time, I had written numerous suicide notes to various people because I didn't know what the next day would bring. The pain and sorrow I felt about my predicament was extremely overwhelming. And I could not see any way out. I felt so powerless—hopeless in the face of so much misery. I was a hostage to the bitter realities that kept dragging my body down inside a bottomless pit.

More than anything, I felt the burning sting of the injustice that had been done to me and I would cry out for some sort of mercy, but it would never come.

Suicide seemed like a logical way out of this living hell, a situation that only seemed to get worse by the day. The reason I thought about harming myself is that I couldn't see being in prison for a crime I did not do and was not involved in at all. Furthermore, I didn't want to hurt or harm my family any more than they already have been as a result of my seemingly eternal incarceration. There are reasons why I am not dead by my own hands.

But as 5 years turned to 10 and now 35, the more I feel trapped in this unspeakable living hell with absolutely no way of extricating myself.

I am not a lawyer nor do I possess a basic knowledge of how to utilize the law. Knowing that, I began to write anyone who could possibly help me find some form of relief in this matter. I silently hoped someone would come forward and own the truth of what really happened to Mr. Edwards.

But once again, no one bothered to take an interest in my case. I must have written nearly 2000 letters that seemed like messages stuffed in bottles that were never discovered by anyone out there. Instead, they simply drifted out into open waters.

Just as I have floated—adrift at sea for far too long!

For 25 years, I wrote the D. A. and never once did he bother to toss me a lifeline. He eventually went on to become a judge in a broader field of influence and power but, rest assured, that no matter how high up the judicial ladder he rises, he will always be flawed and his judgements questionable due to what he failed to do in the interests of justice for Mr. Edwards and for me.

His name is unimportant. Yet, what he had failed to do is exquisitely telling.

Since receiving yet another denial from the prison board, which took place on December 16, 2015, I find it extremely difficult to sleep. It's like they keep opening a wound that has never quite had time to heal.

Maybe I would sleep better had I actually committed this crime. Perhaps then the nightmare would be more bearable. But the truth is, I could never have perpetrated this atrocity on another human being—not for any reason!

My family raised me better than that. I just wish they could have prepared me for the daily trauma that I live with. Till this very day, I have never read my trial transcripts because I get so sick each time I attempt to read through them. The lies and countless humiliations hurled against me simply hurt too much.

Maybe now that I have told my story, something good will come of it. Up till now, it has all been a series of perpetual pain and a lifetime lost inside these catacombs. Maybe the next step will see a "new birth of freedom" for me and the many others who have been caught in this same web of cruel distortions and heartless misrepresentations.

Through it all, however, I still ask God for mercy, not just for myself but for the Edwards' family.

For those doing time for a crime they, like me, never did, I pray their pain will end soon and their freedom will one day be restored.

As for me, I am still waiting!

Juvenile Offenders: From Big Wheels to the Big House

☐ James Howard Meredith, cousin of Ronald Patterson ☐

James Howard Meredith, the first Black student to enroll at the University of Mississippi (Ole Miss) during the Jim Crow South (1962) is the cousin of Ronald Patterson who, as a juvenile offender, entered the California prison system in 1980, at the age of 16. Meredith corresponded with him for over 25 years and even provided two typewriters for his use, actions which ultimately led Ronald to become a better writer. Meredith stated that he is touched by what his beloved cousin, Ronald, has written.

The following picture of James Meredith, a change agent, was taken by 22-year-old Edwin E. Meek, a photographer, on October 1, 1962, on Meredith's first day in class at Ole Miss.

James Howard Meredith Photo by Edwin E. Meek
University of Mississippi, Oxford, October 1, 1962
https://50years.olemiss.edu/photo-gallery/

Meek realized that white students did not want to sit near or appear in photographs with Meredith. Thus, Meredith was the last person in the classroom that day and the photo was taken. At that time, the Kennedy administration asked the media not to interfere with Meredith's educational experience. So, even though Meek took over 800 photographs from 1962 to 1963 of Meredith, Meek did not develop the film. He held the negatives in a safe deposit box for 40 years. His recent book, *Riot: Witness to Anger and Change,* displays a glimpse of an historical period that we cannot and must not forget.

This non-fiction book, ***Juvenile Offenders: from Big Wheels to the Big House***, is also such a book.

To All the Teachers Who Tried To Help Me
by Ronald Patterson

I am here, sitting in prison when I should be out, following the inspirational teachings and high expectations of so many of my teachers who recognized my potential and believed I would accomplish many good things.

I have no doubt disappointed them and I am so sorry for that. But my life is not over and I intend, during my post-incarceration life, not only to fulfill their visions of me but ultimately to go far beyond them in my achievements. In the meantime, let me share with you what some of my teachers did for me:

Mr. Harris actually was my first male role model. The first Black man I truly adored, admired, and looked up to, and wanted to please and be like.

26

When I look in retrospect, Mr. Harris actually was my first male role model. The first Black man I truly adored, admired, and looked up to, and wanted to please and be like. He created an environment for me to learn and excel—that had as a foundation Black history, Black Pride, African culture, and education.

He implanted in me the idea that I had "unlimited" potential and told the youthful me that I could be the first Black President of the United States of America [I missed that one]. When I look back, he may or may not have truly believed this, but that was not as important as the fact that I believed it when he said it. That compliment filled me with pride, and now, as an adult, I understand its underlying message—that I was not limited in potential or achievement because I was Black, poor, and lived in the Public Housing Projects.

Never once did this man acknowledge nor speak to what others may have thought—people who expected so little of people like me who were existing in a place of hopelessness due to our socio-economic environment. And it is because of what he taught me and the pride he instilled in me that, in part, I am the man I am today. And because of his influence, I do not suffer from self- hate nor low self-esteem as so many do who come from the Hood (like myself).

In this sense, he was my first Father-figure. He inspired me in numerous ways, even though I was not conscious of it at the time and maybe was not ready to accept his words.

Mr. Harris was my teacher in South Central Los Angeles, located in the Pueblo Del Rio Housing Projects—known as The Pueblos, and home of the Notorious Blood Street Gang called the 52 Pueblo Bishops. For many of us, Mr. Harris was a Savior (sent all the way from Tennessee), but like the Black Jesus of Biblical times, we did not know his true worth–while he was in our presence.

Perhaps because of his own African roots, he taught us more than the basic curriculum. He taught us to speak English correctly. He was a role model because he spoke English with the same degree of perfection as any scholar. But because he was from Tennessee, we always laughed (because of his accent) when he taught us the specifics of grammar and composition. As an example, when he was telling us about third person, singular pronouns, "he, she, and it." It sounded to us like "he s--t." Just too funny.

Mr. Harris was my elementary school teacher for 4th, 5th, and 6th grades. My sweet mother, understanding the importance of education, made it mandatory that I and my siblings go to school every day—with few exceptions–knowing if we are not there, we can't learn. And daily attendance was so meaningful to Mr. Harris as well.

He wanted to keep some of us with him in his classes over time because I think he felt he could get through to us. On occasion he would take some of us to a movie or a public swimming pool or even take us to his apartment when his girlfriend was there—I think in order to see for ourselves what a different style of life can mean and how it can be possible even for us. Of course, this would not be possible these days with all the concerns about inappropriate behavior, but his innocent actions were not like that at all.

It became obvious to us that Mr. Harris was not your average teacher. First of all, he taught all three classes in one class. He did not restrict learning to the grade level you were in. For example, if you were in the 4th grade but read at 5th grade level, he would provide 5th grade books to challenge us at our level. I actually was studying algebra in 4th grade! As a result, when I was in high school in 10th grade, I was placed in a gifted class for math and science.

Mr. Harris taught me about Dr. Martin Luther King, Jr. and other Black pioneers, like Frederick Douglass, Mary McLeod Bethune, Marian Anderson—to name but a few. He placed pictures and brief biographies of them all around our room. He taught us the Black National Anthem: "Lift every voice and sing, Till earth and heaven ring. Let us march on till victory is won."

His goal was to teach us how to be good African-Americans. He taught us of the glories in African history. He even created a dance troupe. It was more like a combination of modern dance, African dance, and ballet. We danced to African drums-beats and rhythms–as well as to R & B songs. He taught us to appreciate the banjo, conga, and other drums. We wore African dashikis. He taught us how to tie-dye cloths and make our own colorful African shirts.

To us, Mr. Harris was a true Black man. For our 6th grade graduation, he wanted us to sing the theme from Mahogany and other pieces, but the school would not allow it. But I still remember the inspirational lyrics he taught us:

Everything has a
season, Everything has
a time, Show me a
reason,
And I'll surely show you a rhyme.
Cats fit on the window
sill, Children fit in the
snow. Why do I feel, I
don't fit in Anywhere I
go?

Rivers belong
where They can
rumble. Eagles
belong where They
can fly.
I'd like to be
Where my spirit can
Roam free.
I gotta' find my corner of the sky.

Mr. Harris did far more for us. He taught us a sense of responsibility for each other. He taught us–with love and purpose–about discipline. He always wanted to meet the parents of his students. If they didn't come to the school, he, like Muhammad to the mountain, would visit them. For Mr. Harris, showing disrespect to our Black selves and heritage was extremely offensive. As caring and kind as he was, he tolerated no disrespect for himself, yourself, or anyone else.

Yes, as Mr. Harris's evaluations reflected, I was always improving in my educational growth and development under his attentiveness. Even though I never thought about it until today, I guess.   Mr. Thomas K. Harris from Memphis,

Tennessee, was my first father figure and my first Black role model. Mr. Harris always gave the best of himself to us ghetto youth and tried to save us from a life of self-destruction. He was and still is a person worthy of emulation.

Not to be forgotten are some other teachers who influenced me:

Mrs. Blackwell wrote in her evaluations of me that I was "a very independent child. Follows directions well. Gifted in art. Hard worker." She was jet Black and beautiful, spoke like the French and loved art. It was Mrs. Blackwell who taught me to draw and to love and appreciate art. When I told my birth father that I wanted to be an artist, he told me "Artists are only famous after they are dead." Nevertheless, I still draw from time to time and I still love art (despite his discouraging words).

I am also thankful for Mrs. Maxine Lowe who was my 9th grade teacher. She even testified during my trial as a character witness (I think she recognized my potential) Mrs. Sarah Cogshell taught me while I was in Juvenile Hall. She would bring me magazines, like *Ebony* and *Jet*, and would say to other inmates, "I wish more of you were like Patterson." She even entered one of my drawings of Dr. Martin Luther King, Jr. into a contest. I won the trophy—a feat, unfortunately, I never repeated.

Sadly, even these Black Angels (as I call those teachers) could not save some of us and me. They tried to teach me in their own way to believe in myself and that I could soar.

But, unfortunately and foolishly for me, I was being drawn to the street life by that time and thus started ditching classes. Mathematical equations and scientific formulas were far from my daily thoughts. By then, I had been captivated by the life of the street hustlers, players, dope-dealers, and pimps. I was dreaming of Sevilles, Broughams, Fleetwoods, Benzis, pimping, pretty young women, making money, gambling, and hustling. My mind, like other youth around me, was consumed with the conventional "wisdom" and culture of hood life—the life of the streets and those who reigned supreme on them. I truly believed that one day I could live that life–be bigger and better than those I looked up to whose lives seemed so appealing to me at that young age.

My thoughts were far from being "President of the U. S."—the idea that Mr. Harris once dangled over my head. I wanted to have more jewelry than Sammie Davis, Jr., and to "Roll like God."

When all is said and done, Mr. Harris had always said that I am a sharp thinker and enjoy challenges, that I am capable of improving myself, and that I can do good things. Those "talents" are what I plan to pursue and build on once I get that second chance after prison.

Juvenile Offenders: From Big Wheels to the Big House

How Did the Apple Fall So Far from the Tree?
by Mark E. Vigil

My paternal grandfather was Atanacio Vigil Tobias. He was born around the year 1902 in the state of San Luis Potosi, Mexico—the home of most of my family.

Though I cannot say he grew up in the same pueblo which I came to know as our village, it is the place where years ago I came to know my *abuelo* (grandfather). The name of our pueblo is Paso Blanco which is a small, rural community made up of people who live off the land—primarily farmers and craftsmen.

My grandfather was a corn farmer who had three small patches of land known as *ejidos*, land given to him after the Mexican Revolution. He was not an educated man (that I know of) though he was a man who knew many things about the world he inhabited.

To me, he was wise and caring. In the little time I spent with my grandfather, I learned of our family's history and of their struggles to survive off the few things they had.

He was a mixture of Huastec Indian and Spanish blood–though that may be disputed as this region of Mexico has always been a corridor for people migrating through its arid lands on their way to more fertile lands and dreams elsewhere. For whatever reason, he remained anchored there until his death in the year 1995.

When I first visited my grandfather back between 1972 and '73, our village had no running water nor the luxury of electricity to light our nights. The modern elements of life (usually taken for granted in America) had not quite reached our village yet. But the richness and warmth of my family was evident in the way I was embraced by its members and by my grandfather in particular.

My relatives seemed not the least bit bothered by the absence of these creature comforts that somehow have marginalized so many people back home in America.

My grandfather was stern and sincere with me. He expected me to work and help with the planting of our crops and to tend to the few animals they kept—things I never got to do at home.

Because of this, I was able to explore the fields of my father's youth. My grandfather told me stories of my father–stories I had never known before, such as why he came to America. As with most families in our pueblo, necessity made it so that he had to leave his home at a young age so as to forge a new life on the American side of the border in order to help support his family back home. My grandfather provided bits and pieces of our family's history that I would never have known otherwise. Because of my *abuelo*, I continue to feel connected to the two halves of my roots.

I was born in America, but my roots were cultivated in the hard clay and soil of Paso Blanco.

My father was Auscencio Mata Vigil. He was born around the year 1939 in the state of San Luis Potosi, Mexico. He was my grandfather's oldest son and came to America in search of the ever- elusive American dream. He was a complicated man who struggled to understand the way of life on the north side of the border. He arrived here in America—broke and penniless—and went to work in the fields of California.

When my father passed away in 2004, I had already been locked up in Pelican Bay for almost 14 years straight. I was never given the chance to say good-bye to him.

Having no formal education other than the skills as a horseman and farmer (like his father), he followed the crops, much like most other *braceros* (as Mexican laborers were known back then). They were the "arms" doing the labor in the fields of strawberries and grapes, the back-breaking work no one else in this country seemed willing to do.

My father loved to work—it was how he defined and measured his life. He always stressed the importance of being a responsible man—*un hombre responsable.*

From Mexico, he migrated down through Texas and eventually settled in Wilmington, California, where he met and married my mother, Mary Vasquez Vigil. Together they would have five children, I being the youngest of our family.

The earliest recollection of my father was the manner in which he struggled to understand the many differences between life in this country and that in his native Mexico. The food seemed bland; the language, unrecognizable; and the people, strange!

Culturally speaking, it was night and day for him. The notion of *machismo* was also very much in play. At times, during his moments of conflict, it was "Do as I say—not as I do! This attitude caused much division within our home.

In the early years, he used to drink a lot, spending his time working during the days and at night going out to drink with his cousins from back home. I recall seeing him return home in a drunken stupor–falling over himself and us kids in the process. He and my mother argued and fought long and hard over his stubborn inability to be a worthy husband and a good father to his children. These are just some of the things my father found difficult to grasp during those darker moments of my family's time together.

When he stopped working the fields, he took a job in the tuna canneries off Terminal Island in San Pedro, California. This move enabled him to earn more money and eventually to afford to purchase a home of our own. The house was an old, rickety 1920s wooden house located in a part of Wilmington known then as "Ghost Town" because it was in the poorest area of our *barrio* where the people of color lived.

Surrounded by junk yards and the City dumps that were adjacent to numerous factories and oil refineries, the conditions made for the perfect blend of toxic communal blight.

Despite my mother's objections to this move, my father saw it as a step up in his pursuit of a better life for his family. He came from the poverty-stricken fields of San Luis Potosi, Mexico, to the impoverished streets of "Wilmas," where owning something meant everything to a man who came from so little. To us, however, the move was a gamble—not a logical progression.

It wasn't until I visited Mexico that I was able to understand my father's roots. It was then that I was able to understand how big this move was for him—as a man. To him, his decision was huge! As a child, he lived in a one-room shed with a thatched roof and earthen floor next to the corral where they kept their few animals.

Thus, for my father, his new home must have seemed like a king's castle. Yet owning this home also meant acquiring the added burden of being in debt and having to balance a budget.

This was always a major struggle for my parents to manage, as there were few nickels and dimes to go around in order to meet everyone's needs. As a result, there was not always food to eat nor the best clothes to wear, but my father always seemed to find a way for us to get by (but only with the added support of my mother).

My father always attempted to instill in me the lessons of hard work and the value of the dollar. He wanted me to be better than the man he was. Most of all, he wanted for me to take full advantage of the things this country had to offer—to educate and strive to build a better future for myself.

When he passed away in 2004, I had already been locked up in the SHU [Security Housing Unit] of Pelican Bay for almost 14 years straight. I was never given the chance to say good-bye to him. He had gone back to Mexico for a wedding of a cousin where he died in his sleep. His body was frail and battered from all the struggles and hard-fought battles he had won and lost in his lifetime.

Some say his heart gave out, but I believe he died from a

broken heart, partly because of my mother's passing but also from my life spent in prison.

During his life, he tried to give me all he could and since his death, he continues to be the reason. I now strive to be a better man.

Yet, something happened to me despite all those good principles shared. I have spent the better part of my life in and out of prison (I am now 50 but initially became incarcerated when I was 16). I had not valued the lessons my family tried to instill in me and threw away the principles they had tried to impart. Ironically, I embrace as a man all those lessons that I ignored as a child.

So what brought me in both body and mind to the place where I now reside?

Who am I? I am my father's son. I was born in the year of 1963 in the city of Wilmington, California. My name is Mark Edward Vigil. When I was a child, my father gave me the nickname, Pino, which has stuck with me my entire life. I have lived every waking hour of my adulthood locked up in prison since.

I have lived my life inside places barely habitable for human existence and still remain alive. I have managed to survive, not because of how I tried to protect myself here but because of the lessons I was given as a child.

So many things I did not value, such as my beloved family who always tried to teach me right from wrong. But these were lessons I failed to accept as a kid but now hold dear as a man.

I have committed countless crimes in my life—in and out of

prison. On street corners and prison yards, I staked my ignorant claim of dominance—like a pugilist fighting for the prize money that turned out to be only the crumbs lift—but lost at every turn!

I have died and been resurrected each time like Lazurus, only to repeat the same foolish acts of stupidity that have kept me stuck inside this maze called prison.

I am the son of my father who came from the arid lands of his forefathers–so that I might have a better life.

So that I might realize that I am better than the colorless, constricted walls I had built for myself—better than the flaws and weaknesses, the shortcomings and imperfections, the mindless and selfish and mean-spirited failings of my youth.

An apple tree grows from the moment its seed is planted. Time, water, and the nutrients of Mother Earth are required for its branches to spread. Light from the sun will give it life and extend its branches towards the heavens. Once the apple tree matures enough, only then will it render the sweet, golden fruit it is meant to produce.

It is a well-known fact that no tree will bear fruit before it has matured. Clearly, for any organic being to do well, it must be nurtured—something that all children need before they reach adulthood.

--M. E. Vigil

Seeing the Light behind Bars
by Raymond Martinez

I came to prison when I was 16 years old. Getting arrested and sentenced to life at such a young age dramatically shaped my life.

The 34 years I have spent behind bars are the result of the excessive trauma and pain I experienced as a child.

My inability to express the pain I felt caused me to adopt the friends, values, and behavioral patterns that would ultimately earn me a life sentence.

I was born on November 1, 1965, in Phoenix, Arizona, but raised in Fresno, California. Shortly after I was born, my grandparents took guardianship of me and my older brother "M." My mother was only 16 when she had me and not ready to raise children. My father was much older than my mother and was very violent, controlling, and uninterested in raising children. He abandoned my mother before I was born, so I never knew him.

Though my grandparents made an effort to take care of my brother and me—they fed us, clothed us, and kept a roof over our heads—they were alcoholics and could not take care of themselves, let alone adequately care for two small children. My grandparents worked in a winery, so we always had more alcohol in our refrigerator than food.

At the age of 11, I began drinking every day. With so much liquor around the house and no real guidance from my grandparents, I saw drinking as a way of dealing with the feelings of abandonment and neglect from the adults in my life.

Despite being neglected by my mother's parents, I loved my family anyway and could not understand why they didn't seem to love me the same way I loved them.

As a result of not receiving the love and attention I longed for, I grew up feeling confused and withdrawn. Since no one seemed to care, I decided at a young age that talking about my problems would do no good. Thus, I developed many warped defense mechanisms to avoid revealing my true feelings to others.

I could talk non-stop but could never tell anyone what I was truly feeling. The walls I built around me (to keep people from seeing how vulnerable I was) were very high and strong. But those same walls would eventually lead to the self-destructive behavior that caused me so many problems later in life.

After a few years, my mother attempted to reach out to my brother and me, but even so, I never really felt loved by her. Her boyfriend did not accept us and beat my mom. The beatings would occur so often that I eventually became fed up with seeing such abuse, so I threatened to kill her boyfriend to protect her. Instead of understanding how I felt and offering comforting words, she responded by kicking me out of her home! Naturally, I felt rejected and betrayed because I thought I was keeping her from harm. My mother's rejection crippled me emotionally and killed my self-esteem.

I would not understand until much later what these early incidents did to me and how they shaped the way I treated and valued the people in my life.

Since I was always small as a youngster, I would get jumped at school by other kids. I was also considered a loner which didn't help me make friends easily. My negative experiences at school only served to reinforce my developing belief that violence alone commands respect.

So I began carrying weapons to fend off bullies at school and in the neighborhood. As my reputation began to grow, I was introduced to other troubled kids, gang members, and drug addicts. I joined a gang, started committing crimes, and began moving through the revolving door of juvenile hall. Ironically perhaps, doing time became a refuge from my chaotic and discouraging home life.

Once I joined the gang, the homies became my family. The acceptance I received from them and the bonds we formed made me willing to do just about anything for them.

Once I joined the gang, the homies became my family. The acceptance I received from them and the bonds we formed made me willing to do just about anything for them.

The fact is, I felt I needed their acceptance, but this need blinded me to the fact that by doing whatever the homies asked of me, I was giving in to dangerous peer-pressure.

Another reason for joining the gang was because my older brother was already a gang member. I looked up to him because he was respected within the gang and considered a leader. At age 17, however, he was arrested and sent to prison for murder. Since he was someone I looked up to, I felt it was my duty to be like him and copy his idea of manhood—even if it meant following in his risky footsteps.

Although I felt alone and sought the comfort, camaraderie, and guidance from my gang, there were still some adults in my life who tried to help. But the pain and rejection I had experienced with my family kept me from trusting people—no matter their good intentions.

I believed no one could possibly understand how I felt inside. I felt so angry and alone that the gang life filled the void in my life, and my loyalty was only to my homies.

One night, my homies and I went out to a party where we drank and smoked weed and did other drugs. As the night progressed, we grew wild and violent. My homeboy, Fats, started a fight with two guys from another city who were not gang members, just innocent party-goers. Feeling obligated to defend my homeboy, I jumped in the fight and we stabbed both men to death.

Eventually, I was arrested for my crimes and sentenced to life in prison. I was 16 years old, with no hope for a future! Then it hit me — I would have to spend the rest of my life behind bars!

Once I arrived at prison, I was exposed to a completely different world. Everything I'd done outside—the person I thought I was, the reputation I'd earned for myself, my homies, and my gang—none of it meant anything on the inside.

Once incarcerated, "The Cause" was all that mattered (whatever that is?). The Cause now dictated my every action. By that time, I didn't care about my life nor anyone else's.

In the midst of my prison gang-banging career, I heard that my brother had dropped out of the prison gang. My big brother "M"—whom I had looked up to and idolized, the leader of my street gang and my inspiration for joining the gang in the first place—had walked away!

I felt betrayed and abandoned once again. My brother's choice to quit the gang caused deep resentment within me, mixed with hatred towards him that would last for many years.

After 20 years of living the insane life of a prison gang

member, I began to see things differently. I can't pinpoint the exact moment, but my perception of myself and of the lifestyle I was living began to change.

I started seeing my actions, my homies, and the Cause for what they really were. I came to realize how my poor decisions had buried me alive, and how I could have avoided a life of hardship if I'd only found my voice.

I thought, "If only I'd asked for help. If only I had accepted help from the well-meaning adults in my life, then I wouldn't be sitting in prison."

I thought, "If only I'd asked for help. If only I had accepted help from the well-meaning adults in my life, then I wouldn't be sitting in prison."

At 16, I felt unable to express all the pain, anger, and resentment that caused me to hate and not to trust everyone and everything, including myself. But after all these years, I finally had found my true self and let him out!

With all my new-found insight, I decided to take a leap of faith. I sought help from self-help groups and from other inmates who had changed their lives. By seeking the help I have long needed, I was able to process what I had been feeling and learned how to make wiser decisions.

I am now in my 34th year of incarceration and living a better life than I ever have. I can't help but consider all the time I wasted, all the destruction I have caused, all the lives I have ruined. Now I live every day of my life, trying to make amends for the two men who met death from my cold-blooded hands—innocent men who lost their lives as a result of my selfish immaturity and unacknowledged pain.

My hope is that young people who are struggling will read my story and find encouragement. For kids who are headed down the path that I took, I want this story to serve as a cautionary tale for change.

At 49 years old, I'm just now seeing the light. Please don't wait as long as I did to find your true self and to be able to express how you really feel—the pain you now hold inside.

My Hunger Strike
by Mark E. Vigil

On June 30, 2009, I decided to express my discontent with the excessively chronic delays plaguing the THU [Transitional Housing Unit] program at Pelican Bay State Prison in order for an inmate to earn his way out of that lock-up. The process had become so backed up with people waiting to leave C12 (SHU) that the waiting list exceeded double digits.

Since usually only one person can leave the block at any given time, I gradually realized that it could conceivably take me another year—or more—to see any kind of actual daylight for me alone.

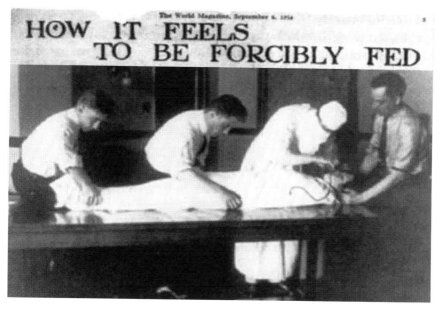

I greatly objected to the way I and most people in the program were led to believe one thing but would find that the reality offered quite a different outcome (in particular, Rule 3378.1 of Title 15 which clearly states that our stay in C12 or the THU program must not exceed one year). The reality for most of us is that that year comes and goes while we remain glued to those bunks in the SHU.

[Editor's Note: Thank goodness, the Federal government and some state governments are presently working to prohibit that kind of isolation that usually extends well beyond a year (when even one year is too much)—based upon the research that shows the deleterious effects of protracted isolation].

Given the arbitrariness of the promise of being released from solitary confinement after one follows the prescribed steps to achieve that aim, I opted to protest the system's prolonged delaying tactics by not eating my daily meals. Hunger strikes are a fairly common practice that inmates use against the prison administration to protest whatever grievances they may have. It's a non-violent means that many use to resolve an issue.

I was not seeking to break my "keepers," many of whom could care less about our concerns, but I wanted to achieve a personal victory—a stand I could take on principle.

Most inmates/convicts don't really favor using this kind of practice for the reason that it does harm only to themselves but not to their keepers. It seemed obvious to me that no one in his right mind would want to do any harm to themselves—myself included. It was, nevertheless, something I had to consider seriously.

I did not want to do anything that would ruin my chances of continuing my involvement in a program that was offering potentially positive outcomes. I also did not want to be labeled a program failure. Nevertheless, I decided that a hunger strike would be the best way to make my point without getting booted—what I thought would be a thoughtful alternative to any other action I might have pursued.

I was not seeking to break my "keepers," many of whom could care less about our concerns, but I wanted to achieve a personal victory—a stand I could take on principle.

It is true that my efforts were merely symbolic, but I am not against using symbolic methods to prove my point. I felt this was my best alternative, especially after I had tried the now-defunct 602 process–which is basically a waste of time and effort because the system generally denies the vast majority of our appeals—even when we, unquestionably, are in the right!

Consequently, at the time, a hunger strike seemed the right way to attack the issue without further burying myself in this place of isolation. Initially, I was told by prison staff that my efforts were pointless (even childlike or those of a spoiled child) but as I told them, it's not they who must sit inside these cells and deal with all the b—s— that keeps the program running at a snail's pace. So while I understood their point of view, to me the right thing to do was to take a stand (childlike or not). After all, to do nothing would only net me the same results that I'd already experienced for some 15 months in my hellhole!

There was just too much "nothing" going on within these nightmarish confines. Hell, I had spent the last 18 years of my life fermenting and aging inside this place without doing anything. But each year during this time, I was repeatedly told my only real option was to debrief.

[Editor's Note: a step that must be taken to convince prison officials that an inmate has truly reformed and wants to escape from his earlier involvement in gang activity and crime (separating himself–inside and outside of prison–from his previous life of crime in order to evolve into a person who can eventually be given that second chance once parole is approved].

Once I committed to and began that lengthy and rather arduous process, I believed the system should have done its part based upon its own promises—to move me forward in the program which would at length release me into the world I had missed out on for so long—a commitment which I felt I truly deserved. When this did not happen, I chose to do a hunger strike.

On the first day of my strike, the staff reacted in disbelief (as though we aren't supposed to behave in such a manner), but I reassured them that it was not to be taken personally but merely my way of making it known that I was frustrated with the program.

On the second day, they came to search my cell to see if I or my cellmate (who did not participate in this civil act of disobedience) had any store or canteen in our cell. They even threatened to feed my cellie in the holding cages outside the pod to insure that he not share his food with me, but they opted not to follow through on that tactic when another inmate filed a 602 against that illegal move—they even gave my cellie my dinner tray to get me to eat but I rejected it straight out!

However, on the third day, after coming off the yard, I was finally removed from my cell and placed in a holding cell (minus any personal belongs which would have included my reading and writing materials and hygiene products) and was told I would have to stay there until I decided to end my hunger strike.

That response was another questionable move on the part of

the staff because they are not supposed to remove me from my cell to monitor my eating habits (since it is possible for medical staff to simply check my vitals to determine whether I am eating or not). Thus placing me in the cage was merely done as a means to break me and to play the obvious psychological card which, perhaps unfortunately, worked because I ultimately opted not to proceed with the strike out of fear that I might lose my place in the program, an act which would have been counter-productive and not at all close to what I was trying to achieve.

So I returned to my cell (now fully aware of the consequences and extent to which my keepers would go to keep me from bucking the system). However, I promised myself then that I would not rule out another attempt at getting my point across, especially because I believed I was being wronged by their deliberately denying me the rights to which I was entitled from Title 15—the opportunity to exit that notorious and dreaded isolation unit at Pelican Bay called the SHU (Security Housing Unit).

Interestingly enough, during my appeal process, a sergeant was sent down to see me in an attempt to get me to withdraw my appeal, a filing which was meant to move the process forward along an acceptable timeline—he had used every method in the book to persuade me. When he failed at everything he tried, he came right out and threatened me with being labeled a program failure (which was totally inappropriate and rather frightening) because all I was doing was exercising my right to appeal their chronic delays.

Furthermore, when my appeal was finally heard, the sergeant in question was so frustrated by the hearing procedures that he stormed out of the proceedings. It became apparent to me that his sole role in all this was to coerce me into withdrawing my grievance, but he had failed at that. I learned from this that there existed and still exists little room to maneuver within legal channels– measures that take time to put together and that often bare little fruit.

But I also learned that civil disobedience has its place, is worth the while, and can and often does produce meaningful results—lessons for us all.

I am not in the SHU anymore and will never be again!

The above is a small testament which demonstrates the extent of my journey and what it took to arrive at the point where I am today (ready for my Parole Hearing and an eventual parole date).

I did eventually leave the SHU in December of that year and finally made it to the THU where I was put in limbo once again while the Powers-That-Be decided what the fates of those SHU inmates would be.

In 2010, the entire THU program was shut down in Pelican Bay and transferred to Kern Valley State Prison where I would do another 14 months—undertaking a process that would insure prison staff that my change was sincere.

Since that time, I have explored and become an active part in every kind of program that would help me grow. As a result, I can honestly claim that the problems I once faced and even created are no longer and will never again be part of the person I have become. It is because of my ability to recognize my past wrongs and because of my genuine and sincere willingness and eagerness to change, that I am ready for my second chance.

I am a better person now, ready for the world to accept who I am—the new me.

Juvenile Offenders: From Big Wheels to the Big House

Editor's Note:

The SHU at Pelican Bay State Prison in Northern California (near the Oregon border) was designed as a super-maximum security prison. It was, in fact, intended "to minimize human interaction. The windowless, 7.6-feet-by-11.6 -feet cells were built to face concrete walls. Doors opened and closed electronically. Correction officers spoke to the inmates through intercoms."

What were the expected results of such incarceration—a confinement which, at best, was meant only to be used for short periods of time and for only the worst of the worst persons who were too dangerous ever to interact with others (though even for such persons, the use of this kind of facility is questionable). Certainly, the results have been counter-productive.

Due to the SHUs (shall we say) overzealous employment of harsh and heartless tactics, it has caused many formerly sane inmates to suffer from various forms of short- and long-term insanity.

A case was filed in 2012 (now working its way up to the U. S. Supreme Court) to redress the grievances of those who have become victims of the SHU. Some have been left, for as many as 28 years, in solitary confinement, having been further victimized by being denied their rights guaranteed by the Eight Amendment.

Many of those who found themselves in the SHU had been convicted of very serious crimes (which included murder) but there are also many who had simply been identified as gang members (inside or outside of prison), for whom solitary was considered a good thing to keep them separated from the rest of the prison population. Really? What kind of justification is that?!

These are people who cannot receive personal phone calls or even receive simple personal contact (like a hug) by those who have been allowed, during certain designated times, to visit them. Even guards are expected to limit any kind of contact with them—rarely touching or speaking with them.

For those who have been incarcerated in this way, they have lost connection with reality and lose the humanity within themselves. How in the world can we then expect them to reintegrate successfully into society once they are eventually released from their prison walls?

One SHU inmate was observed as speaking to family pictures placed on the walls of his cell, hoping to hold on to a small bit of reality and with the hope of someday being able to hold and hug one of those friends or relatives. Another, who was formerly housed in this dungeon-like hole, has been quoted as saying, "It was a concrete tomb!"

Incidentally and perhaps coincidentally, President Obama is currently advancing ways not only to reduce maximum minimums, particularly for victimless and low-level crimes, but he is also actively pursuing a path to re-integrate former prisoners (in productive ways) into their respective communities.

One way, in particular, is the Ban-the-Box Initiative which would remove the "Have you been convicted of a felony?" question on employment applications. In that way, the formerly incarcerated have the opportunity to demonstrate who they are (offering supportive letters of recommendation along with proof of in-prison training that has often led to certifications and degrees) before the eventual and dreaded background question is asked during a subsequent interview. Statistics have demonstrated that when this process is utilized, the newly released applicants have a much better chance of being hired and becoming valued as an employee of the companies for which they work and, ultimately, as a contributor to (not a detractor from) society.

Editor: Rosemary Jenkins

□ In Memoriam □

Johnny Martinez passed away far too young. He had been released from prison for only five months before his passing in March of 2018. He leaves behind a child who will have to grow up without him. I wish he had had more of a chance to make his mark on society and on his family – something he had wanted so badly to do.

by Rosemary Jenkins

Turning a New Leaf in Prison
by Johnny Martinez

At the age of 16, while committing a robbery, I murdered Reno Koncz, a Hungarian immigrant who was just trying to make an honest living for himself and his family in this country. I was arrested the following day. Due to the serious nature of my crime, the court found me suitable to be tried as an adult. A jury of 12 found me guilty of first degree murder, and I was sentenced to 29 years to life in prison.

Today, I am 40 years old and have spent the last 24 years of my life in a prison cell, contemplating my past actions and why I committed this callous crime. How could I have taken the life of an innocent human being?

It was easy for me to live in denial by blaming alcohol, drugs, and other people for my crimes. However, facing the truth by searching for the answers within me was an entirely different matter.

Many years would pass before I fully accepted responsibility for taking Mr. Koncz's life. Accepting responsibility meant developing remorse and empathy, not only for Mr. Koncz and his family, but for every other innocent life that became the collateral damage of my careless and self-centered actions.

I came from a pretty good home. My mother and grandparents raised me as an only child. They did not raise me to be a killer. I never knew my real father, which always left a void in my life. My family understood this and did the best they could to make up for my father's absence.

As much as they tried—try though they might—they could never make up for the deep sense of loss and abandonment I felt because my father was not a part of my life.

Deep down, I longed to know my real dad. I longed to know who he was, to be loved by him, and to be taught what it meant to be a man.

When I was a child, I was molested by a childhood friend, and later by a distant cousin. The experience left me confused and ashamed. I didn't know how to express those feelings, so I didn't talk about it—something that caused more harm than it did good.

Being an only child, I was spoiled and always allowed to get away with every form of negative behavior. Thus, without accountability or proper guidance, I gravitated toward negative influences in search of the father figure I always wanted, and the brothers I felt were missing from my life.

I found the father figure and brotherhood I was seeking in a group of street thugs. Eventually, I joined a gang and began using drugs. The first drug I used was marijuana, followed later by heavier drugs such as cocaine and PCP.

At first, I used drugs simply to fit in with my friends and not to be "the odd kid out." In those
days, I would do just about anything to be accepted and belong to my gang.

As time went on, I realized that when I was high, I didn't feel the underlying emotional pain I had been suppressing from having been abandoned by my father, or the feelings of anger and rejection I felt from other childhood friends who had pushed me away, or the feelings of guilt and shame that I harbored from being molested. I didn't know how to express those feelings, so, at the time, it was hard for me to trust people.

As my addiction progressed, I started selling drugs to support my habit and carrying a gun for protection. I'd recently been shot, so I believed having a gun would protect me from robbers and rival gang members.

By the time I was 16, I already had a child and another on the way. Unfortunately, not even the realities of parenthood could slow me down. I was too young and too reckless.

At the time, if someone were to ask me who I love most in the world, I would have answered, "My parents, my girlfriend, and my baby." However, my actions told an entirely different story. At every turn, I chose the homies and my destructive lifestyle over my family.

In my mind, I believed that because I was hanging with an older crowd, using and selling drugs, having sex, and living life on my own terms, I believed that I knew everything there was to know about life!

I would soon find out how wrong I was! In the meantime, I still felt like an adult, like no one could tell me what to do. Back then, I defied every form of authority, including my parents.

Though I was making what I thought were adult decisions, I certainly wasn't ready to face the consequences of those decisions, much less accept responsibility for them. I was irresponsible, reckless, and selfish, and refused to be held accountable to anybody.

When I entered prison, I played the role of a "tough guy." But that was only a mask. I was really afraid, lost, feeling hopeless, in denial about my crime, and looking for guidance.

The first place I turned for guidance was the veteran inmates. The old inmates embraced me and I became "one of the fellas." But it wasn't long before I was taking orders from the older homies. I'd become a follower—making my decisions based on what others thought of me and how I wanted to be perceived. This was the extent of my insecurities then.

Just like when I started hanging around gang members on the streets, I wanted to fit in with the crowd in prison. Even on the inside, I was still seeking that sense of brotherhood (a false brotherhood, I realized later) that led me to joining a gang in the first place.

During my first week in prison, I was given the Southern Mexican prisoners' code of conduct. Though I never obeyed my own parents, in prison I found myself obeying other inmates. No longer could I live life on my own terms!

Eventually "homies" introduced me to heroin. And so began a new addiction. Over the next 12 years, my life continued to spiral out of control with drug use and violence. Throughout that time, I dragged the people who loved me the most through an emotional roller coaster of lies, betrayal, pain, grief, and sadness.

I used and manipulated anyone to support my habit—my mom, grandma, girlfriend—it didn't matter. I did anything to keep myself numb–anything to avoid acknowledging my conscience— that nagging, persistent voice in my head, saying "You killed someone! You deserve to be in prison! Start doing the right thing!"

I still had all of the unresolved core issues going on within me, those things which stemmed from my childhood. What I didn't realize is that at the center of my addiction was a vicious self- centeredness which kept me running from reality and reason for as long as I could.

But my day of reckoning would finally come. Ironically, I'm thankful for the Institutional Gang Investigation officers (IGI) who did their job in labeling me as a prison gang associate— an action which resulted in my receiving an indeterminate SHU-term (Security Housing Units). To me, being categorized an SHU was the means God used to really shake me up and bring me to my knees!

My options were clear: Either go to Pelican Bay SHU and spend the rest of my life playing the "tough guy" role and living the façade or turn over a new leaf and get right with myself, my family, and God.

After much hard work and self-examination, I eventually came to understand the importance of making amends to my victim, to his family, and to all the people I had harmed while living a violent and reckless lifestyle.

Unfortunately, it took getting a life sentence and many harsh lessons in prison for me to change my ways. I pray that what occurred in my life doesn't happen to anyone who reads this article.

I didn't change on my own. Few people ever do. I had to want it, and once I began to seek change, I found there were people who had been willing to help me all along.

I've shared this portion of my life to send a message to anyone
who is listening, to those who are looking for a way out and a better way of living. No matter who you are, what you've been through, what you've done, or where you are–know that there is hope. Know that there are people who care.

Know that you are valued, and that with effort–healing and change are possible. The question is, are you willing to embrace such a future?

An Inmate's Word to the Wise
by Ronald Patterson

I'm Ronald, but the Streets know me as "Duke." These days I'm called Brother Shabazz, due to my Muslim faith.

I was born in South Central Los Angeles, raised in the Pueblo Projects, home of the Notorius 52 Bishop Blood Gang.

Though we lived in the city, my mom (born in Alabama in 1929) and dad (born in Mississippi in 1916) instilled their Southern values, traditions, and beliefs in us. Neither parent had a criminal background. When I was only 6 months old, however, my parents divorced (I was the youngest of all the siblings). My mother raised me and my siblings in a loving home with strict Christian values.

We were on welfare, yet my mom was able to raise other people's children in her home, while my dad worked for Lockheed Aircraft, from which he retired in 1980 after 35 years.

Ironically, the year 1980 would also be the year my life changed forever, for this was the year I came to prison at age 16.

From a young age, my surroundings were limited to certain

types of people, places, and things. My associations outside my home began to shape my beliefs, so I adjusted my behavior accordingly. As a result of allowing negative influences to dictate my life, I disobeyed my parents and messed up in school.

Although always considered "from my Hood," I did not officially start gangbanging until I went to prison. But long before getting locked up, I began experimenting with drugs, drinking, sex (at age 11), fighting, gambling, etc. I adopted the lingo, mannerisms, and fashion that allowed me to fit in with criminals, gang members, hustlers, dealers, pimps, and players. All of these people embraced me and accepted me as one of their own.

My friends and I were fascinated with players, hustlers, gamblers, dealers, and gangsters because they played by their own rules, despite the law. Ignorantly, we admired and emulated them and would eventually turn into monsters who killed people and destroyed our community.

When it came to crime and mischief, if you can name it, I've done it or knew someone who did. I coveted the objects and trappings of what represented success in "The Life"–clothes, money jewelry, guns. My friends and I were fascinated with players, hustlers, gamblers, dealers, and gangsters because they played by their own rules, despite the law. Ignorantly, we admired and emulated them and would eventually turn into monsters who killed people and destroyed our community.

Lack of vision and hope caused me to be more susceptible to the destructive codes of the streets. So, abandoning my parents' teachings, I embarked on a criminal journey that resulted in my taking someone's life.

I couldn't see nor understand how my way of thinking and behavior was impeding my intellectual and spiritual growth. I began to accept the negative, destructive aspects of my environment as normal, adopting these rules and conditions for survival and success, while applying them to all aspects of my life. Rules such as "The G-Code"–don't run, don't back down, get money, power and respect at all costs. By the time I committed my crime, those "values" had been instilled in me at that young age–they had become embedded in my personality, character, and conduct.

On August 10, 1980, I went to the store to cash my Summer Youth check. Once there, the owner kicked me out because he remembered that I used to steal from his store and from the delivery trucks that serviced it. I was no longer into petty theft (and was then a part-time student, dealer, hustler, gambler, who had moved on and up to "bigger and better things"), so the owner refused my entry.

I returned home, gave the check to my Mom and returned to the store with a friend. Without my knowledge, someone had just robbed one of the employees. The owner and employee approached me and accused me of the robbery. I denied the accusation, and we began to argue. The owner told his employee (a 21-year-old boxer), "You know what to do to him." The employee, in turn, said, "The next time I see you, you better have something." I later learned that he had secured a knife to stab me and a gun to shoot me.

In survival mode and sensing danger, I ran to a homie's house, where my brother was. They had just gotten into a conflict with some Crips and wanted me to go with them to confront the rival gang. They gave me the gun. Still upset, I headed back to the store. I spotted the person who I had argued with and who'd threatened me earlier. I said, "What's happening?" He came towards me. I pulled out the gun and shot at him. He died from a gunshot to the neck, the bullet travelling to his heart.

Upon hearing what I did, my mother immediately took me and my brother to the police station and turned us in. I was tried, found guilty, and sentenced to adult prison.

Being the youngest person (16) in the California Prison System, not to mention one of the smallest (120 pounds soaking wet), my transition to prison life was not easy. Almost immediately, someone tried to rape me. Thankfully, I fought back and prevented it. That experience led to me becoming a full-fledged gang member with many years of rebellion and disciplinary problems ahead of me.

My prison lifestyle became a continuation of my life on the streets. I looked up to criminals and adopted their behavior and way of thinking—something which not only prevented me from seeing the error of my ways but also prevented my release. As a result, I have served 35 years on a 15 to life sentence—that's 23 years past my minimum release date! You can see how my mentality led to many extended years of incarceration!

It took many years, negative experiences, and numerous disciplinary reports before I finally began to reject the influences of the negativity around me. Change has been a constant struggle for me! I continue to develop my identity as a mature, responsible person. Now I attend self-help groups and apply principles—concepts like empathy and respect—that I had once disregarded as "soft" and "for suckers." The 12 Steps of Criminals and Gangmembers Anonymous (CGA) have become part of my everyday life. By living according to these principles, I've learned the value of positive living.

Today, I'm comfortable with the person I've become. The joy

and peace that comes from engaging in non-destructive behavior is worth more than all that I thought I was getting from criminal activity.

Now, I'm viewed as a positive role model (even in prison). And I want the chance to do something positive on the outside to help make up for all the destructiveness of my prior behaviors—the things I should have done before I allowed myself to be led astray!

For me, self-development means internalizing the teachings my parents tried to instill in me: Faith in God, respect for myself and others, and being a good man. I no longer fit into other people's view nor definition of who I am, but strive to be the best person I can be.

To struggling young people out there, I'd like to say that if you've made mistakes, you are not a monster, despite how others may make you feel. Many people called me a monster for killing someone at age 16. But I've changed. I'm not the scared, insecure, misguided little kid anymore. And if you're a young person reading this, just know that you can change. Please do so.

I'm guilty of a horrible crime, one that did not have to occur. My crime was the result of accepting faulty principles and destructive ideas. I was a product of my environment, but that doesn't diminish my guilt, nor the need for me to be held responsible for what I've done. I accept full responsibility for my crime.

Each new day brings the potential for success, as well as challenges. As you strive towards change, set goals and when things get tough, pray and keep trying. Believe in yourself.

Juvenile Offenders: From Big Wheels to the Big House

Overcoming My Pride
by Eved Romero

My story starts 29 years ago in a small town called Presa la Villita, just outside the city of Lazaro Cárdenas Michoacan, Mexico. I grew up there for most of my youth until I was 15. That's when my family and I came to the US. Though my father was living in Springfield, Tennessee, at the time, I stayed in California in search of a job to help provide for my family.

I was raised in a good household with good parents and siblings. I am the third-born of my parents' four children—two older sisters and my baby brother. Thus, I'm the oldest boy.

Although we were poor and didn't live in the best environment, my parents did the best they could in raising us. They taught us right from wrong and how normal, law-abiding people were supposed to behave. Nevertheless, as young kids, we were exposed to a lot of violence, drugs, and injustice and that framed our existence—the way we viewed the world.

Where I was from, people who were "soft" simply didn't make it, so I adapted to my situation. I put on a mask to guard my true self—the mask I would wear for many years, a mask of toughness, heartlessness, and ruthlessness.

I'm from a place where police and law enforcement were rarely seen. In fact, crime was so high that we used to joke that the law might as well not even exist. Everybody took the law into their own hands and lived according to the rule that stated that a man should do what he has to do to provide for and protect his family.

That meant if a person had to rob, steal, sell drugs, or even kill to survive it was okay, as long as you didn't do it to the wrong person (someone who would retaliate). We all knew it was wrong, but we justified our actions by saying that we didn't have any other choice. It was what we *had* to do to survive.

I remind myself that in my early years, I was a good kid. I listened to my parents and stayed out of trouble. Despite what should have been a good foundation, however, my criminal behavior began when I was 7 or 8. That's when my cultural environment—the people, places, and things in my life—began to influence my conduct in a negative way.

As I mentioned earlier, my family was poor, so my brother and sisters would get teased by the other kids because we didn't have as much money or as many clothes as they did. Once, when I was about 8 or 9, an older kid made fun of my little brother for being poor. That incident caused a lot of resentment within me. I felt helpless, vulnerable, and angry.

Being teased and seeing my siblings teased gave me the motivation to survive their tauntings, to prove to everyone who put me down that I too could have what they had. It was a catalyst for what I became, but what I became was a completely different person, almost unrecognizable from the good kid I had been and had been taught to be.

Where I was from, people who were "soft" simply didn't make it, so I adapted to my situation. I put on a mask to guard my true self—the mask I would wear for many years, a mask of toughness, heartlessness, and ruthlessness. Out of fear and insecurity, I created a new persona that would allow me to do what I had to do to provide for my family and protect it. I started stealing and selling drugs, and my behavior progressed until I became involved in taking someone's life.

I was scared, but I gave in to peer pressure from the people and circumstances that surrounded me. I was dared to steal money from my own uncle. I remember being so frightened and insecure, but I just had to do it, just to prove myself and fit in with the crowd and earn that all - important RESPECT.

Once my "homies" saw that I was willing to go to extremes, I started gaining that respect, and the respect I got from my peers felt good. It gave me a sense of gratification. Soon, though, all the money that I was making from my "ill-gotten gains" was not enough (sort of the way people need more and more drugs to get that same high). At the same time, all the attention I was getting fed my ego and made me even more self-confident and pleased with myself.

So, in order to continue feeding my ego, I felt that I had to do bigger, more impressive things. I went from stealing and selling drugs to getting involved with people who were planning and performing murders.

Looking back at my life, I now realize that my need to prove to people that I was more than just the poor kid and that my family was just as good as everyone else's allowed me to justify my actions to the point that I no longer felt the guilt that I should have.

But look at me now. I am in prison for the horrible crimes that I committed!

On April 25, 2005, I was arrested and accused of a murder-for-hire. I was 17 years old, facing life in prison, but all I could think of was how I was going to survive in that new environment awaiting me. On the one hand, I felt ashamed because I would no longer be able to provide for my family, yet, on the other hand, somehow I really didn't care. I was convicted of murder and sentenced to 25 years to life.

When I arrived at Salinas Valley State Prison, there was a war going on between the Mexican Southerners and the whites. I was young and afraid (all over again). I did not know what to expect. I was not a tough guy (in reality), but I had to develop a tough exterior in order to survive. It was my first time ever being locked up, but instinct told me not to let anyone know that I was afraid—that would be a death sentence for me!

So I did what I now realize what most people do when they first come to prison. My go-to response for every situation was violence (a reaction so common for most newbies). Developing that kind of defense mechanism brought me a lot of problems during my first few years of incarceration—including many write-ups for hurting people in my "new neighborhood." I had felt the need, once again, to prove to people that I was not a "punk."

After I began to gain the respect I craved from other prisoners of my race, I did what I was used to doing to support myself—I resorted to selling drugs (believe it or not, something very easy to do behind prison walls).

After about 4 years of being a prison "dope man," I got caught. As a result, I lost my visiting privileges for three years. I could not see or talk with my family during that entire time!

The time I spent in the "hole" as a result of all my absurd actions, did cause me to reflect— maybe this self-inflicted punishment was a blessing in disguise. When you are in the hole, you have a lot of time to think. And, boy, did I think!

I thought about the fact that, while trying to do what I thought I needed to do to provide for my family, I ended up separated from them. I thought about all the damage I'd caused and all the victims that I had created by doing what I thought was the "right" thing to do. Not one time when I was selling drugs did I stop to think about the effects of what I was doing nor did I think when I got involved with people doing murder-for-hire that we might get caught. Perhaps worst of all, I had given no thought about the pain and suffering the family and friends of my victims would go through.

The more I came to grips with what my actions were doing to me and to others, the more I became disgusted with myself for the way that I had been living. I was tired of going back and forth to the hole but I did not know how to change. But I did what had always been so hard for me to do: *I sought help!*

I looked at the people, now older and more experienced, who were now surrounding me who I knew had once lived the type of criminal life-style that I had lived. Over time, I had come to respect them. When I recognized how they once lived and how they had now changed their lives, I began to think that it was possible for me to change too. I often wondered why I had done a lot of the things that I did, but when I began attending self-help groups, I started to gain the necessary tools and insight to fully grasp the reasons for my behavior and how I could truly change for the better.

Having attended numerous self-help groups for the past few years, I must admit things for me haven't been easy. But it feels good to live my life without feeling like I have to hurt people or get over on others in order to get by. It also feels good to not have to pretend to be someone that I am not.

I soon began to take seriously the groups and courses I had signed up for. I began to gain an understanding of myself that I never thought possible. I have overcome my fears and insecurities and have finally found a purpose and meaning for my life. I know who I am, where I come from, where I am now and where I'm going.

I hope that my story helps anyone who is struggling with a destructive life-style to see the light. For those who want to take a different path and can't seem to find their way, a good place to start is taking a long, hard look *within* yourself. Then try to recognize how the *outside* pressures in our lives influence our behavior.

For me, I did eventually follow my own advice (because it was not and can never be too late). It is, therefore, up to you to consider your own options–but only once you truly know what you want out of life. I hope you decide to choose right over wrong.

I am thankful for the opportunity to share my story. If my words can be the wake-up call that causes someone to change, then I will have done my job of helping others avoid making the same mistakes that I did.

Juvenile Offenders: From Big Wheels to the Big House

Seeking Redemption
by Louie Gomez

My involvement in crime escalated very quickly from when I was a 12-year-old petty thief to when I became a teenaged, street-gang hoodlum almost overnight. One day while hanging out in the neighborhood, drinking and smoking, three homies and I decided to commit a robbery to make some easy money. Sadly, the robbery went awry and an innocent man was killed. A few hours later we were all  arrested and charged with murder. To make a long story short, we were convicted of second degree murder and sentenced to 15 years to life.

This was 1982; I was 16 years old.

Initially, it all seemed like one big adventure in a movie—cops and robbers. Reality didn't actually set in until my preliminary hearing (when evidence is presented against you and all the witnesses get to take the stand to testify against you) and then you start to realize that play-time is over. In the process, ironically, I got a lot of attention—something I had craved all my life—but not like that!

One of the witnesses that testified was the murdered victim's older brother who needed a translator. The district attorney began to ask him questions, such as when was the last time he saw his brother alive. After about the second or third question, he just broke down and began to cry as a very small child would do. Never once did he look at me with any hate or hostility—as I had expected. He just tried to cover his face with his hands and arms—perhaps out of embarrassment for showing a weakness. He just sat there, continuing to cry while looking so humble and meek.

I was a little disturbed because I'd never seen a grown man cry like that. I immediately turned around to gage the effect the brother's obvious emotional despair was having on my parents who were sitting right behind me. They certainly must have felt some sort of twisted blame for being the parents of such a wicked person, someone who could commit such a heinous act. I'll never forget my mother's and father's faces. They looked so sad and full of grief—mesmerized, it seemed, by the poor man whose brother had been murdered by their son.

I have never in my life felt so much guilt and shame. I realized then that I was a monster! I just wanted to dry up and crumble like a dead leaf and let the wind scatter me in all directions of the known and unknown worlds–to dissolve into nothingness. In that instant, if I could have taken it all back by replacing my life for the victim's, to bring him back, to bring him home, I would have done so without hesitation. I just wanted to yell at the top of my lungs, "I'M SO VERY SORRY, SO ASHAMED! I DIDN'T MEAN TO DO WHAT I DID! I AM STUPID! I DIDN'T THINK! I'M SORRY!" But I didn't have the courage.

In prison, I've played the bad guy, the victim, the revolutionary, and the good guy—nothing seems to be the perfect fit.

Fast forward, several decades later. Still behind bars, I'm a mature, middle-aged man of about 50 years–with many regrets and unresolved issues. I spin between two worlds of purpose and meaninglessness. In prison, I've played the bad guy, the victim, the revolutionary, and the good guy—nothing seems to be the perfect fit.

Maybe I am a little bit of everything or maybe I am nothing at all. I just know that I'm tired of playing. I have wasted thousands of hours being bored out of my wits—being around the same old people, the same old food, the same old rules—just thinking about the same old shit— thinking about how things were, were not, could have been, should have been. I have come to realize that if life has any meaning, then suffering and dying must also have meaning. Sometimes I see myself as a deep thinker yet at other times, I feel so shallow.

Recently, I began participating in self-help therapy groups. One of these groups is called Victim Awareness. It has helped me to see or perceive crime from the victims' perspective and to develop a better sense of empathy. It assumes, rightly or wrongly, that criminals lack a certain ability to connect with or relate to the feelings of other people—no matter how long they've been incarcerated.

In the group, I was asked to perform an exercise. I had to write an essay describing how I believe the victim felt the day of the crime, the day I robbed him and murdered him.

I wrote the following essay:

"In My Victim's Shoes"

It's a Tuesday. I'm walking home after a long day's work. I'm tired and hungry. I'm almost home. I wonder what my brother's doing right now.

Who's in that car driving by real slow? They're looking at me. Do I know them? I don't think so. They look like *cholos* (Hispanic street-gang members). I hope they don't mess with me–I'm almost home. My heart is starting to beat really fast. I try to keep up with the beats by walking faster. I'm almost home–I'll be alright. Oh no! The car is stopping by the curb in front of me.

Three *cholos* are getting out. They're walking my way. What do I do? What do they want? I hope they are just looking for someone else. Wait! One has something in his hands. It looks like a rifle, a gun. I think they are going to try to rob me. Many of my friends have been robbed by *cholos*. They almost got me one time, but I ran and got away. That was a long time before.

I'm starting to panic–my adrenalin is running. Should I run? I have a little money, but I can't afford to lose what I have. I worked very hard for my money. I need to pay bills, and I need to send some home to Mexico for my family who depends on me. Without me, they can't make it.

The *cholos* block my path. The one with the gun points it at me and starts yelling.

"Give me your *feria* (money)!"

"I don't have any," I say.

I keep moving forward. I'm almost home. I can make it. They are just little punks, but there are three of them. I don't think I can take them all at the same time, and one has a gun pointed at me, demanding money, yelling profanities. I turn to the right, but another *cholo* starts blocking my way and also starts yelling.

"Give up the money, *baboso* (slimy one)!"

And he pushes me. "I have no money," I say to him.

He begins to throw punches at my face, but I block them all. I have to keep moving before they shoot me or all jump on me. I'm more scared now. I have to keep moving. Should I run? Yes! I can run into that apartment building. People will come out. They know me there and will help me.

It's dark in the building. I can barely see anything. I hear a bang, like a fire-cracker. I instantly feel a kinda' funny, forceful impact just as a sharp pain hit my side. I don't know if I'm shot or just grazed. I just don't know–I really don't want to know. I can still stand and move though.

I turn and see the *cholo* with the gun; he's at the door. He is pointing the gun at my face, coming towards me, and demanding money. I grab the gun hard with both hands. If I can take it away, I can defend myself. Why doesn't anyone hear us?! Why doesn't anyone come out of the apartments?!

There is something wrong with me. It hurts inside. Here comes another one of those cholos through the door. I have to get the gun or they are going to kill me. The other cholo starts yelling.

"Let go, *pendejo* (stupid)!"

I ignore him and struggle harder to get the gun. I then feel two hard blows and a stinging sensation to my stomach. I pull even harder. I need the gun. The gun will scare them away.

Where is everybody? Why doesn't anyone come out to help or call the cops? I feel two more hard blows to my back–they hurt worse than the first two. They knock the air out of me. I feel like I'm suffocating. I immediately drop to the ground. I can't run or fight anymore. I'm terrified now. I have to give them my money before they hurt me some more. I pull out my wallet and hold it as high as I can and then yell.

"Here! Take my money! Here!"

One of them takes my wallet. Finally, all of the *cholos* run away.

Finally, it's over. They leave me alone but I can't breathe right. There is something seriously wrong with me. My lung is making a weird noise. I try to command my body to get up. They're gone now, so it's alright.

"Come on, breathe," but it does no good.

My heart is beating faster than ever now. I feel all wet. Is that my blood flooding the hard floor beneath me? I feel saturated. What is that wet, warm slush? But I don't really want to know. I can't breathe no matter how hard I try.

Oh, God! Don't let me die. It hurts so bad. I've never felt this much pain before. Please God, help me. I'm only 27. My family in Mexico needs me. They depend on the money I send. I worked so hard to come to this country to try and make a better life for my family. I have so many hopes, plans, and dreams. I want to see my children grow up and be happy. It can't end like this. This isn't fair!

Where's my brother? I hope the *cholos* don't get him too.

It's almost impossible to breathe now. I'm getting nauseous. I think I just threw up clots of blood. I'm getting very cold. Oh, God! Please forgive me for all the wrongs I've done. Please bless and protect all my family. I love them so very much. I'm so cold. I can't feel my body any more. Now I just want to let go.

I tried to be as sincere as possible in writing this vignette, trying to put myself in the victim's place, but for some reason it doesn't seem to be enough. I want to do more. It did get me thinking. In truth, I've never before put myself in the victim's place like this as I did in this story.

I mean, I've thought about it, but not like this.

Another group suggests that people, like me—people who do wrong to others–should make direct amends to the people they've victimized (unless doing so would injure them or others even more). So I decided the least I could do in that respect was to sit down and write a letter of apology to the victim's family. It began like this:

To My Victim's Family:

I don't quite know exactly how to start this letter, which has been so long overdue—33 years by now–without the fear of causing old and hurtful memories to resurface for you.

No matter how reluctant I may be or fearful of causing more harm, my conscience compels me to address your terrible tragedy–one that I had no right to cause.

In 1982, I was a sixteen year old, no good street punk. I had no respect for myself, and thus, I had no respect for other people. Yet, more than three decades later, I am nothing like the troubled kid, or hoodlum that I was then.

Your loved one was an innocent human being—someone I never knew on a personal level. I never knew his struggles in life or his responsibilities to his family. I did not know all the fine qualities that all of you loved about him and which made him so unique–a person that you will always miss so very much. I feel such guilt knowing that my actions left children without their father. I take full responsibility but I don't ask for nor deserve your forgiveness.

I acknowledge the despicable crime I committed against your family. I cheated all of you, but I especially cheated the late Mr. Hernandez by ending his life long before his time. No matter what I do or what is done to me, I can never bring him back nor reverse the chain of events that led to his death.

The best way that I can ever hope to redeem myself for my acts is to swear off all forms of violence and never hurt another human being again (in or out of prison)If given the chance someday, I hope to become a productive member of society, helping rather than hurting people.

The sorrow and regret that I feel I can't put into words. I simply cannot express strongly enough how very sorry I am for all the grief, pain, and loss that I have caused your family.

I don't know. It seems to me that no matter what I try to do in order to better myself or to make amends, it's just not good enough. Maybe it's more of an art than a science or maybe there is no redemption for murdering a human being. Still, I must make the effort and maintain hope. When I start to understand that I may never reach that place of redemption, I remember an old Chinese proverb: It is better to travel with hope than it is to arrive.

You know, it's funny, but I never used to think about other people's feelings, hopes, and dreams–I just didn't care. Not caring or thinking all the way through about the ultimate effect of my actions made it very easy for me to hurt others in the worst ways possible.

Now, after spending most of my life in prison and not likely to ever get out, I realize that that kind of indifference has been and is my greatest failure. I hope this column can show others the paths to avoid and the ones they should take.

Letter from Inside: Learning the Hard Way, Part I
by Anthony Andrew Ferguson

For the past 13 years, prison life has been the only life that I have known. It is sometimes difficult to see past the unending grind of daily life here and the constant indignity of

bearing the label of "felon" as a result of my crimes. But my incarceration did have a beginning and a cause.

I was raised by my mother and my grandmother in a very loving environment. They taught me all of the basic values that every involved, law-abiding citizen should live by. Because my mother had five children to raise, keeping track of everything we did was a difficult task. Fortunately for her, I was the only child who gave her any significant behavioral problems; thankfully, my grandmother was there for my mother to pick up the slack in raising me.

When I was four, my mom met my stepdad. Mom thought that a male presence in my life (I never knew my biological father) would give me a better chance at developing as a mature, responsible adult. And while my stepdad did make an attempt to impart what little he knew at the time about being a man, I was unreceptive to his attempts to connect with me. The values that he taught me — more from deed than from any conscious effort, such as the importance of having a strong work ethic — still resonate within me today.

But my stepdad's lack of parenting experience, coupled with a sense of being overwhelmed by the responsibilities of raising someone else's "problem child," made his attempt to take care of me inadequate to the task of keeping me on the straight path.

My mother and grandmother taught me to love God, respect others, and follow the rules. None of my immediate family members had ever been to prison or had ever been in any real legal trouble, so it was not my family that subjected me to the criminal or gang lifestyle. However, the worst aspect of my family life while growing up was my mother's alcoholism which caused many verbally violent arguments between her and my stepdad and affected me very much emotionally.

It wasn't until I ventured out during my late elementary and early middle school years that I really began to rebel and stray from the values that my mother and grandmother had instilled in me.

It wasn't until I ventured out during my late elementary and early middle school years that I really began to rebel and stray from the values that my mother and grandmother had instilled in me. During this time I was given a large amount of autonomy by my mother who had her hands full with raising four other children besides me. The allure of the world (that I encountered outside of my home and my desire to fit in with that world) led me to manipulate and take advantage of my mother's inability to supervise large portions of my life when I wasn't with her.

The more I was away from home and out playing in the streets, the more I was exposed to unwholesome values. The streets are where I learned to steal, vandalize, and sell drugs. Eventually I was running wild and being indoctrinated more from the streets than I was at home with a family that had no part in a criminal lifestyle. Thus, the streets became the primary source for acquiring my values. I gravitated toward what appealed to me the most, which was the instant gratification that I got from running the streets (as opposed to what I then viewed as a mundane, uneventful life at home).

As I got older and entered high school, I began smoking marijuana and drinking heavily, mostly because my friends were doing it. Also, my criminal behavior became more frequent and more destructive. Every chance I got, I stole everything from candy and money from peers' backpacks at school to cars and appliances from people's homes. I even joined a gang to fit in with the people I was trying to impress. The criminal lifestyle that I'd adopted continued unchecked until the day I committed the crime that landed me in prison.

On January 25, 2002, at age 17, I was arrested for the attempted murder (with a firearm) of three police officers. During a long, hard night of drinking and smoking weed and PCP, I went on a crime spree–stealing from stores, breaking into cars, and burglarizing businesses. Armed with a gun, but without common sense, I encountered a marked police car and thought it would be a good idea to shoot at the unoccupied vehicle as a prank. When I was arrested and informed of the charges I would be facing, what had seemed like a joke and a stunt that I could brag about to all of my friends the next day, turned into a real-life nightmare. I was 17 years old and facing life in prison for a dangerous, meaningless, and senseless prank.

Fortunately for everyone involved—the officers, their families, my family, myself, and the entire community—none of the officers were injured as a result of my actions. I eventually pled guilty to two counts of assault with a firearm on peace officers and sentenced to 34 years in prison [having pled down from the original 103-year proposed sentence].

Juvenile Offenders: From Big Wheels to the Big House

Letter from Inside: Learning the Hard Way, Part II
by Anthony Andrew Ferguson

At age 19, I entered New Folsom Prison. I didn't know what to expect, but I did know one thing: I was afraid and could barely hide my fear. The racial and regional politics; the hateful and degrading treatment from the guards; the constant lockdowns, and the endless violence took a great toll on my psyche. Having gone from doing whatever I  wanted (with all of the opportunities afforded by being free) to having my every decision (when to wake up, eat, sleep, come, leave, sit, stand, dress, undress) controlled by others, devastated me.

Before coming to prison, I used to think I was tough. However, prison quickly taught me how tough I wasn't! Because I've always been more comfortable living as an individual than as part of a crowd, I was often forced to defend myself against gang members who didn't like the fact that I wouldn't associate with them. Before coming to prison, I'd decided that the gang life wasn't for me and that I wouldn't spend my time incarcerated as a prison gang member. Thus, I was forced to become tougher in order to maintain my individuality in the face of constant attempts to recruit me into an even more criminal lifestyle than the one that landed me in prison.

I have learned a great deal from my prison experience. Early on, I made a decision to educate myself by reading relevant books which made me more conscious of the world around me. By seeking the knowledge that I'd consistently rejected before, I was able to grow intellectually, something which gave me a better understanding of my past and a foundation from which to build a better life.

It didn't take long for me to figure out that I didn't fit into the prison environment. The treacherous culture of the inmates and air of superiority among the guards made day-to-day interaction with others very difficult. Thus, I isolated myself as a coping mechanism. In other words, I became a "loner." Since I felt that I didn't have much in common with the people around me, I spent most of my time reading or writing, activities which kept me away from the drama that surrounded me.

However, while my self-isolation and preoccupation with books kept me (for the most part) out of trouble, my maturity level hadn't really changed much. My method of staying out of trouble was more a way of avoiding danger than any sort of genuine display of a change in my ways of thinking. As a result, I still harbored the same resentments and hostility towards authority; had the same drug and alcohol addiction; and the same criminal ways of thinking that led me to prison. The only real difference between me and the people I isolated myself from, was that I didn't revel in acts of violence.

It took me almost ten years to fully realize that if I was really going to change, I had to evaluate and challenge the mentality that allowed me to justify committing so many crimes.

It took me almost ten years to fully realize that if I was really going to change, I had to evaluate and challenge the mentality that allowed me to justify committing so many crimes. But despite a growing awareness of my problems, I still held onto the drugs and alcohol as well as to my old resentments toward authority. But through constant self-reflection, attending self-help groups, and seeking positive role models was I able to break free from my various addictions. I no longer value or rely upon criminal thinking, deception, or drugs and alcohol to cope with life. Nor do I feel the need to resist authority in order to feel powerful or validated, I am confident that by living an upright life (whether in prison or on the outside), I will have more peace, greater joy, prosperity, and personal fulfillment–those elements that my criminal lifestyle was unable to provide.

If I could go back and change the behavior that led me to prison, I would do so in a heartbeat. For kids who are struggling with the same issues that I struggled with growing up (the anger and self-esteem issues from not having a father and the need to be accepted by my peers), I would urge them to remember what really matters in life.

For kids who are fortunate enough to have family members who love them, they should know that the homeboys, the drug money, and the fast life will come and go. And when they go, they undoubtedly will leave behind negative consequences. The gang and criminal lifestyle may seem fun and even glamorous right now, but nothing good ever comes of it.

For those who think that their criminal lifestyle won't land them in prison, I can only say that I was the kid who thought that I would never go to prison—that I would never be shot, that no one close to me would ever die. I was wrong about all of those things.

I cannot truthfully say that I didn't have opportunities growing up. Many people tried to help me turn away from the lifestyle I was living. Unfortunately, I refused to listen or to accept their help. And I suffered greatly for my stubbornness.

Although I take full responsibility for my actions, I believe that many juvenile offenders would be better served by being offered alternatives to prison-time for their crimes. Providing youth offenders with an opportunity to be held accountable for their crimes in a meaningful way would go a long way toward preventing juveniles from re-offending. I definitely could have benefitted from a consequence other than prison time for my crimes.

But, as it turns out, prison has been the ultimate deterrent for me. My intense dislike for the prison environment has forced me to delve deeply into myself to gain a better understanding of who I am, of my motives, and of the potential consequences of my actions. My determination to stay out of prison and to keep others from coming to prison is a direct result of my experience in prison.

When I first came to prison, I felt hopeless. Though I didn't have a life sentence, a 34-year sentence at 19 years of age seemed no different from having life. I can honestly say that I've struggled through those years of hopelessness and can now see light at the end of the tunnel. And though I am still far from perfect, I take solace in the fact that I now have a sense of purpose and direction that motivates me to do better, think differently, and encourage others to do the same.

Juvenile Offenders: From Big Wheels to the Big House

Letter from Inside: An Apology for Past Action, Part III
by Anthony Andrew Ferguson

On January 25, 2002, I committed an assault with a fire arm on Santa Monica Police officers Richard Lewis, Scott Matsuda, and Danny Smart. For my actions, I was sentenced to 34 years in state prison. For years, I have sought a way to express my remorse to the officers for my crime against them.

As state law prohibits me from directly contacting them, I have decided to post this public apology as an acknowledgment of my wrongs against both the officers and the community-at- large.

Officers Richard Lewis, Scott Matsuda, and Danny Smart:

This letter is intended to express my sincerest apology for all

of the danger and suffering that my actions put you and your families through. No amount of words can adequately convey my regret and sorrow for how my crime has affected you, your family, friends, colleagues, and the community of Santa Monica as a whole.

I was a clueless and impulsive teenager who desperately wanted to fit in with the wrong crowds and knew nothing (and didn't care to know anything) about life. I blatantly disregarded all notions of right and wrong and failed to foresee the consequences of my actions.

I will not attempt to waste your time with "woe-is-me" sob stories about how I wasn't loved as a child, or about how "poverty made me do it." Such excuses neither justify my actions nor are they true. The fact is, I acted out of self-centered foolishness. For that reason, I do not seek your sympathy or your forgiveness. The goal is to acknowledge my offense against you (both as officers of the law and as people) and to express my commitment to living a productive, law-abiding life.

For what it's worth, I am ashamed of what I've done. Every day since my crime, I have tried to understand what really motivated me to grab a gun and shoot in your direction. After much reflection and self-examination, I have realized that my desire to fit in with a peer group, my enormous need for acceptance due to feelings of isolation and low self-esteem, and my willingness to receive such acceptance from the worse segments of society all helped shape my thinking. Back then, everything I did and every thought I had was a result of influences in my life and of the beliefs that I chose to adopt.

My family did not raise me to be a criminal. At a young age, I chose to become a criminal. And now I have chosen not to be one.

My family did not raise me to be a criminal. At a young age, I chose to become a criminal. And now I have chosen **not** to be one.

Today I live my life, trying to amend for my many faults. I try to make up for what I have done to you as well as to my own family and to everyone in the community who have suffered because of my past actions. To demonstrate my commitment to change, I have dedicated myself to ministering to others by working to help at-risk youth (like my former self) to turn away from drugs, gangs, and crime. In addition, I am an active participant in the Victims' Awareness Offenders' Program which draws attention to the impact of crime through the concept of Restorative Justice.

I understand that my current activities will not erase the past. No amount of good deeds and change-talk will change the fact that my actions were dangerous and reckless and caused you and your families harm. If, after reading this, you are still skeptical about my sincerity, please know that my commitment to change myself for the better will remain constant.

I will live every day with the intention of being responsible and productive and encouraging others to do the same. Regardless of whether I am ever released from prison, my obligation to you, my community, and my family is to contribute in a positive way–even if society does not change.

Never for one second have I questioned whether I deserved to go to prison for what I did. I deserved to go to prison as much as you deserve this apology.

I get it now. I have accepted and continue to accept responsibility for my crime. My hope is to communicate my genuine feelings of remorse to each of you.

From the bottom of my heart, I am sorry.

Sincerely yours,

Anthony A. Ferguson

How Do I Express Regret?
by Ronald Patterson

As I write to my beloved mother (my Beautiful Black Queen), I express many thoughts that I have contemplated over the years and yet did not have the courage to write. Here are some of those meditations:

"As always, you remain in my prayers, and I hope God will continue to bless, protect, and guide you. I also pray God will use my experience to spread my words to all the others who need to hear them. Though I have not always understood it, nor been able to explain it, I know there is a reason and purpose for my life and some day it will be revealed to me.

"I am ashamed to say to you that in the 35 years of my incarceration, rarely have I thought of how my actions not only led to my arrest and separation from you but how it also affected you and victimized you. To see your child violate your teachings and the laws of God, humanity, and society must have been and still is some of the most difficult tribulations you have had to encounter.

"I can only imagine the many tears and sleepless nights you have had, possibly wondering, "Where did I go wrong?" thinking of how you prayed for me, sacrificed and tried to teach me and guide me along the right path.

I am in prison, not because you failed as a parent, but because I failed to live up to your expectations as a son. I am in prison because of my own choices which you had no control over.

"I write this letter today to ask your forgiveness, for any pain my crime caused you and to release you from any guilt you may feel. I am in prison, not because you failed as a parent, but because I failed to live up to your expectations as a son. I am in prison because of my own choices which you had no control over.

"I am sure as a mother, nothing could have prepared you for the shock of seeing your child being handcuffed, shackled, tried and convicted, and led to a place so far away and, yet, unable to do anything to make things right. No parent should ever have to witness such scenes nor should she have to become a victim of her own child's doings. In my thoughtless, senseless act, I took the life of HR's mother's son, but, at the same time, took your son away from you.

"Never having had the chance to be a parent myself, I can only imagine the pain I caused both mothers. The shame I caused you in church and in the community because I chose a path that led to me being responsible for ending someone else's life.

"For a long time, I did not think of the sense of the loss, misery, and shame I caused you. I only thought of myself. For many years, I felt wronged and looked at myself as a victim too and that an injustice had been imposed upon me. One

Parole Board Commissioner even told me years ago that I was always feeling sorry for myself. What a self-centered person I was then.

I had not really thought about how I had victimized you with my actions–because you never once mentioned to me your own pain, loss, or suffering. Instead, you always showed me concern, compassion, strength, God's glory, and, especially, your unconditional love. I indulged myself, taking you for granted because of your awesome demonstration of non-judgmental love for me.

"Beloved Mother, if I do nothing else with this letter, I want to let you know that you taught me right. And it is totally because of my own actions, thinking, and choices that led to me being in prison today. I accept full responsibility for my crimes and criminal lifestyle.

"You have been blessed to be on earth over 85 years, so I ask that you don't waste any more energy blaming yourself in any way for my actions. Yet, I thank you for loving me despite my atrocious behavior. Thank you for standing by me these past 35 years of my incarceration and the 50 years of my life. Thanks for believing I can learn from my mistakes and change my life.

"And, Moms, even if you do not live to see me released from prison, rest assured, I will leave prison some day with a sense of purpose and determination—to become the son you can be proud of with plans to touch someone else's life in a positive way, just as you have touched so many in your attempt to serve God and others.

"Know that it is inside me now to try to make amends to everyone, anyone I have in any way wronged. That is why I finally wrote the mother of the young man I senselessly murdered in order to express my true remorse and regret—even though my expressions will in no way bring him back or make amends for the horrors I caused.

"So I want to share with you part of the letter that I wrote the mother of my victim.

"As I write this letter to you, I sincerely hope you find the grace to open it and accept it from me. We are strangers, yet we do know each other because I have affected your life in the most horrible way and have been the cause of the greatest pain imaginable.

"Even as I attempt to introduce myself, I am ashamed to do so because I don't feel worthy enough of the right to address you.

"For over 20 years, I have wanted to write to you, and I have struggled with the decision to do so. I have searched the very depth of my soul, and after each search, I still felt unworthy, lost, and anxious. As I write this letter, I am moved to tears, but even so, I feel I don't deserve the right to express my personal pain after the pain I have caused you. It has taken me so long to write because, initially, it was from selfish and cowardly reasons and out of plain ignorance.

"I was selfish about not writing to you as soon as I found myself incarcerated in San Quentin State Prison. On my mind was the fact that a fellow inmate had written to the mother of his victim, asking for forgiveness which she offered. I did not want to write to you asking the same thing because my motives would not have been pure. I would not have been thinking about you, then, but myself, motivated by trying to make myself feel better (and even hoping you too would write a letter on my behalf to the Parole Board—as the other man did). For me at that time, it would have been a truly selfish motive and so, despite my feelings, it would have been wrong to write to you and so I did not.

"I have chosen to write to you today, ready to say I am sorry for the pain I caused you and how much I regret your loss. The only thing I can offer you now, as a symbol of my sincerity, is to try to become a better person by helping others become aware of the true destructiveness of their actions. I want to encourage others to think first of the victims and their families before acting– but, if the wrongs have already been committed, to seek atonement by attempting to make
amends to all the victims.

"My own 17-year-old brother was murdered when I was 16, so I do know something of the pain and anger over such losses. Why I did not learn from that, then, is unexplainable and perhaps unforgiveable. I don't want to blame the environment I grew up in (though I know it was a factor) even though retaliatory murders were the way things were handled by all the people I
knew. I realized only later just how much I was affected by those who had the power to influence me.

"If by sharing with you how sorry I am and if by asking for your forgiveness causes my own death (through future pay-back), I am ready to accept whatever comes as a result. I know my words can do nothing to bring your son back, but I am no longer a coward. I have the courage now to apologize to you even though no apology can come close to what you need and deserve.

"I sincerely hope that the act of writing this letter is in no way considered disrespectful of you and your memories. In no way do I want my words to dishonor you or your son.

"I was at a workshop not long ago when I heard from a

mother of a murdered son. She talked about all the wounds that had been inflicted upon her and how that one dreadful, irrevocable act had forever shattered her life. I realized then the long-term consequences of all our actions, and I am so sorry for mine.

"But while I listened and saw the mother's tears, I also thought of you and my own mother and all the mothers who have lost children to such senseless violence. For the first time I understood that no circumstances can justify such dreadful crimes nor lessen the grief felt by all those related to the victim.

"You and your family members remain always in my prayers. If it is possible for me, I want to do something to honor your son and help you in some way. I know how that must sound, but truly I am sincere in all that I have said.

Sincerely,

Ronald Patterson

****

Editor's Note: And so this 48-year old man writes to each of us to offer some insight into what can transpire within the hearts and minds of those who have committed such crimes. This is not an anomaly among inmates who have had the time to mature and learn about what drove them to their actions. In fact, so many of them (and it is a surprisingly large number) now realize that they can be transformed and, for many, they are ready to be approved for parole and get that second chance that all of us deserve—to get that second chance to leave a positive mark behind.

--Rosemary Jenkins

My Struggle with Redemption
by Eric Ardoin

"Fear can hold you prisoner. Hope can set you free."
--Stephen King's *Rita Hayworth and Shawshank Redemption*

For years, I lived in denial about my lifestyle. Due largely to the nature of my destructive, arrogant actions, I believed I had built air-tight justifications for my crimes. Fact is, I just didn't want to take responsibility for what I had done to others–and how I, my family, and my victims have suffered for it. My background and family history could have provided the obvious excuse for everything that I said, did, and became. After all, my mother met my dad while he was locked up in Federal prison. Soon after meeting, they were married, and were divorced before I was 5 years old.

My mother did her best to raise me the right way, but the streets became my main teacher, and "the block" became my home.

When I was young, my family moved around a lot, so the only consistency I found was in the life of the streets. Eventually my mother began using drugs, so I turned for support and guidance to the chaos, violence, and destruction that surrounded me. Wherever we lived, crime was everywhere, and wherever I lived, the Crips had become a symbol of respect. I became for them what you'd call a stick-up kid. Put simply, I robbed people for a living.

I started off by robbing my "rival gang members"—my perceived enemies. But as time went on, my crimes progressed to "bigger and better" targets.

Eventually, I was arrested for robbing a check-cashing place with a firearm. I was charged with three robberies, arson, felony evading, and drug possession—in addition to special gun enhancements.

When all was said and done, I was convicted of one robbery and sentenced to 17 years in prison. I was 17 years old at that time.

It took me years to realize the amount of damage I had perpetrated upon the victims of my crimes—people who were innocent but just happened to be in the wrong place at the wrong time.

As I stated in the beginning, it took me years to realize the amount of damage I had perpetrated upon the victims of my crimes—people who were innocent but just happened to be in the wrong place at the wrong time. Many were affected psychologically and had to seek counseling afterwards. Such after-effects are things I never ever considered prior to committing my crimes.

My arrest devastated my family. My mother blamed herself for the way I became and started using even more drugs as a result of my behavior. As a consequence, she was badly injured in a car accident.

On top of that, my sister had really needed me by her side to help her raise her three kids. I helped her raise her two oldest kids–though I was just a kid myself. I felt an obligation to shield them from the violence and negativity we were surrounded with. But then, look what I did! I abandoned them—though it was not my intention—because of the acts I did that put me in prison, away from all of them.

Since I have been in prison, my sister caught a life sentence and one of her sons is now serving 6 years in prison as well. I see this outcome as a direct result of my committing my crime and going to prison. I also see how this kind of dysfunction goes on and on while the vicious cycle is rarely broken.

On the other hand, sometimes I think that, on the scale of things, not much was lost by my imprisonment. Looking back, my being locked up was exactly what the community needed– to be protected from my very own stupidity!

Eventually, my introduction to prison was pretty rough. I was 18 years old by that time and placed in a level 4 (Maximum Security) ward. I had a release date that was far in the future, so I joined a prison gang to get on. After all, I had been a gangbanger from a small town, so doing this same thing (so I thought) would make it easier to fit in.

But soon after my arrival, Blacks and Mexicans had a riot. Some Bloods had a problem with some Southern Mexicans. The Bloods never told the other Blacks about their conflict. As a Crip, I and other Blacks were in the dark about the dangers we were in.

Suddenly, one day when we were on the exercise yard, the Mexicans took off on all the Blacks. We were all caught off-guard by this surprise attack. As for my reaction, I didn't have time to be afraid or to think about anything else, besides fighting for my life.

I made sure I was not separated from my homies, to stay safe. I looked around the yard that day and saw another guy who had separated from our group and was being stabbed repeatedly. By
the time the chaos had subsided, 7 people had been stabbed or cut very badly and one guy was so severely injured that he

had to be air-lifted out of there by helicopter.

The incident affected my psyche so much that I called my family and told them that "*I may never come home!*"

Needless to say, the way I had grown up made me think that I had to have a chip on my shoulder and go along with the violence that surrounded me in prison. That I had to be tough in order to survive the prison environment is an understatement!

To make it, I had to become crazy, angry, and pay no mind to reason or to the excuses of other people for what they did or said. In other words, I learned how to conduct myself in a continuously hostile manner in a continuously hostile environment. I learned to be respectful, yet stern, and assertive, and I had to have discipline (but at the same time, I was scared).

I honestly believe that for a long while after my imprisonment began, I became a worse person because I had been incarcerated at such a young age. Since I was locked up as a teenager, it was difficult for me to see a future beyond prison. I had no long-term ambitions other than living in the turmoil of the moment. I became paranoid, believing that everyone had an ulterior motive and an angle to do wrong and to wrong me.

Thus, I was forced to learn how to be a "man" from people who didn't know how to be men themselves–people who taught me that fighting and stabbing people was normal behavior.

Unfortunately, when you're playing the political game in prison, you have to live by certain rules. And being the rebellious kid that I had always been, I would intentionally break those rules just to prove a point.

Although I was part of a big, so-called Crip "club," I never let anyone get close to me. For me, to let people know the real me–to allow them in–meant becoming vulnerable. In prison, you never want to show vulnerability, so I learned to become a good liar, to tell people what they wanted to hear, and *never* to let my true feelings show.

It didn't take long for me, though, to figure out that I had become caught up (before I knew it) in a cycle of drugs, alcohol, and violence. And as a result, I extended my sentence by 3 years!

Because I came to prison at such a young age, I've never had to deal with any real responsibilities. I have always had something or someone to fall back on, whether it was my family, my homeboys, or the State.

I have never been on my own or done anything to take care of myself without an element of crime behind it. I have a long road ahead before I am truly where I want to be as a son, brother, and especially as a person.

Though I have since left the gang life and no longer engage in prison politics, I still have much work to do to make myself a better person and to put my bad history behind me. I believe that co-dependency is my greatest problem. In short, I have become a co-dependent of the State when once I had been a co-dependent on my gang.

But I know that I am getting closer each day to achieving my goals because I am working hard to put my old ways behind me. I know I have hope, and I know that I am fortunate not to have been given a life sentence for all the things I have done.

The time I was given has, in fact, provided me the chance to reflect on my life and to begin the process of cultivating a better future. This thinking may sound odd (because people should not have to come to prison to find redemption), but that is what happened for me.

Maybe if I had had the good fortune of encountering better role models in my youth, my life would have gone in a different direction.

In the meantime, I hope my story can be used as a learning tool for how *not* to lead your life. The block, the street, carrying glocks—these paths are not the ones to follow and do not produce the kind of life that people really want to live. Prison is full of people who think like that. I see them everywhere I go in here, and their stories always end the same way. I understand now that I don't want that for me!

A trail of broken dreams is what can be found behind prison walls, but for some at least (and hopefully for me), there can be second chances! I like to think that there is another future waiting for me.

I am thankful for the opportunity to share my story with those concerned about this grievous issue.

Testimony of a Juvenile Offender Part I
by James B. Elrod

My name is James B. Elrod and I'm writing this as a juvenile offender in the sincere hope that in walking the reader through my story, I can shed light upon why I committed the horrendous crimes of which I am so guilty.

In NO way is this story an excuse for the choices I made. There are NO excuses for such acts—I really wish to stress that up front. I'm also writing this as part of the amends I wish to make for my own misdeeds with the hope that through sharing it, I can effectively intercede on behalf of young people (who are faced with childhood experiences similar to mine) to keep them from spiraling into self-destructive behavior and ultimately harming others.

My life began in a small town in East Texas. It was a culture that believed in the value of hard work, looking out for your neighbors, and seeking justice. But it was also a culture still struggling—even in the 1980s to overcome its Jim Crow past.

We lived a strict socially segregated way of life, something which was hard to understand for me as a child. It was normal to hear the most decent, respected, and hard-working adults in my community speak about the value of a man in one breath and refer to him as a "nigger" in the next. We all had Black friends in school, yet none of us were welcome in one another's homes, churches, or social events. There were clear class distinctions that could not be overcome—then and perhaps even now. That way of handling things was the norm. Even through my child's eyes, I could see that Reality was contrary to all the values our community claimed to embrace.

I would like to say that I grew up in a perfect home, but very few of us ever do. I can say that I was blessed with two parents who loved me and my siblings without question. They were there for us early on and worked hard to provide for us. We never went without and they instilled in us the solid principles of honesty, love of family, and hard work. They also really valued education. I credit them for creating a healthy foundation during my early childhood which, sadly, I would reject as a teen and young man but would later, through time and healing, return to as a grown man.

Unfortunately, I was also exposed to very destructive actions within my home. My mother was raised in a very violent home where my paternal grandfather severely beat my grandmother, mother, and my mother's siblings.

My mother in turn learned this same angry and violent behavior and raised us in a similar manner. She loved us but was clearly trapped in the same cycle of abuse and violence she'd experienced herself—blind to what she was passing on. Thus, violence became the norm in our home. She didn't use the more accepted discipline of spanking. Instead, her punishment was terrifying, filled with out-of-control screaming, slapping, hair-pulling, pushing, and shoe-swinging ferocity. Later, it became natural for us to adopt this same pattern of behavior for every aspect of our own lives.

Equally as destructive as the violence in my home was the fact that, from my earliest memories until I was around eleven or twelve, my brother (four years older than myself and the recipient of most of my mother's violent attention) sexually and physically abused me.

Equally as destructive as the violence in my home was the fact that, from my earliest memories until I was around eleven or twelve, my brother (four years older than myself and the recipient of most of my mother's violent attention) sexually and physically abused me.

I can't remember exactly when I came to understand that his actions were wrong but I know I was still pretty young. At that point, I began to resist and threatened to tell my parents but that's when he convinced me that it was my fault, that my parents would know that I was "weird" and a "faggot." The thought that my parents or anyone around me would think bad of me paralyzed me. And this manipulation of my childhood-thinking kept me locked into an abusive cycle for years.

My brother would also physically abuse me with kicks, punches, shoves, and hitting me with objects. For me, the emotional torture was worse than the physical. Any time I resisted, and his violence against me would not work, he would destroy something I loved—a favorite toy, a school award, trophies from Little League, and then even killing our family pets—and all the while threatening to tell our parents or my friends what a "faggot" I was. At 8, 9, 10 I couldn't see just how upside down that was, but I was too frightened to go to my parents for counsel and help.

It's hard to put into words how negatively this abuse impacted every aspect of my lie. It completely altered the way I saw and interacted with the world. I equate it to looking into a large mirror and then trying to see yourself in the same way after the mirror has been shattered.

I write this with the hindsight of an adult, now capable of seeing what all of this did to my life. I rarely felt "normal." I was convinced that that kind of treatment was my fault. I always felt as if I had something to hide. I felt different from my friends and worst of all, I took all of that fear, pain, and awkwardness and channeled it into anger and ultimately into violence. But it was through violence that I ended the abuse. A good thing–yet a bad thing—because it re-enforced the idea that using ugly behavior could solve my problems.

Prior to ending the abuse, I was introduced to drugs at the age of eight or nine. My friend had stolen some marijuana from his mother and asked me to smoke it with him. The abuse I was suffering made me very insecure and needy for friendship and acceptance. Although I didn't really desire to smoke anything or to know what getting "high" was all about, I said Yes. By 12 or 13, I was getting high every chance I got. By 14, I was doing every drug I came across—from LSD to smoking crack. The neighborhood hangout became my safe place where my low self- esteem was pushed into the background, a place where I was accepted and even "cool." My life soon revolved around nothing but getting high—a path that led me all the way to I.V. use.

At around 15, my mother caught my dad cheating on her, so

their marriage ended rather bitterly. I was incredibly hurt by and angry with my dad. I had always looked up to him and had felt closer to him than any other member of my family. But I used this betrayal on his part as validation that all the basic principles of being a good person (ones that he had taught me) were crap! I cursed him (in my mind) as a hypocrite. I was filled with self-pity and thus abandoned any hesitation about staying out of trouble.

I had by then committed petty crimes in order to feed my addiction, but after that, I escalated to serious burglaries of homes and businesses, sinking myself ever deeper into addiction. And the more crimes I committed, the more I rejected my conscience. It was all about ME and MY pain and MY anger.

Kids are naturally self-centered and I was no different. I was so selfish at that age—without really grasping the effect of what I was doing. I felt almost nothing at that time for all of the people I was hurting. I was so incredibly selfish and wrapped up in my own unresolved issues that I had no empathy for others!

When I turned 16, a friend of mine asked me to come stay with him in Bakersfield, California. I jumped at the chance to leave home. By then, my parents had had enough of my behavior and had begun to act indifferently toward me. They had no idea how to deal with me and did not fight me on my decision to leave. I did want to go, but since they did not resist, I also internalized their reaction as proof that they did not care about me. On the other hand, after all these years I still continue to believe that they viewed my leaving as a good opportunity for me to get a fresh start (even though it didn't work out that way)—I guess it is my way of rationalizing their indifference.

My first few months in California were great. I got a job and my friend's mother helped me get back into school (I had dropped out in Texas after a suspension for fighting). I felt good about my fresh start but I was a teenage drug addict by then, and it wasn't long before I got my hands on some meth and had a needle in my arm again.

My friends didn't like my doing drugs, but I didn't care. My addiction was stronger even than my need for their acceptance. I just found other "friends" who also used. Meth took my life. All I wanted was to get high and the more I used, the worse I became as an addict and as a person.

One of the friends I met (who also used) was Scott. He too was an addict. We had so much in common—youth, anger, parents we believed didn't care, broken homes. But what really connected me to him was (at that point in my life) how he was the only person I could confide in about my sexual abuse. He also shared with me that he had been through a similar experience with a relative. This one moment of honesty on our parts bonded us. Because of the neediness from my low self-esteem and from the bond we had created, I felt like there was nothing I wouldn't do for him.

A few months later, he needed some money to fix his van in addition to the money we always needed for dope. So we came up with a plan to rob the very place where I worked. The plan was, I would go in with a mask on and do the robbery while he and an acquaintance of ours would wait in the car. We did not realize at the time just how incredibly reckless and stupid the plan was. When I tried to enter the shop, the doors were locked. It was at that point that I knew I had to identify myself to get in. I could have run. I could have left, but between not wanting to disappoint the others and my selfish need to feed my addiction, I knocked on that door.

Testimony of a Juvenile Offender, Part 2
by James Elrod

A young woman I worked with, named Susan Perry, heard my voice and, trusting me, opened the door. I still had a mask on and upon seeing that, she screamed. Panicking myself, I

grabbed her by the shoulder, shoving her into the store and immediately shot her point blank. In the instant before the reverberation of that shot finished sounding, I knew I had just made the most horrendous choice of my life. Yet, I still ran to the back room and checked the safe, which was locked. I saw her purse on the desk, grabbed it, and ran out the back door.

Writing that down all these years later is devastating for me. Facing the ugly fact that I was so cowardly, sick and uncaring, and knowing the pain and shame I continue to experience is NOTHING COMPARED TO THE UNSPEAKABLE DAMAGE I CAUSED TO HER AND HER FAMILY. She had a five year old son whom I robbed of a lifetime of his mother's love–a lifetime of memories and experiences. . . . I did that!

I was arrested for murder on February 8, 1991, and by the

end of that year, I was justly convicted of first degree murder, second degree burglary, and a gun enhancement. Judge McGillivray could have sentenced me to life without the possibility of parole but chose instead to sentence me to 29 years to life. A sentence I knew I deserved for a crime for which I was (and am) so ashamed that I never pursued an appeal.

My story does not end there. I would compound these horrific choices with equally bad decisions as I began my incarceration. Upon my initial arrest, I went to Juvenile Hall and was quickly indoctrinated into the juvenile gang culture.

As a young white kid, I had no clue as to where I fit in at the Hall which claimed White Pride or Supreme White Power. Looking back on it now, the options were pretty pathetic, but in a system dominated by gang culture, all that most white kids (24 years ago) had to identify themselves with was race. And with my cultural background growing up in East Texas, it was easy to seize that racist identity as my new incarcerated identity. I took that attitude into the County Jail California Youth Authority and on into the adult prison system, getting into trouble every step of the way.

I was floundering in serious, unresolved issues and too scared and immature to seek help. Being so self-centered, all I could see was MY pain, MY fear, MY hopelessness over my sentence, and MY shame over MY past abuse and the senseless crime I had committed. All I saw was one big, black hole with no future and no hope.

Having no real concept of what honor really is, I resolved in my own twisted logic and rationalizations that I would be the toughest, "downest," and most loyal white gang member I could be.

112

In that mindset, I was desperate to do anything I could to repair my own personal sense of honor. Having no real concept of what honor really is, I resolved in my own twisted logic and rationalizations that I would be the toughest, "downest," and most loyal white gang member I could be. And so the cycle of doing anything I could to find acceptance through destructive, violent behavior, just as I had in my youth, perpetuated itself. Thus, by 22 I found myself in Pelican Bay SHU (Security Housing Unit—otherwise known as solitary confinement) around older and equally dysfunctional gang members.

The White gang members in the Aryan Brotherhood overlooked my past and spoke to me with pride about my willingness to represent our race behind bars. They viewed me as an asset to furthering their own violent, criminal ideology and agenda, and so I became genuinely proud of their acceptance.

Even at 22, I still wasn't mature enough to take an honest look outside of my own pain or to see the big picture with any clarity. I didn't question the ideology of the A.B. or the widespread use of violence in prison life. I was accepted . . . and that's all I cared about. So when I was ordered to kill Philipe Cruz for the A.B., I did so without any thought about the value of his life or the terrible pain I was to cause his family. We held no value for our own lives–apart from how we could ease our own pain through self-serving actions. In an existence where our own lives have no value, there's certainly no value for the next man's life.

Murdering Philipe Cruz spoke volumes about my lack of character and just how lost I was. I'd do anything to take these choices back, but that's not how life works. Some choices are forever and can never be made right. I live with these horrible decisions day in and day out—even now at age 41. I am sick at heart and filled with remorse over my actions and will take that knowledge and self-awareness to my grave.

I had become a member of the Aryan Brotherhood at the cost of Philipe Cruz's life and the immeasurable pain suffered by his family. I sat single-celled in the Pelican Bay SHU for over 16 more years in a small, windowless cell. I only saw my family through thick glass twice during that time. Equally hard, I only received two phone calls during those years to inform me of the deaths in my family. My nephew, Christopher was born, lived, and died during that time. I lost friends, one of my uncles, and all of my grandparents–never being able to be there for anyone because I sat in the SHU, "staying down for the cause." I chose to stay "loyal" to the A.B. whose purpose is racial hatred and criminality. All of this as I watched my own family members and real friends pass away–along with everything else good in my life.

All of those years alone in that cell afforded me the opportunity not only to mature but to take a deep look at my life, to finally reach a place where I could see the big picture and to understand the causative effects of how my childhood abuse directly led to my fear and anger which fueled my addiction, criminality, and violent behavior. And it's in really understanding why I ended up making the horrific decisions I made that actually gave me the power to finally take control of my life and break the destructive cycle that ruled my thinking and behavior.

I consider myself to be blessed by God in that I was able to see my life with an honest eye, no matter how painful it is to live with. I left the A.B. and debriefed in 2012-13, a choice I can tell you without hesitation that I am proud to have made. I made the concrete decision to stop running from my past; to stand up and deal with my character defects and addiction; to take advantage of every class, group, or service offered to us in bringing us to a better understanding and healing; to never again allow my pain to lead me to destructive behavior.

I have finally found the real meaning of honor while working every day to be the very best man the Lord created me to be. I'm living every day dedicated to helping others while at the same time trying to make amends for the lives I've destroyed and to all the countless people I've hurt.

As a juvenile offender, this was my road. With all of the trouble I got into after my conviction (I was sentenced to an additional 16 years for manslaughter), I don't know what the results of my upcoming Parole Board Hearing will be. But my sincere prayer is that my story gives the readers a little more insight to understand why and how such crimes can occur. I also wish to stress that SB 260 will, without question, save lives behind bars. If we can identify these young juvenile offenders, who may only see that same hopeless black hole that I and so many others did so long ago, we can bring real light to their lives with genuine hope for their future—before it is too late.

I am thankful for the opportunity to share my story with those concerned about this grievous issue.

My Journey to the Special Needs Yard
by Esteban Tabarez, Jr.

At the age of 21, I was convicted of a terrible crime and given a 26 years-to-life sentence. I had been a "good" kid, a role model, a straight-A student, attended church regularly, was a picture-perfect son, community leader, and outstanding citizen, and yet I was given this severe sentence.

How did this happen?! I grew up in a dysfunctional household. My dad was an alcoholic and drug-user and was hardly ever home. He stopped using for several years but, sadly, relapsed recently. My mother is a hard worker. She was a strict but loving parent but, at times, an extremely harsh disciplinarian. She often verbally and physically abused me. I tried to tolerate this treatment for myself but would not allow it for my siblings.

At the age of 8, I was sexually abused by my uncle, cousin, and a next-door neighbor—at different times but more than once by each. This left me confused. Later I realized I am a homosexual but still have no idea whether those early experiences had anything to do with who I am now.

Growing up, I bottled up my anger, hatred, resentment, and other negative feelings–becoming a loner without the ability to relate to others. Hiding my sexuality from my family (who simply would not understand it) and from many of my fellow students and friends took a big toll on me. At the time, it seemed like a smart move for me to turn to alcohol and eventually to other drugs (like marijuana and Ecstasy).

However, when you mix any drug with the psychiatric medications that I was prescribed (I have been diagnosed as bi-polar), it is inevitable that the outcome will prove dangerous. For me, the tragic consequence was my killing a new friend (RIP) during a time when I was not taking the proper medications (sometimes, as some of you may know, the side-effects can be worse than the "cure"). I actually called the police on myself after my terrible act and was soon arrested.

I was charged with murder and booked into the Los Angeles County Jail. I was placed in a psychiatric ward—I never would have made it in General Population. The experience was my first time in prison and I did not know what to expect (except I was very scared). I was repeatedly stripped naked (something I dreaded due to my sexuality) each time I went to and from court. I was yelled at all the time and felt intimidated and frightened. I often felt suicidal and sometimes tried to end my life.

I spent two long years appearing in the San Fernando Courthouse and then returning each time to jail. After I was convicted, I was sent to prison. At first, fellow inmates and guards were friendly and helpful to me (but I soon realized they were only trying to size me up). Many inmates were trying to figure out how they could take advantage of me, to extort from me, and use me for sex.

Being gay on the outside is hard but is even harden on the inside. Many inmates or even guards do not accept or tolerate you—many automatically believe you are in jail because you must be a sex offender due to your sexuality.

I was placed in the Sensitive Needs Yard (SNY) due to my "alternative" lifestyle. Being gay on the outside is hard but is even harden on the inside. Many inmates or even guards do not accept or tolerate you—many automatically believe you are in jail because you must be a sex offender due to your sexuality.

The prison where I now reside used to house the worst of the worst and, therefore, conditions continue to be exceedingly harsh. Food portions are small, medical services are frequently inadequate, heating during cold nights is usually turned off. Correctional officers encourage fights and, believe it or not, sometimes (through their constant taunts) even urge suicide attempts through their constant taunting.

For me, being imprisoned has not helped me and I don't feel that I am currently on the road to rehabilitation. For me, each new day is merely another day I have survived. I have tried to take classes and make other self-improvements but so far it has been far too difficult for me to succeed because of how hard it is to concentrate and focus and be diligent about those efforts.

My life was destroyed by drugs and alcohol. Not taking my

meds intermittently certainly was a contributing factor to the person I became.

I have learned that drugs and alcohol are a temporary solution to the many pressures and sadnesses a person feels. Masking your feelings about who you are and what you think and believe is not going to achieve anything positive either. If you have experienced abuse (sexual, verbal, or physical), seek help—it is really out there to be taken for the asking. I have learned one big thing since I arrived at prison, Love yourself because no one will love you as much as you can love you, and if you do not love yourself first, you cannot help yourself or others.

This is my journey but it does not have to be yours and the story is not over—perhaps it is only the beginning!

Barrio Stardom
by Joey Vasquez

For almost two decades, I've been confined to a cold, dark, and gloomy prison cell as I pay my pound of flesh and soul for the choices I made as a youth.

I currently reside in a facility located on the outskirts of a rural California town, a facility designed to rectify the failures of society. But, instead of rectifying Society's ills, my residence is nothing more than a graveyard of broken lives and fading dreams.

As I reflect upon the dark parts of my life, it's taken a large

amount of strength for me to muster the courage to share my story and message with you. I share this message because I care deeply for you and don't want to see you follow in my footsteps and down a path of self-destruction.

You see, I'm what they call a *barrio* (neighborhood) kid. I grew up in the ghetto of a city we call Longo and raised by my *abuelitos* (my grandparents). They loved and cared for me and wanted only the best in life for their *hijo* (son). My *abuelitos* were first-generation Mexican-Americans who believed in the virtues of hard work, education, and struggle to realize one's dreams—in a society where brown-skinned people have to work twice as hard to succeed.

My *abuelitos*'s message sounded good, but my idea of success was different from theirs. For me, the *veteranos* (older homeboys) in the *barrio* (neighborhood) held the keys to the type of life I wanted. I idolized and looked up to the *veteranos* because they possessed what I thought was respect, loyalty, and honor.

I followed their example because I honestly believed that I was destined for a life of "*barrio* stardom." Being a hurt kid who felt abandoned by my parents, I thought I had to prove myself to others for my self-worth. And becoming a *barrio* star seemed like the best way to prove my self-worth.

By proving myself in the *barrio*, I thought that I would be empowered, respected, and feared—that way no one could ever hurt me emotionally as my parents had. My parents were themselves caught in a web of criminal addiction. My father spent most of his life in prison and was absent a lot during my childhood.

While my mom was constantly struggling to support my younger siblings, she was a slave to the game of selling drugs which she must have believed was the best way to support her family. All of this caused me to develop deep resentment toward my parents because I felt alone, confused, rejected, and abandoned.

Every child deserves to have parents who love and support them—parents who raise them to become productive citizens in a society where the odds are often stacked against them!

Growing up, I didn't know how to express what I felt inside, so I learned to suppress my emotions and used violence to demonstrate my disregard for others, which was only a mask to hide my internal pain.

Being a hurt kid who felt abandoned by my parents, I thought I had to prove myself to others for my self-worth. And becoming a barrio star seemed like the best way to prove my self-worth.

It was in grade school when my life took the turn which would eventually become a nightmare. During this period of my life, I began to learn the unwritten rules of the streets and picked up "game" from my *tios* (uncles), who were from the *barrio*. They were the ones who laced me up with the tools necessary to survive on the mean streets of a city where racial tension between Mexicans and Blacks would eventually erupt into an unending street war which destroyed countless lives on both sides.

I, along with other kids from the Eastside of Long Beach, had strong family ties to the *barrio* and wanted to fight in the war, but was too young to take the vow of an "Eastsider," so we formed our own crew at school, known as the *Lokitos* (crazies) and began emulating the broader, more violent patterns we witnessed in the *barrio*.

However, my time as a *Lokito* was short-lived because a friend betrayed me by telling on us kids for a burglary we committed on school grounds. The betrayal of my "friend" confused me because in the *barrio* you learn not to tell, show weakness, or cooperate with the police. In short, you had to show *corazón* (heart) and be down for your homies.

I also felt ashamed because now my *abuelita* (grandmother) knew of the evil deeds I was doing behind her back. While she thought I was an angel, I was out committing crimes. I knew my actions hurt her, buy I refused to acknowledge it and blinded myself to her pain. At this stage in my adolescent life, everything was all about me!

After hanging around with my uncles and his homeboys for a while, the time had come for me to make a choice. I remember that summer night well. They asked me if I wanted into the *barrio* as I was already tagged with my uncles' moniker, "Sharkie," and didn't want to let them down.

With a simple "yes," the choice was made. There was no going back. I began a life of crime that led me to commit two execution-style, gang-related murders at the age of 16. Because I was too young to be executed, I was convicted and sentenced to life in prison without the possibility of parole!

Fortunately, I have a chance to regain my freedom one day. Through what I can only describe as a miracle, my case was overturned on a legal technicality and I was given a second chance at a "new" life.

This second chance has caused me to take an honest look at myself. I knew I had to change the beliefs I had that made me a cold-hearted gangster who didn't care about anyone, least of all myself.

Now I realize that, not only did I deprive my victims' families of happiness, peace, and love, but I hurt the very people who had tried to love me. *Mis abuelos* (my grandparents) loved me with all their hearts and tried to raise me the right way, but I didn't listen.

What hurts the most is that they have passed on without me being able to say, "I love you"–to offer them an apology for the harm and suffering I personally caused them and my victims.

Don't listen to the lies and the poison your so-called homeboys put in your head. I made that mistake and learned through time and experience that the very things I thought I was against—betrayal and deceit of those I love—I wound up doing myself. I hurt my family—I did wrong by them! In the gang and criminal lifestyle, everyone is expendable, including any one of us. The homeboys will use and abuse you until there is nothing left to use.

I conclude my message by saying that if you are hurting inside, find someone who will listen to your troubles—whatever they may be. Don't hesitate to seek help for the things ailing you inside.

You should know that your life matters to the world and to those around you. I wish I had had the opportunity that you do have right now: to make better choices and avoid coming to prison—or worse, like being killed in the streets.

It simply is not worth it, little brothers and sisters!

Change is possible. It might seem hard right now, but remember: A journey of a thousand miles begins with the first step. So take that all-important step and maybe your life wont' be like mine.

Juvenile Offenders: From Big Wheels to the Big House

On Incarceration, Rehabilitation, and Re-Entry

by Juan Moreno Haines
San Quentin News office

Anthony Kline, a California appeals court judge, came to the *San Quentin News* office to talk about incarceration, rehabilitation and reentry with about a dozen incarcerated men whose personal histories included gang-banging, drug dealing and even murder.

The incarcerated men were lead facilitators for several self-help programs that enable participants to deal constructively with anger, criminal thinking, victim awareness, early childhood trauma, and lack of education.

Two prisoners recently transferred out of Pelican Bay after spending a combined 36 years in its Security Housing Unit (SHU) were in the audience. Each said they were impressed and looking forward to this opportunity for rehabilitation for the first time in their incarceration experiences.

"I grew up around a lot of violence and a broken family," said Chris Gallo, describing how he gravitated to a criminal element of "skinheads" and committed "many acts of violence," adding, "I'm not proud of that.

"I began to see things differently after attending a Restorative Justice seminar," Gallo said. "When I was there, I kept my head down, not looking at the person speaking. However, the speaker said something that really connected with me. When I looked up, I saw an African-American man talking about everything I went through. I began going to the sessions, and today, me and that guy, Darnell 'Moe' Washington, are best friends."

James "JC" Cavitt talked of how two inmates serving life sentences helped him understand his role in the crime he committed. Cavitt said when he first began his sentence he thought he was in prison for a crime he didn't commit.

"Okay, if you think that way," one of the lifers said, "Think about what *you did.*"

Cavitt said when he slowed his actions and considered everything that happened he began to understand "that merely by what I did, made me responsible for her death."

I challenge you to come up with a curriculum that would

show youngsters how to stop from developing the habits that send them to prison.

"Since that moment, 16 years ago, I've taken every kind of rehabilitation available to help me understand *who I was* in order to answer how I got to the place where a human being could be brutally and savagely beaten to death."

Cavitt is a facilitator for the juvenile diversion program, SQUIRES.

"The boys who come through have a lot of trauma that they are carrying around with them," Cavitt said. "They don't have the space to talk about what they are going through. SQUIRES gives me the opportunity to give back. It is a huge blessing to give back. The reason it works is that my truth is their truth, and we are able to relate."

Another SQUIRES facilitator, Tommy Winfrey, added, "SQUIRES lets young people know that they are part of a community. It's about sharing empathy. We don't speak in a position of authority but as a place of shared experiences and of taking off the mask.

Judge Kline suggested that "people on the outside" need to hear the inmates articulate how and where their lives went bad, along with their suggestions on how to prevent others from making the same mistakes.

Kline acknowledged that the definition of insight is difficult for the courts to determine.

"I'm shocked at the level of insight needed to get out of prison, and nobody knows exactly what it is," Judge Kline said.

"It is talking about reasons for the commitment offense. Most people cannot do this. I don't think judges and lawyers can do this. However, I'm impressed about the level of insight in this room."

Julia Posadas-Guzman of Santa Clara County Probation has

been coming inside San Quentin for nine years.

"What affected me is the honesty and sincerity," Posadas-Guzman told the inmates.

"You have a model here that is working.

"I keep seeing lambs go to the slaughter," Posadas-Guzman continued.

"I am wondering how to stop it. I don't see the magic key. I am learning that overcoming trauma and poverty are important factors. I challenge you to come up with a curriculum that would show youngsters how to stop from developing the habits that send them to prison. I want to take what you're doing here to the next level so that young people didn't have to come here to get it."

Restorative Justice facilitator, drug counselor and adult educator Jen Slusser added another request. "I challenge you to make a series of videos showing people that they are capable of doing things productive. You should come from a place of embracing these young men. I can't do this. It has to come from you guys."

Later Judge Kline said in response to the forum, "You need to send *San Quentin News* to all judges. Judges are major players in reform."

Kline is the presiding justice on the First District, Second Division of the California Court of Appeal. He was appointed in 1982 and took office in December of that year. He was most recently retained by voters in 2014 to a 12-year term expiring in January 2027.

PRISON CODERS: 7370 MEDIA DAY or How to Get the Outside World to Listen to Prisoners' Ideas
by Juan Moreno Haines

It's hard to imagine an investor going inside a prison to discuss putting his money into a business idea dreamed up by an inmate, but that's exactly what Jason Calcanis did on June 22 when he visited one of the most innovative prison programs in the world.

"If you're a great coder, you win. The world needs great coders," Calcanis told the inmates.

"Nobody cares about the background of successful people. They care about the great product. Get up every day, making great stuff. You have the time."

The program, Code.7370, teaches inmates how to develop apps based on their inspirations that have a socially conscious component. The program is the brainchild of venture capitalist Chris Redlitz and Beverly Parenti, who established the coding program in conjunction with California prison officials.

The program, Code.7370, teaches inmates how to develop apps based on their inspirations that have a socially conscious component.

Redlitz and Parenti invited Calcanis along with podcaster and author of *Unmistakable, Why Only is Better Than Best,* Srinivas Rao, to hear the inmates pitch their ideas.

The ideas included a mobile app that helps parents and teachers track students' educational and athletic progress, another that follows the recovery of substance abusers through a fitness regimen, and one that uses technology, sensors and fire-retardants to fight wild fires.

"I had a family member who lost a beautiful home in San Diego, and I also worked as a firefighter. I always wondered why technology wasn't interfaced with wild fire protection," said Azraal Ford, 44, who has been in prison for 18 years. He said that he's been in and out of jail since he was 14 years old.

Ford's app, *F8 Fire Protection Systems,* stores 1,500 gallons of water along with a smaller unit of a fire-retardant substance. The system is controlled electronically through sensors that are programmed to douse wild fires that get too close to a home.

"The fact that F8 uses sensors, and they are cheap, and if each person in the community installs sensors, and they were linked, that could be something relevant," Calcanis said.

The next presenter, Jason Jones, is finishing the last 10 months of a 12-year sentence. His app, *Getting Parents Attention* (GPA) "would make parents more aware of what's needed toward public education and sports," he said. "Younger people need to be aware of the value of education, if they want to succeed in life."

"You are a good communicator, because it's personal to you; it sounds exciting," Calcanis told Jones.

"There's a gem of an idea in there because the app brings the parents closer to the children. The features need to be tested. Since it has a bunch of features, finding the one that grabs users will be the challenge."

Chris Schuhmacher created his app, *Fitness Monkey*, because he said, "16 years ago, drug and alcohol addiction led him to prison."

"*Fitness Monkey* allows recovering addicts to track recovery and relapses in real time," Schuhmacher said. "And, it allows its members to connect with each other for support."

"Treatment centers could pay commissions if *Fitness Monkey* delivers clients," Calcanis told Schuhmacher.

"Build the platform and allow recovery centers to place their names on it. Plant a flag, and then it'll be like clockwork."

Later Calcanis took on questions from the class.

In recognizing the advantages of taking prison programs, he said: "You guys made a mistake, and now you're paying a big price. However, I've seen a lot of people make mistakes and recover. Being an entrepreneur is the most rewarding thing you can do because everybody begins in the same place when it comes to creativity. You guys are starting with the world against you. You are counted out. But the truth is, your product will speak for itself."

To keep the inmates motivated and focused, Calcanis added: "A lot of people are going to try to stop you from being successful. Don't listen to them. You've got to use the fact that [when some] people count you out, [it is a way of motivating you] to be successful. To the extent you can do it, take the hand you were dealt and go [forward]."

Calcanis gave his take on failure: "Failure is something you have to deal with to be successful. As an angel investor I have to try a lot of things, and some don't work. But I'm going to continue to keep knocking on doors. You have to have that mindset, even being in prison. We are running around at light-speed out in the free world, while you're running with a huge brick on your ankle and still being successful."

An inmate asked Calcanis if he would come back: "How can I not? I want to hear how it turns out. There is strength in numbers. Entrepreneurship is a team sport. Work together."

Juvenile Offenders: From Big Wheels to the Big House

Death In San Quentin
by Juan Moreno Haines

For the second time in eight years, San Quentin State Prison almost killed me. What bothers me the most about getting a deadly disease and not knowing I have it is that it took healthcare providers nearly a month to officially tell me (and only through a letter) that I had Legionnaires' Disease. Adding insult to injury, the origin of the bacteria was the cooling towers on the $136 million hospital built in 2010 where I was being treated for high blood pressure.

When I had the sickness, my lungs were filing up with a deadly fluid. I was walking around ignorant that I was succumbing to this degenerative disease. I felt tired and had a slight headache. I lost my appetite and stayed in my cell, in the dark. I thought that my old migraines of 10 years ago had come back to nag me. I thought that rest would revive me and I'd recover in soon. However, I looked terrible and several people told me this.

Can you believe that some people on their websites have even declared that maybe Legionnaires' Disease at San Quentin is actually doing the public some good by killing off criminals who are worthless anyway?

After a few days, I didn't feel any better. And, I couldn't muster up the energy to go to important meetings. I went to work late the following Tuesday and Wednesday. My friends and even a correctional officer urged me to see a doctor. Finally, I did. I was bed-ridden for days with a fever that climbed to 102.7 degrees!

Many might have said, "Good riddance to that scumbag! He's done a lot of damage to our community." Can you believe that some people on their websites have even declared that maybe Legionnaires' Disease at San Quentin is actually doing the public some good by killing off criminals who are worthless anyway? I do seem to understand this attitude shared by lots of people—even good people—and yet it is so misguided. It's our criminal past that seems to interfere with their thinking with more clarity and prevents them from seeing us as human.

Although I've committed grave misdeeds, I've never stopped being a human being and that is how I (and my fellow inmates) deserve to be treated. It's funny that, at the ripe old age of 57, I've finally grasped what it truly means to be human and that includes understanding the importance of relationships, community, and the powerful simplicity of empathy.

In large part, realizing who I am at my core came from reading the likes of Viktor E. Frankl's *Man's Search for Meaning*. Frankl taught me what it means to suffer and to face death while still preserving one's dignity. The following is an excerpt (in paraphrase) from his book that has inspired me:

Death in Teheran

A rich and mighty Persian once walked in his garden with one of his servants. The servant cried that he had just encountered Death, who had threatened him. He begged his master to give him his fastest horse so that he could make haste and flee to Teheran, which he could reach that same evening. The master consented and the servant galloped off on the horse.

On returning to his house, the master himself met Death and questioned him, "Why did you terrify and threaten my servant?"

"I did not threaten him," Death said. "I only showed surprise in still finding him here when I planned to meet him tonight in Teheran."

At the height of having Legionnaires' Disease, when I was feverish, I became delirious and could not figure out what was happening to me. I was headed towards Teheran and I didn't know how to stop. Even though I dodged Death, I suffered a devastating and crushing psychological awakening: Death had a chance to take me and I barely escaped it.

It was by returning to Frankl's descriptions of his own suffering in *Man's Search for Meaning* that I was able to rediscover what all of it entailed. After getting well, I returned to rising each morning to do my job, but I had been given the gift of a new insight to life—something which made all the difference in mine.

When I first began to engage in criminal activity, I could not find purpose to *my* life and did not know how to respect the lives of those around me.

It is different today. Checking off my second decade in prison, I have grown increasingly fixated on the mistakes I've made. And God knows I've made a lot of them. There's something important that I've learned: I am connected to every human being on this planet because, simply put, I too am human.

I have done my best to turn my incarceration experience into something positive and fulfilling. I am proud of my accomplishments and proud of the work I do on a day-to-day basis. Prison can kill people, physically and emotionally. Nevertheless, with all that I have and all that I have built for myself, I am still vulnerable, like the younger version of myself who had committed all those unforgivable acts.

I made the decision to create a life of purpose for myself even though I was still in prison. I became a journalist inside this place—a job giving me a way to tackle so many of my unresolved issues.

At San Quentin, I report through the *San Quentin News* about what inmates are doing with their time from a boots-on-the-ground perspective. Many here are people making remarkable transformations in spite of so many obstacles. This evolution has been made public via the *News* (which I edit) and through other reporting agencies. County sheriffs, district attorneys, judges, and teachers have come inside this place and are surprised by the range of humanity and productivity they find.

I bet that even the average American would be astonished by the resilience of the men inside San Quentin State Prison—many of whom are better now than they ever were before. They have experienced humility and have accepted accountability to the larger public for their past misdeeds. For many, they are seeking forgiveness from others even when it is hard to forgive themselves. For others, they seek not forgiveness for the unforgivable but, instead, work toward redemption through their own works.

For everyone's sake, the conditions inside prisons in America must be of universal concern. We need to move away from the 18th century practices we are stuck in, to a modern system that treats prisoners (in California's 34 prisons and countless county jails) as people worthy of rehabilitation and reform and not destined for recidivism.

In the meantime, here I am, awaiting the chance to demonstrate to the parole board that I am no longer the bank-robbing bandit I was in 1996—that I am a new person, finally deserving of a second chance and a new start.

Get on the Bus 2016
by Juan Moreno Haines

In celebration of Father's Day, dozens of children, many with painted faces, spent the morning of June 17 in a prison visiting room, laughing and playing with their incarcerated fathers. The event, held at San Quentin State Prison, also accommodated 35 adult sons and daughters.

"Children and incarcerated people don't have a voice. They

are some of the least powerful in society," said co-coordinator of the event, John Kalin. "That's what draws me to Get on the Bus."

The <u>Get on the Bus</u> project was founded in 1999 by Sr. Suzanne Jabro, CSJ.

The program does all the paperwork for the visit. It provides chaperones for children who have no adult to accompany them. It charters the buses to and from the prisons, and provides all the meals during the travel.

For the last six years, John and his wife, Catherine, have coordinated the Get on the Bus event at San Quentin.

"It's so rewarding to see children hugging their dads. They don't get to do it as often as children living in other places," Catherine said. "One 47-year-old woman said, 'He's still my dad and I still want to give him a hug.'"

This year, 11,000 children will be reunited with their parents in the visiting rooms of seven men's prisons and three women's prisons across the state.

Get on the Bus, in conjunction with the California Department of Corrections and Rehabilitation, has held the annual event for16 years. This year, 11,000 children will be reunited with their parents in the visiting rooms of seven men's prisons and three women's prisons across the state. Next year, the program is scheduled to expand to High Desert State Prison.

Keya Banks traveled from Los Angeles with her son, Demauri Williams, so that he could meet his incarcerated grandfather. Travis Banks has been incarcerated since his daughter, Keya, was 16 years old.

"I want them to get to know each other," Keya said. "I want my son to have that bond that I didn't have growing up."

"My father has always reached out to me and stayed connected, even when he was in and out of jail," she added. "At first, I didn't want a relationship with him, but when I got older, I realized people make mistakes, they learn from them and grow from them."

Keya acknowledged that "it's important to be with your family. Things happen and we have to move on." Keya's mother added, "It feels good to be connected. As long as he's here, we'll keep coming back."

A 2013 study shows more than 1.75 million children under the age of 18 had a parent in a state or federal prison in the United States. Nationally, about 53 percent of men and 61 percent of women in the U.S. prison population are parents.

This represents nearly 810,000 incarcerated parents.

"It is joyous to see families reunited," said Philip Haik, one of the 22 Get on the Bus staffers assisting the San Quentin event. "It's good to give back, especially when you have been so blessed." Haik also volunteers in feeding the homeless and makes contributions to the Navajo nation.

For the last four years, inmate John Vernacchio, the visiting room photographer, has worked during the event.

"I look forward to this every year because the sponsors are some of the nicest people you can meet," he said.

Uniting children with their mothers and fathers in prison.

2014 Annual Report

www.GetOnTheBus.us

Jason Jones has about 10 months left to serve on his 10-year sentence.

His wife, Katy Flood, and his step-children Kiley Lyon and Rappor Lyon made the three-and-a-half-hour trip from Visalia, California, to see him.

"Getting time to spend with Jason is good," Kiley said. "We get to do things that we don't do on regular visits," Jones added, referring to the face painting and games, Subway sandwiches for lunch and photos.

"They had all kinds of refreshments on the bus and blankets. They made us pancakes and bacon for breakfast," Katy said. "They did a great job. Next year, I'll have to make the pancakes," she added, while looking at Jones.

"I can't wait for that," Jones replied, smiling.

Breakfast with Arnulfo
written for Carmen by Juan Moreno Haines

"Let's go, Juan," Arnulfo Timoteo Garcia chanted as he passed my cell every morning.

He took long strides to stay ahead of the hungry walkers making their way along the third tier of North Block in San Quentin. The fast moving amoeboid cluster would round down a set of stairs, out a large steel door in the back of the housing unit and line up in front of the chow hall. I tailed the mob to join Arnulfo where for more than eight years we ate breakfast together.

Most of the hundreds of mornings, Arnulfo waited for me at Table 122 - one of about 200 in the sprawling establishment of chattering men, bound by obvious similarities and places, places tied to identity, like race or city or gang: Northern Mexican, Crip or Blood, or White or Asian. Everyone enjoys the sameness of familiarity - familiarities that are as constant as the daily menu. Scrambled eggs begin the week, followed by pancakes on Tuesday, coffee cake on Wednesday, creamed beef on Thursday, more eggs on Friday and pancakes again, with the week closing out on Grand Slam Sunday.

The men pick up their trays and go to the same seats day after day. It's the same at Table 122. Yet, Arnulfo resists prison normality. He brought us together to challenge institutionalizing markers. At Table 122, there is Mike, the white guy and hardest working person I've ever met; me, the black guy, better known as the sidekick, and Arnulfo a Mexican vato who was always doing something good. We liked talking, joking, eating together as men of

142

faith.

Breakfast always began by me putting my empty cup on the table. Arnulfo had this huge plastic coffee mug with "Hard Time Cafe" printed on it. He told me that he could only drink about half of the coffee, so I'd always get the other half of the flavorful Taster's Choice brand he liked.

When we first started eating together, I'd wait for him to give me the okay to pour my coffee as, back then, my mind was only just emerging from the old prison thinking that different races don't do this kind of sharing. But Arnulfo went against prison - made rules every chance he got. He didn't like that I would wait for him to give me the okay. The coffee was for us. The way he got me out of that old penitentiary thinking was this: he'd go ahead and pour my coffee, but when he poured it, he'd fill it to the brim-to the point that I couldn't pick up my cup without spilling some on the table. If I hesitated and Amulfo had to pour it, my cup would run over. That happened from time to time-me hesitating to pour my own coffee, and Arnulfo making me pay with a smile. We'd laugh, with me exaggerating a pretend frustration if I picked up the overfilled cup and spilled some, or if I had to spoon a little out to make it manageable. The joke would never cease to be funny to us. Arnulfo did all kinds of things to make our table special.

Through his wheeling and dealing with the kitchen workers, fresh tomatoes, onions, bell peppers and the likes would find their way to our table. The kitchen workers knew very well that their fresh foods would turn into all kinds of things, from canteen to art supplies, anything they might want. Arnulfo would get these ingredients, cut them up, and toss them into a small plastic bag. Next, he'd sprinkle a little black pepper, a touch of olive oil, and spice it up with some jalapenos. He'd add some water, put it in a bottle, shake it up, and pour the mixture over his eggs - it's good on everything. He'd bring this concoction to our table.

"Try it. It's good," he'd say, putting the bottle on the table with a grand gesture.

"You're going to need more than that. I'm going to make more." Arnulfo was the kind of person who'd never take small bites into what he liked. He'd be so cheerful that people at other tables would reflect in kind.

"Would you like some?" he'd ask, offering the bottle already as if he was certain they would say "Sure."

I stayed numb and stunned for weeks hearing that Arnulfo was killed in a car accident, two months and two days after he earned his way out of serving a life sentence in prison.

I met him at a San Quentin News Journalism Guild meeting. He saw that we shared something important: we wanted the rest of America to know more about the state of incarceration in the country. We wanted to talk about people who transform themselves inside these prisons. In the beginning, I was somewhat timid. Still, I got Arnulfo's attention. He came by my cell and asked me to go to some event held at the prison. I think it was a graduation for one of the self-help programs. After that, he'd come by any time something was happening or somebody important came inside. When we worked together, I'd do the interviewing and he'd take down everything that was said. Occasionally, he'd chime in by asking a question that was on his mind, adding to the piece. Lots of times, after I thought I had it right, Arnulfo read over it and added some special details that made the story better. On top of that, he was the best proofreader I'd ever experienced. He would go over something I wrote and question things that were unclear. It came to a point where I gave him everything I wrote before it was finalized. He used to love finding mistakes in my work. Later, I learned that Arnulfo had written more than 16,000 pages about his life. He'd turned about five or six into short memoir stories. He was most proud of the one called, "The Tour," a story about what was on his mind while taking a prison bus to San Quentin. I felt honored that he asked me to write its foreword.

Arnulfo believed that everyone on the yard had a story, and he wanted to hear it and have it told. He dreamed of giving everyone at San Quentin, including those on Death Row, a pen and notebook to write about themselves. He maintained that it's important to let people tell their own story; he believed that deeply.

His other obsession was feeding everyone at the prison. He believed that breaking bread together was the key to family and unity. On all of his ideas-and they were abundant-he worked tirelessly.

There would be times when I'd be sitting in the newsroom, head stuck in front of my computer, working on something important for the next edition. It would be dinnertime. I wouldn't stop. The dinners aren't so good-plus, I'm a fussy eater and I change my diet a lot. One month, I'm vegetarian, the next no red meat the next month, all burgers and hot dogs. But Amulfo didn't like when I changed eating habits so much.

"Eat everything, pork and burgers and fish and beans. Eat it all," he said.

When I went on one of my Uno meat" rants, he made more meals with meat, waited until one of those times when I was hungry as hell and then put a big fat burrito, full of meat and with a side of chorizo, right in front of me. He stood there beaming, as I salivated with a grimace. I gave into my hunger, feasting on the meal my friend made for me.

From him I learned what it means to take an interest in another human being. Arnulfo saw value in everyone. There are so many life lessons he taught me - like what it means to be a father from behind bars, how to make a difference no matter where you are, how to dream and make it happen. He especially taught me what friendship is - that will never leave me.

I remember what it was like for Arnulfo to come to breakfast after seeing his daughter, Carmen. After a weekend of seeing her in the visiting room, the next morning he'd show up with a pocket full of pictures, pull them out, and hand them to me. No matter how I was feeling, seeing him with Carmen wrapped around him made me gleam like him. Sometimes I'd clown him by putting my thumb over his image, saying, "Now that's a nice - looking picture!" He'd look back at me with a little frown.

He told the story of Carmen as his final life-changing moment: it was the combination of the promise he made to his mother that he'd never use heroin again and the birth of Carmen that gave him a new life. Amulfo talked

146

about Carmen to everyone, including judges, prison officials, fellow prisoners, advisers, **anyone--he was so proud of being** a father of such a beautiful little girl.

However, there was one time when Amulfo came back from seeing Carmen that he was upset. She must have been 13 or 14. They'd been battling back and forth. "Carmen thought I didn't see that her ears were pierced," he said to me.

He'd told me earlier that they'd agreed that she could have her ears pierced when she got older. To him, that might have been age 25 or 30. He wanted to let her know that he was her father, he was doing his fatherly duties, and they were connecting as father and daughter, which meant that they would come to agreements as she grew into a young woman. "It is important to keep agreements," Arnulfo said. But more importantly, he wanted her to talk to him about what was happening in her life. He wanted to know everything, which meant he talked to her about boyfriends and how important it was for her to get a good education. I knew how he felt about education because of Lucia de la Fuentes. She was the role model that he ter to follow. Lucia was so influential to Arnulfo. She is a Mexican on a mission to bring culturally relevant teaching to incarcerated people. She had been working on her graduate degree. She used an unconventional kind of peer review method for her dissertation, and asked Arnulfo to be an expert to validate parts of her thesis. Arnulfo was extremely proud to help Lucia, and he prioritized education similarly for Carmen.

To all the news staff, Arnulfo was our hero who had made it happen. In the newsroom, his smiling portrait keeps us company and reminders of him stay on my desk.

He was at one point a life-term inmate with decades of incarceration ahead of him, and day by day, little by little, he worked to show that incarceration is not right for a rehabilitated person. When he was inside prison, he told stories about incarceration, rehabilitation, and reentry, and continued to tell the same stories once he got out. We stayed in touch by telephone. Once when I called him he was, of course, with Carmen - taking her shopping for school clothes. I was asking him questions about a speech he was going to give to a church in San Jose. He was going to take another formerly incarcerated man, Aly Tamboura, who had worked for the newspaper, too.
"You know what I'm going to say, Juan," he said. "Just write about incarceration, rehabilitation, and reentry, like we always do."

We laughed and then he told me that he was reuniting with Olivia, Carmen's mom. Carmen had her view of how the world should be, and one crucial piece was that her mother and father should be together, and she did everything she could to make that happen. It was kind of funny how he gained freedom but was still being bossed around by his daughter.

"Someone wants to talk to you," he said and put Carmen on the phone.

"Hi," she said. Carmen sounded so sweet. There was a long pause and I could tell she wanted me to say something. I imagined Carmen smiling and feeling secure while standing next to her father.

"Are you happy now?" I asked Carmen. I could feel her bubbling with joy over the phone.

"Yes," she said. I could hear the spirit of the young woman who had used everything in her power to "defeat" her father with the zeal only found in the Garcia family.

It was not unusual for Arnulfo to hand me the phone while he was in conversation with his family. The phones are on the first floor, and to get to the staircase to the upper tiers, you had to pass the row of 12 booths. I'd be on my way to my cell on the third tier and he'd stop me and hand me the phone. He pulled me into his family, as if I belonged. The Garcia family has influenced my life very much--even to the point that to this day, other inmates address me as Juan Garcia. When I'm down and out, and looking depressed, it has often been a Garcia to ask, "Juan, are you alright?"

Arnulfo knew I wasn't all right when in 2013, my close friend Lizzie, an advisor for San Quentin News, left the newspaper abruptly. She was frustrated with the way it was being managed and with how arbitrary some of those management decisions appeared. The administration didn't like her sharp perspective and commentary and in the end, that was that. Amulfo could see how disheartened I had become. I couldn't hide it. He knew how her friendship sparked life into me. I felt like I had no support, but how wrong I was.

He took me on walks around the Lower Yard and told me how important Lizzie was. He told me that the kind of changes and directions Lizzie and I wanted had to be approached more cautiously. We were a little too extreme in our ideas. Arnulfo knew how to read the tea leaves far better than I do. He taught me that most people in government really do want a better community and value the work we are doing, but can get intimidated by the

149

power of the press, even the little power San Quentin News has. Arnulfo figured out how to bring these confrontational issues slowly. He taught me how to engage that way - to bring ideas to the table from all sides without malice. I still feel Arnulfo's presence guiding me to take his approach in doing things important for the betterment of the community.

During breakfast at Table 122, we still talk about the things we used to when Arnulfo was there. It seems strange that the seat mostly remains empty. Everyone in the chow hall knows that it's Arnulfo's seat, and no one is ready to fill it. Eventually, though, someone will take that seat. When they do; I hope that they bring something of what Arnulfo brought.

I still arrive at the table with my empty cup. Mike looks at it and says that it's not going to fill itself. He doesn't realize that the spirit of my friend, Arnulfo, fills it every morning.

CHAPTER TWO

*Thinking about the Meaning behind Juvenile Crime, the
Conditions which Produce It, Other Issues which Affect It*

"The purpose of life is to make ourselves better people and to
make the world a better place."

--articles in this section and the above quotation
by Rosemary Jenkins

The goal of her articles included in this and other sections is to demonstrate how there are a multitude of reasons that are contributory to turning far too many youthful people (often living a poverty-stricken existence) to crime: bullying, ethnic and religious bias, immigration status, gender and appearance discrimination, mental health issues, humiliation, dysfunctional family life, homelessness, neighborhood and peer pressures, poor role models, drug and alcohol abuse, sex trafficking, incest and other sexual acts which were perpetrated upon these miserable (but once naïve and innocent), defenseless, and impressionable victims.

In addition, once these young people are incarcerated, it is how they are treated that makes all the difference in their rehabilitation. Furthermore, the question remains, Is it counter-intuitive when young people (whose brains have not been fully developed) are tried as adults to sentence them to serve lengthy terms in adult prisons?

For the most part, her articles refer in the main to male prisoners. However, it should be understood that what applies to them also applies to female offenders.

Justice Matters
by Rosemary Jenkins

"Justice matters!" This exclamation is an echo of, precursor to, or parallel with today's many unfulfilled demands/ appeals/petitions. These, in turn, mirror the needs and expectations of the countless millions among us who are far too invisible to far too many. Black lives do matter as do Brown and Gay. As do those of immigrants, the impoverished, and rank-and-file workers. As do all those who cannot earn a living wage despite working one full-time job, let alone two!

The reality is that presently we are faced with a multitude of pressing issues. No sooner than we concentrate on one than another pops up—not to replace but to add to. Soon there are dozens, all of which demand our immediate attention—all of them with a layer of urgency attached to them.

But for our purposes here, let us concentrate on one that is prominent and persistent–one that simply cannot be ignored by those we elect to represent us and our most paramount interests. Just last week, the Los Angeles City Council made the long-awaited and courageous decision to raise wages for nearly all employees within City boundaries (incidentally, but not coincidentally, the County is currently considering required wage hikes within our unincorporated areas and most likely will come to a determination that will closely align with LA City's rulings).

After a 14-1 vote, City Council sent the wage resolution to the office of the City Attorney, Mike Feuer, for the final draft wording which will then be put before the full Council in June for the final vote.

Important to note, Mitch Englander, District 12, was the sole Councilmember voting to defeat this very popular and widely supported motion—clearly siding with business interests over the welfare of the people who make their businesses profitable in the first place. His recent newsletter to his constituents falls far short in explaining his reasoning.

Many of us (including the 15 women who fasted for 15 days for $15 an hour) have been demanding that the higher wage be phased in more quickly and thus are disappointed with the timeline that is now being developed.

Yet, there is a very positive and promising side to the ultimate compromise that was made:

My fear, in the meantime, is that by July 2020, $15 will be worth much less—leaving workers to be challenged by the same deflated buying power they are facing now.

Beginning in July of 2016, minimum wage will rise to $10.50 ($1.50 more than the State requirement as of 2014), followed each year with a varied increase (averaging one dollar) until $15 is achieved by July of 2020. What is particularly impactful is that wages will then be increased, beginning in 2022, according to the COLA and, thus, workers will never again have to fall behind because of inflation. My fear, in the meantime, is that by July 2020, $15 will be worth much less— leaving workers to be challenged by the same deflated buying power they are facing now.

Furthermore, the new law will punish wage theft which is so rampant among businesses (large and small) that use lower-paid employees. Wage theft and other discriminatory decisions (including retaliation) are crimes that must be confronted head on and dealt with in so meaningful a way that such business practices will not only be discouraged but prevented altogether now and into the future. It is anticipated that this new law will include such provisions.

It should also be noted that small businesses with 25 or fewer employees will be given an additional year at both ends to produce the required increased wages. Although many such businesses have already voluntarily begun paying their employees at more equitable rates, most such enterprises are also concerned that without a tax break to help offset the increases, their companies will no longer be viable.

To counter that claim, these smaller concerns in most cases do not currently pay enough in taxes, in the first place, to make giving them a further tax break a logical or pragmatic way to offset their additional costs for higher salaries (the extra year should be more than enough for them to make necessary and logical modifications in their management style).

Some individuals have suggested that, in lieu of a tax break for the smaller businesses, the City could offer free workshops to teach proprietors how to run their establishments with such efficiencies that they can achieve both higher wages for their workers and ongoing viability for themselves.

In my opinion, no one should even consider being in business if the employees cannot be treated in a way they need and deserve. When employees thrive, so does the economy, crime goes down, and acceptance rises, discrimination decreases. When people are treated fairly—with dignity and respect, invited to be genuine and contributing stakeholders in their communities—it will become evident that all people do matter and, at that point, justice will prevail for far more than what we see today—regardless of appearance, background, thoughts, practices, beliefs, and morés!

Keep in mind that just because we did not at this time get from City Council everything for which we asked, the final draft will include a number of momentous stipulations, one of which will be a rule regarding enforcement provisions (with meaningful penalties for violations). Unfortunately, paid earned sick leave, for which advocates have relentlessly been pushing, was separated from the main motion (though it is believed to be a point which will be reconsidered sooner-than-later).

This latter provision is especially necessary so that workers are able to stay home for their children or themselves when there is illness. It would be nothing short of counter-productive to expect to keep sickness at bay in the greater community when ill employees and their family members are up and about spreading disease (think of the recent measles outbreak that circulated so quickly). Thus, it is critical that the earned paid sick leave requirement be enacted without delay.

Let us also remember that parallel protests are being made among our brothers and sisters in the drayage profession. For many, if not most, they are driving "sweatshops on wheels" and yet there is still not enough public awareness to produce greater outcries about the continued abuses these drivers endure every day. We can appreciate the recent progress being made to help alleviate these concerns but cannot be complacent. There is still much more ahead of us to attain.

We can no more tolerate their poor salaries and unconscionable conditions than we can for any other worker in Los Angeles (let alone anywhere). And that is why we often find ourselves marching together, supporting each other's causes (which in many ways are the same) and are gradually achieving varying degrees of success—the train (or the track or the march) is moving inexorably forward.

It was stated at the recent Giants of Justice—CLUE event, "Working people deserve more than modest aspirations." And thus "we cannot run away from adversity but must run toward it to overcome it."

In doing so, we shall discover a remarkable truth-that "the opposite of poverty is not wealth but justice!" And so we come full circle. Justice matters—with liberty and justice for all!

RESTORATIVE JUSTICE: Save the Prisoners, Save the Neighborhood
by Rosemary Jenkins

Restorative Justice—an interesting term about which most of us know very little. Very simply, it "is a theory of justice that emphasizes repairing the harm caused or revealed by criminal behavior. It is best accomplished through cooperative processes that include all stakeholders."

I have been working with the incarcerated within the California prison system for quite some time. I constantly hear of inmate abuse—incessant beatings, indeterminate punishment in solitary confinement (a situation well-known for causing or increasing mental deterioration—remember **Hurricane Carter** in the eponymous movie), refusal to provide needed medication as a punitive action (it has been reported to me that because some people were selling drug contraband, the inmates from the entire section were indefinitely refused their prescriptions).

Such conditions, and many more, have resulted in eventual **recidivism** because of the anger and resentment held inside by these prisoners and acted upon once they are released.

The purpose of prison is not only to **punish** but also to **rehabilitate**, to teach inmates how to take responsibility for their past actions, to provide education and training opportunities for eventual return to society where they can be contributors. For those who are lifers, they can still be taught the same pedagogies and apply them by helping other inmates who will eventually be released.

Too often, that is not happening. A large proportion of prisoners are not learning how to re-integrate into their respective communities upon their release but, through varying degrees of neglect and indifference, are devolving into recidivists rather than becoming productive.

In some prisons, however, the concept of *restorative justice* is **now** being seriously contemplated. **Incentives?** The inmate can learn to transition from a state of brokenness to integrity again. If inmates participate in and graduate from these classes and groups, earlier parole will be considered.

Part of the philosophy is really no different from many of the self-help steps taught to recovering alcoholics or gamblers.

What are some of these steps?

- efforts to **restore** (repair, mitigate) the harms perpetrated on victims and/or their families and to help make both offenders and victims whole again

- provisions for participation by victims in **resolving issues** regarding prisoner treatment as well as parole issues affecting their prison terms
- **guidance** in designing the government's role in maintaining a peaceful and orderly community

Among the programs are **Alcoholics Anonymous; Narcotics Anonymous; Criminals and Gang Members Anonymous** (a 12-step process); **Enhanced Out-Patient Program**; and the **Victims Awareness Offenders Program**.

What is expected?

- taking daily moral inventory, recognizing wrongs and admitting it—using meditation and prayer to produce a spiritual awakening (something from which we can all benefit)
- "helping criminal offenders to understand the true nature and effect of their crime"
- understanding that there are no victimless crimes—all crimes have ripple effects, like falling dominoes
- discussing the **arc of crime**: activator—reactor—consequence
- placing themselves in the shoes of the victim (perpetrator, victim, victim's family and friends)
- learning "how to dig deeper into root causes" of the "bad" actions; among these are childhood bullying, propensity to destructive behavior, learning how to understand themselves and how to change for the better
- addressing the past which produced the present which can lead to a better future
- learning how every action has a consequence for others even if one never knows what they are (for good or for bad)

One inmate courageously stated, "One problem I see with the EOP is the inability of the correctional system to deal adequately with many of the patients who are housed . . ." in a prison.

Guards (some with an axe to grind) are frequently ill-prepared (often despite good intentions). The numbers they guard and the issues they encounter can be overwhelming. Ineffective interaction with the extremely mentally ill (who often should be in "regular" mental-health facilities in the first place—not prison confinement) can make matters even worse.

Another inmate adds to this discussion that when **then-Governor Reagan** closed many of the State Mental Hospitals (think of Camarillo) or substantially reduced services, many of the mentally ill found themselves out on the streets without any help at all. Such people often turned to crime in an effort just to sustain their tragic lives.

Right now, most restorative programs are implemented **post-imprisonment** (think of **Jericho** and **Shields for Families**). They do provide easier access because they are community-based. Law-makers generally support this concept whose outcome reduces court time, prison overcrowding, and recidivism.

More recently, however, many principals are recognizing how effective the **restorative justice program** would work if it were initiated while the offender is still *in prison* and has demonstrated a sincere desire (through a variety of personal behaviors) to take an active part in it.

Another issue that must be addressed is the **right to vote** by former prisoners who have successfully served their time. As it is, the formerly incarcerated for felonious crimes are in most cases not allowed to vote for the rest of their lives. If we truly want them to re-integrate fully into their communities and be productive there, the franchise must be restored to them.

We know that too many have been incarcerated unfairly or for low-level crimes. People (particularly in their youth) make mistakes, sometimes egregious, but ought not be punished 'til the end of their lives by taking the vote from them. It sends a message that they are forever tainted.

Having the "Mark of Cain" placed upon the formerly incarcerated can only lead to ruinous consequences, the unintended consequences that we should be loath to make happen. If read closely, the mark was supposed to protect Cain. The very least we can do is protect and support the people who have recognized and taken responsibility for their past and want to create a better future for themselves and others. Imprisonment is supposed to be about redemption and rehabilitation, not unending punishment.

Restorative justice and other such programs are at least part of the answer.

CALIFORNIA'S JUVENILE DIVERSION PROGRAM: *Fantastic*
By Rosemary Jenkins

There are so many prisons and so many programs within each one that I cannot possibly tackle in a single column all the issues that each one presents. However, if you have been following some of my articles on juvenile justice, ban-the-box, "justice—not jails," and so forth, you know where my heart is.

Recently, Californians passed the somewhat controversial **Proposition 47** about which I wrote very recently. Many in the field of policing opposed its passage for fear of unintended consequences. But I believe our voters saw the wisdom in giving thousands of inmates a chance at a fruitful life **after** prison by reclassifying many "minor," but felonious crimes to misdemeanors (along with making certain other adjustments).

Building on that, today's column is addressing one of the outstanding programs that our penal system offers. This one, **the Juvenile Diversion Program** (JDP), is located at the **Mule Creek State Prison** (MCSP) in Ione, California, and is run by truly dedicated, compassionate, sincere, and highly-qualified leaders.

Each prison institution offers a version of this program but I am particularly impressed with the one at MCSP. Under the umbrella organization is a variety of smaller programs that are geared to meet the diverse needs of the incarcerated. These groups include *Alcoholics Anonymous*; *Narcotics Anonymous*; *Anger Management*, and others that address the causes of the mistaken and misguided behaviors that put these inmates in prison in the first place. They also receive instruction which teaches them how to take responsibility, to reflect on the concomitant ramifications of their actions, to learn how to choose better relationships, and so forth.

JDP representatives often go into schools, or community or church clubs to meet with those who can gain the most from participation in the program (frequently school or other counselors refer young men whom they recognize would greatly benefit from the one-on-one "face time" they would receive). The two organizations with which MCSP works the most are the **Stockton Peacekeepers** and **Lodi GRIP** (Gang Reduction Intervention Program). Participants learn about choices, decisions, and consequences and build on that knowledge.

The following is a quote from a passage that accompanies a 5-minute video that briefly explains the program. You can catch it on-line (Google MCSP Juvenile Diversion Program), from which you will get a feel for the program from the words of youthful visitors, their in-prison mentors, and staff:

"A group of 13-17 year old boys from Lodi took the first step to change their lives. They spent the day at Mule Creek State Prison as part of the Juvenile Diversion Program or JDP. All of these young men have ties to gangs, and like the mentors who are trying to steer them in the right direction, it's important that they know what that [risk-filled] life can lead to, and what the consequences are."

I recently spoke with **Eddie Escobar**, *Community Resources Manager*, and **Karen Heil**, *Lead JDP Sponsor*. They were both so helpful in taking me through the program and in helping me to understand its various facets. I was especially excited when Karen told me that she knows and admires the young man there with whom I have been corresponding and working on his behalf. I am urging him now to write an article for this site, sharing his own experiences. He is essentially self-taught and demonstrates a brilliance and articulation that I have rarely seen even among my own students.

The JDP classes take place on Saturdays for eight hours and offer a number of workshops. Six to twelve young men are brought to the prison at any one time and receive orientation upon arriving. This program, by the way, must not be confused with *Scared Straight* (from what I have been told, it really does not work that well in the long run because the teens involved have been scared almost since birth and have become inured to the yelling, cursing, threats, dysfunctional family issues, and minimal living conditions about which these often-hardened criminals share).

The Diversion Program matches up **volunteer mentor inmates** (who have met certain criteria) with **at-risk youth** (in this case, from Stockton and Lodi—high-crime areas). The latter are taught skills about the importance of staying in school, being a productive part of the community, and learning how to respect themselves and others (such as parents and teachers and those in a leadership capacity). I was moved when I heard some of these young men state, when asked to share something important that they had learned from the outreach program, "I want to make my parents proud of me!"—so few youngsters seem to feel that way these days.

Mentors have been taught how to **role play** effectively, putting themselves in the shoes of those whom they have volunteered to help. These inmates are well-trained and disciplined. They frequently find themselves working with young people (often like themselves) who are suffering from a form of *post-traumatic stress syndrome*—very similar, but in some cases worse, than what many returning fighting soldiers have experienced.

So many of these youngsters are damaged already (nearly irreversibly). At their young ages they have often heard and seen (and, sometimes, experienced) it all: murder, robbery, rape, beatings, foul language, threats, constant fear, abandonment. Thus, the goal of these programs is an attempt to turn these young people around--before it is too late!

One to two mentor inmates are assigned to each visitor at which time they learn a little bit about each other (earlier, the inmates have received a biography of their mentee and have prepared, through team meetings, how best to connect with the young person and his needs).

The visitors are taken to **A Ward** (which contains Level 4 and Level 3 inmates—those who are serving time for some of the worst crimes, including murder). After that, they visit the housing units and share lunch together in the assigned mess hall. They also have the opportunity to walk the A yard. They talk together and really "hear" each other.

All-in-all, the visitors get a clearer understanding of what jail life is really like—dispelling the "glamorous" images they have gotten from movies and songs. They have interacted with murderers, lifers for various crimes, and gang members (past and present)—never sex offenders—and, believe it or not, have frequently become changed from that brief interlude in their lives.

Many **graduates of this program** have already seen great improvements in their lives—choosing to jump out of gangs (about 80% of prisoners in California are gang members), making new friends whose goals reflect their own, concentrating on school performance and matriculation (some participants have already graduated from college). Because they recognize just how beneficial and influential the program had been for them, they frequently choose to go back on Saturdays to share their successes with others and demonstrate how anyone who genuinely wants a different pathway for their lives can "come out on the other side" (as John Steinbeck has so poignantly stated).

It is heartbreaking that some are not so lucky. One young man named **Julio**, a 14-year old (whom I mourn though I never knew him), was on the right track and was anticipating a Saturday visit when he was ruthlessly shot dead while trying to hide in the bushes (to stay out of trouble) during a wild gunfire rampage. When he thought it was over and stuck his head out, he was shot in the back of the head. We must cry for him and all the others that were never able to take advantage of this program long enough to see its positive results.

You may remember a relatively recent movie, based on **Antwone Fisher's** life. When I heard of Julio's story, I was reminded of this touching piece of literature that Fisher wrote.

> Who will cry for the little boy?
> Lost and all alone. . . .
>
> Who will cry for the little boy?
> The boy inside the man. . . .
>
> Who will cry for the little boy?
> He died again and again.
>
> Who will cry for the little boy?
> A good boy he tried to be.
>
> Who will cry for the little boy
> Who cries inside of me?

Many of our young men, in particular, can no longer picture themselves living beyond 20 (if they are lucky enough to live that long). Many on the outside are seen wearing *in memoriam* shirts of loved ones they have lost—with birth and death dates on them. Yet some of these young people often wear shirts *depicting themselves* with their own birth and death dates (their next birthday). One young man wears a shirt that reads "In Memory of Me"; another says "RIP." How heart-wrenching is that?!

When there is a feeling of hopelessness, futility, and despair among these inmates, they are taught to cherish and celebrate their successes in prison because there is so much they can do to help themselves and their fellow inmates to choose a different and better path, let alone to help the young people who visit there, though temporarily, to find the support and succor they so desperately need. Such instruction has been and continues to be profoundly palliative.

Escobar shared that some highlights of the program include keeping at-risk young people out of the prison system altogether, and, very importantly, offering the opportunity for both mentors and mentees to **give back**. One prisoner with whom I correspond and has been in prison for decades (but has learned much and has become a changed person) says he does not want to die in prison because he wants the time to **make his mark** in a positive way on society.

Keep in mind, on the other hand, that all is not lost for many lower-level inmates. *There is light at the end of the tunnel.* Many can take courses through approved partnerships, such as **Folsom Lake College**, to earn AA degrees and/or certification in certain careers, such as drug counselling. The downside of obtaining that educational advancement, however, is the cost to the inmate—not all can afford it! If he has no one to offer financial assistance, then obtaining his educational goals may be beyond his reach (with the exception of the possibility of earning one of the very limited scholarship opportunities).

Between these programs and changing laws, there is promise for those who feel unrelenting hopelessness. We as a society are certainly much better off when such programs succeed in rehabilitating inmates to become productive in their outside lives (or when the incarcerated can help others to achieve-- even when there seems to be *no light at the end of the tunnel for them*). We need to support the maintenance and expansion of such programs **and** challenge the current institutionalized and systemic shortcomings that must be ameliorated within the penal system.

Juvenile Offenders: From Big Wheels to the Big House

Why We Must Support Prop 47

Rep. Karen Bass, ACLU Executive Director Hector Villagra, and Prof. Kareem Crayton

In case there is any confusion over dubious advertising, I must go on record urging all of you to Vote Yes on 47 (let alone to place your mark on the entire ballot—many of us sometimes inadvertently forget to do that).

In a separate article, I am going to write about the cover-up regarding the misguided (and deliberately deceptive) war on drugs. But for now, I must offer clarity to what passage of this proposition (with all its ramifications) will establish.

I was at the recent "Turn the Page" conference, led by a number of prominent speakers, that addressed this and related issues. Karen Bass (former Speaker of the Assembly and current Congresswomen from the Los Angeles area) launched the panel session, which was moderated by ACLU Southern California Executive Director Hector Villagra. She reminded us that the drug war, carried on over far too many unsuccessful years and dating back at least to the Reagan Administration (remember, Just Say No!), led to massive incarcerations. Caught in the web was a disproportionate number of people of color convicted of mostly non-violent crimes, such as possessing an ounce of marijuana or selling drug paraphernalia or stealing a slice of pizza (the latter of which infamously placed the offender in jail for 25 to life under the mandatory-minimum laws).

In fact, the infamous 3-strikes law led to building 12 more prisons in our state, many of which were profit-driven, private enterprises whose operators urge Sacramento to pass more laws (with very broad, wide-sweeping parameters) which would, in turn, populate our prisons with ever-larger numbers. As President Eisenhower once said upon leaving office, Beware the military-industrial complex! Well, Attorney General Eric Holder is similarly warning, Beware the prison-industrial complex! Holder is further urging prosecutors

across the country to be more lenient with those who have committed victimless crimes and to be more compassionate with how sentences are meted out. There is great need for sentencing reform, but this can only happen when lawmakers are willing to change policy or, short of that, when voters support reform through the Initiative Process. Again, we must Support Proposition 47!

As a consequence of the current irrational, illogical, myopic process, low-level offenders (after release from prison) are forever relegated to the lower rungs of the socio-economic ladder for a variety of reasons:

- They would never be able to vote (and hence would not have the ability to participate in decisions for their own communities).

- Often they would not be permitted to go back home to take up residence there because a member of the family may have had a criminal record in the past.

- At present, they are precluded from being hired in more than 50 job categories because of laws that were passed by uninformed, often intolerant, and seemingly biased "lawmakers."

When the formerly incarcerated return to their home communities, too frequently they are forever stigmatized and humiliated (often because of youthful, non-violent transgressions). It becomes harder for them to fit back in and contribute in a positive way to society, let alone to their immediate neighborhoods.

Disproportionate Sentencing

Don't forget the concept of plea-bargaining. Often the real criminal rolls over on a naïve accomplice (maybe someone waiting in the car). The actual perpetrator gets a minimum sentence while the "friend" gets 25 years. And what about proportionality? Why do people of color get far higher sentences than others do for similar "crimes"? For instance, those caught with rock/crack cocaine get far heftier sentences than do wealthier, white offenders who were arrested with powder cocaine? So unfair and so unjust—yet, perpetrators of relatively minor crimes continue to get caught in an unforgiving, tangled legal web.

What recourse do we offer these "felons" who were convicted under questionable laws? It is true that while in prison, some can take advantage of certain available programs in order to obtain their high school GED diploma or get a college degree, but I have found in working with prisoners that many who attempt these endeavors do not have families that can furnish the money to pay for the course-work, books, and supplies (yes, there are some ways to obtain stipends but such financial support is still not across the board—a little like the haves and the have-nots all over again). What is more, quite ironically, is that many of the in-prison training programs, such as barbering, are training the incarcerated for jobs for which they are not allowed to hold after release.

What Will Prop 47 Do?

In part, what Proposition 47 will do is decriminalize specific infractions or reduce certain convictions from felonies to misdemeanors. Instead of building more prisons or shifting overcrowding from the more notorious penitentiaries to County jails, this proposition would provide over a 5-year period about $1 billion for K-12 school programs, victims' services, mental and drug treatment programs, and so forth.

In so doing, law enforcement can concentrate on the kind of offenses that really affect our safety and security—not on petty, generally harmless, victimless crimes. More officers and better programs can help mitigate the type of crimes we all fear—murder, rape, armed robbery, child abuse, and so on. It just makes no sense to ruin forever the lives of those who have committed youthful indiscretions!

According to Professor Kareem Crayton (originally from Montgomery, Alabama, and now teaching at the University of North Carolina Law School), society as a whole seems to expect that the majority of prisoners will be people of color and oversee to them "accordingly"—it appears that most prison wardens and guards are Black and are often responsible (perhaps from self-imposed pressure) for enforcing rules more harshly for ethnic prisoners than for other inmates. Such offenders are frequently on lock-down for inconsequential infractions and are often denied essentials on a regular basis, even medications.

The fact is that one in three Black men between the ages of 18 and 35 will find their way into prison. If we do not offer attractive alternatives within their home communities, before they even think about committing a crime, these numbers will continue and are bound to increase. Crayton says that what transpires in adulthood is based on the paths we choose, and we can only choose the "right" path if our home and neighborhood environments make positive choices possible.

As was unambiguously declared, "We can't incarcerate our way to a better society!" We must invest in our communities and we must change our attitudes as to how to address the issues that produce and nurture a criminal climate. We must also convince those who are wary to look at solutions differently.

How do we avoid recidivism if those released come back to families who are very poor (and cannot help them) and to

neighborhoods where they can find no jobs?

How do we avoid recidivism if those released come back to families who are very poor (and cannot help them) and to neighborhoods where they can find no jobs? These realities are just some reasons why we must change current laws. The formerly incarcerated (who have paid for their offenses) need to become a genuine part of a welcoming community where their spiritual as well as their educational and employment needs are met.

The fact remains that reading scores taken at the 4th grade level generally determine which young people will eventually turn to a life of crime. We cannot, therefore, afford to wait until children reach middle or high school to teach them their foundational skills (because many, by then, have already been introduced into the criminal milieu). We must begin to concentrate our efforts at the pre-school level (it is my wish to see universal-preschool a mandate across the nation)—where we can teach, even then, the three R's and other significant skills. And at the same time, we must make sure that good health and proper nutrition programs are part of any education.

We can only turn around our crime statistics if we turn around our young people at the earliest possible age. We must offer parenting classes and hold parents and guardians responsible for laying for their children a foundation that will produce positive results.

Our Neighborhood Justice Program

Mike Feuer, our City Attorney, talked about his Community Justice Initiative which oversees the Our Neighborhood Justice Program in the second panel session, moderated by Drug Policy Alliance California Executive Director Lynne

Lyman. He has partnered with a number of civic leaders here and elsewhere, such as Cyrus Vance, Jr. (New York County District Attorney), to make such programs possible. Some of the goals of these plans for low-value offenses are as follows:

- Perpetrators who are willing to take responsibility for their actions will be eligible for participation.

- The offenders must help effectuate change in their respective communities, like mentoring other would-be offenders, tutoring those in need of educational help and guidance, volunteering in nursing homes or for construction of community projects.

- If they follow through and complete their obligations, they will not be subject to prosecution but will become part of alternative programs.

- The idea is to get at the root causes that lead young people astray.

Thus, programs that address mental issues, home dysfunction, drug and alcohol use, and gang involvement are unquestionably essential. If a person understands what drives him or her, such people can turn their lives around if given the opportunity and are nurtured and guided along the way.

175

Too many of us are just not aware that children who witness horrible, gruesome crimes tend to be the ones who will later enter the criminal world themselves. Studies are showing that their brains simply do not develop properly after such encounters become part of their mental pathology. There is no question that we must intercede before such tragedies can transpire and provide help for those who have already had these scenes burned into their memories.

Some schools are already part of such pilot programs whose aim is to create safe pathways for walking to or returning from school; addressing child truancy issues; and focusing on minimizing gun violence (sometimes holding parents and guardians responsible and trying them as accomplices if their own guns are used in a felony).

Cradle-to-Career Attention

Assemblymember Reggie Jones-Sawyer, Sr. added that we must provide cradle-to-career attention for all our young people, whose formative years will shape them forever after. And might I add that before pregnancy, parents (both mother and father) ought to be taught how to follow good health and nutrition practices if they expect to give birth to a healthy child.

Interesting input was offered as well by Assemblymember Steven Bradford. He reminded us that we are becoming increasingly aware that prison time is often a matter of economics—those with money to hire the best legal advocates get the "best" justice. What is perhaps worse is that low-crime, "soft" offenders who enter these penitentiaries come out as hardened criminals who have been jumped into gang membership and are often covered with gang tattoos for identification. For them, such actions within the prison walls were a matter of survival; unwittingly, however, these same associations generally follow them outside where they are provided with few positive options for a fruitful future.

The bottom line is that we must support Proposition 47! If we really want to eliminate the root causes of many crimes, we need to recognize how this initiative will mitigate many of the issues that create them. If all people are created equal (as our Constitution clearly mandates), then we must produce legislation that will fulfill that declaration and treat all our people accordingly.

Finally, the privilege of voting must not be taken for granted. We must get out to Vote on November 4, 2014 (unless you vote by mail and have already voted). And don't forget to vote the entire ballot, from top to bottom.

VOTE YES ON PROPOSITION 47!
Gun Control: Whose Ways and By What Means?

Gun Control: One small step for Los Angeles. One giant step for sanity!

The decision this week by the Los Angeles City Council was unanimous in supporting its gun control measure prohibiting possession of large-capacity ammunition magazines (11 or more rounds). In addition, owners will be expected within a time-certain deadline to turn over those larger magazines to the police (or other appropriate agencies) or to other organizations with the authority to receive them.

There is one caveat, however: Mitch Englander—CD 12 (the same member who is the only one to have voted against raising the minimum wage in Los Angeles) asked for consideration of an amendment (to be taken up next Tuesday) to exempt retired police officers and those with concealed carry permits from the regulations by which everyone else must abide. I got the feeling when I attended the session that the other Councilmembers present were not all that enthusiastic about his request but were willing to have it heard.

This concern must receive careful deliberation:

Retired officers are rightfully concerned that ex-felons and/or their cohorts might seek to retaliate against those who put them in prison in the first place (and/or at least managed to cut down on their nefarious "enterprises").

Next Tuesday will be another Council meeting which not only will hear the amendment but will vote on another measure that involves safety and protection: proper and safe storage of firearms.

I happened to see a *Dateline* episode last night that was a perfect example of the problem. It coincidentally dealt with the very conundrum this measure would present:

A judge was caught on video stealing three computer monitors from the courthouse and was appropriately punished for his indiscretion. In retaliation, he shot the prosecutor in the face and two month later shot and killed the DA and his wife. He was eventually caught and sentenced to death.

Although LA's measure might not have prevented these gruesome events from transpiring, I can understand the concern by retired police officers and other concealed-carry permit citizens who might also be subject to similar retaliation because of the jobs they used to hold.

On the other hand, the rest of us might argue that we also have the same right to protect body and home from such violent attacks. Why exemptions for the "privileged" few?

Next Tuesday (try to attend or at least offer your input through your Council offices) will be another Council meeting which not only will hear the amendment but will vote on another measure that involves safety and protection: proper and safe storage of firearms. Too many of our residents have become victims of gun violence in the home or at a business— whether intentional or accidental. It looks likely that this proposal will pass as well (hopefully with unanimity).

A summary of this second ordinance is relatively simple: owners must "lock up handguns [and/or] use trigger locks when the weapons are not being carried which could prevent accidental discovery and shootings, particularly by children."

I believe that Mr. Englander (and perhaps Mr. Buscaino) will offer a similar amendment to that motion for the same reasons.

At the same time that last Tuesday's meeting was taking place, LA County was hearing testimony regarding imposing greater oversight over the Sheriff's Department, one whose violations have been a blight on our County (a Department which has become notorious across the nation for what can be called its felonious conduct). Final decisions will be made in the near future

As a phrase often used, these are issues whose time has come. History has repeated itself in too many instances. Whether it is Sandy Hook or military venues or movie theaters or churches and synagogues, there is always a lot of chatter over the horrors of these events and a demand to do something. . . until the words finally die out in a distance echo.

It is time to move beyond our city boundaries to nearby cities and counties and ultimately across the nation to serve as models for what can and should be done to mitigate the dangers of these weapons. Surely, Congress will recognize the will of the majority of its constituents (including large numbers of NRA members) to regulate arms (not "a well-regulated Militia").

Forget the NRA! Once an organization set up to teach gun safety, it has distorted the true meaning and intent of the Second Amendment and has cleverly convinced thousands, if not millions, of others to believe these misrepresentations. NRA is beginning to lose its influence and will continue to do so as long as we stand up to them! We, as citizens, must retake our ability to make reasonable decisions that affect all of us.

It is time to take our country back (as so many ultra-conservatives like to rant)! Guns can be used for hunting for food (with strict adherence to the rules), not for trophy hunting (think of poor Cecil). Conservationists, however, do say that careful and judicious hunting to cut back certain animal populations actually saves the herds. Rarely, though, are guns actually utilized for self-defense (though many people make the claim that they need a weapon for protection–more often, these guns wind up being used to kill an innocent friend or family member).

Our Constitution was never meant to afford us freedom to do anything we wish (we all accept that a person can't cry "Fire!" in a theater when there is no fire). We must be rational and logical in our thinking and in our decision-making.

This is the time for Los Angeles (both City and County) to stand up and be counted. Hurray for us!

Murder Is a Serious Crime But ...

I have always been under the assumption that the **purpose of imprisonment** is two-fold: to make one *pay for one's crimes* and to *rehabilitate the perpetrator*. I have also held close the concept that **crime and punishment** must be carried out with **justice and mercy** in mind.

It is time ...

We can go back millennia to find the many discrete ideas that divergent societies discovered to pursue and implement this challenging and often controversial goal. Interestingly enough, the *Old Testament* speaks of **Cities of Refuge** where criminals could live (under protection and supervision) and be able to support themselves (but could never leave the confines of those special communities). This notion is certainly a paradigm for mercy.

Furthermore, the more modern interpretation of "an eye for an eye" is really a perverse reading of the dictates of God to Moses and of the *New Testament* rendering by Matthew. It was never meant to insinuate that a murderer should be murdered—rather, it strove for a **logical, sensible balance.** It also strove to accomplish the reasonable and pragmatic goal of **restitution** (our contemporary idea of **Restorative Justice**)--an essential ingredient for making amends.

Even *Old Mother Russia* enacted similar measures by sending many of its convicts to **Siberia**—a god-forsaken place and far from the madding crowd—but also a place where families could join them, where the convict could work and live but not be able to leave until his term was finished.

I mention these examples because it seems to me there was an effort, a consideration that the punishment should be equal to the crime and that rehabilitation was possible.

. . . that we consider . . .

What I am seeing now is how perverse our prison system has become. It is not (if it ever was) about justice and mercy. The **blind-folded Lady Justice** (through no fault of her own) seems to be tipping the scales favoring some but censuring others.

Periodically we, as a Society, deign to discuss (when there seems to be no other choice) the inequities and disproportion in arrests and sentencing in certain communities, especially when we see a major and "obvious" injustice being perpetrated. Maybe because of social media and the news media and their instant, often incessant, reporting around the clock, we simply are more aware of the ugliness from which we too often try to hide or even deny.

If we are not already jaded, we are on occasion astonished and enraged. Then we demonstrate and try to change laws to make them and their enforcement fairer—actions that make us feel better about ourselves. Yet, too often, there is not follow-through and the rage of the moment evaporates with time.

... a more humane way ...

Despite all this, there is one part of the "justice system" which still seems disparate. I have long been working with prisoners and have become increasingly enlightened—though I have much more to learn. In doing so, I have helped start a prisoner-written series (which is being published) that offers the kind of insight of which we, for the most part, have been unaware.

I have seen a **repeated theme**. Young boys, in particular, have grown up in dysfunctional homes where they have witnessed and been victims of unspeakable acts to which no person, let alone a child, should be exposed—alcoholic, drunk, drug-addicted parents; one or both parents having a prison record or serving time in jail; parents willing to introduce their own children to a life of crime; physical and psychological abuse of their mothers and themselves; being victims of incest or other sexual abuse and exploitation.

Many such young victims leave these homes, seeking a "family" in which they are esteemed and cared for, where they feel important, where they can rise to an enviable position, and where they know their "brothers and sisters" will gladly have their back--but also where there is **a price to pay**! Many of these young people come to idealize their surrogate fathers and are eager to emulate their ways in order to feel loved and to fit in—to belong. The consequence for such idolatry is their unquestioning, unflinching obedience and allegiance—they must be willing and ready to do whatever they are ordered to do (even if it is against whatever conscience they have left).

... of treating those ...

One-by-one, these young perpetrators find themselves in a gang, robbing a liquor store and killing the unwitting cashier who resists their criminal advances; or, under other circumstances (perhaps at a party), they jump in to defend the friend who is being confronted and kill the "evil" assailant.

Then they are eventually caught and punished for their indefensible crimes, given 25 years to life, and face the reality of the life they have thrown away. Once in prison, their behaviors frequently follow them. Many feel the same need to fit in and thus join a prison gang for the sense of family and protection.

Eventually, however, (surprisingly or not) greater and greater numbers of such inmates find themselves rejecting the "life" with all of its ramifications (often after many years of incarceration during which they have been victimized all over again--by being raped or stabbed or extorted or threatened and in fear of their very lives—or all of the above).

... who fill the leagues ...

It is these people with whom I greatly empathize and sympathize. Incarcerated at 16 or 17, many have spent years on the road to rehabilitation (instead of further destruction)—a road on which they find their true selves, understand the nature of their crimes, and become genuinely remorseful and contrite. They have learned how to be accountable for the transgressions of their youth and no longer blame others for their offenses, regardless of their own earlier circumstances.

. . . of the reformed incarcerated, . . .

I have gotten to know so many young men who fill this category. They fully subscribe to the concept of **Restorative Justice**; they are mentors in the **Juvenile Diversion Programs** to help at-risk young men (their former selves) follow a better path, filled with honesty and integrity. Many turn to religion and even minister to other inmates to help assuage their mental suffering and to offer hope.

Many have become **Certified Drug Counsellors** and/or have earned **advanced college degrees** (we often hear of the prison lawyer). Many, in fact, *have* become attorneys with plans to advocate for young people on the outside who deserve a second chance.

. . . deserving their own second chance!

What about the **victims** and their families and friends? you may well ask. Part of **Restorative Justice** is the genuine effort by the offender to make amends for the crimes perpetrated *without* asking for forgiveness (which is so gratuitous). It is about taking responsibility and being given the opportunity to make better the circumstances in which the remaining loved ones find themselves.

History cannot be changed and the deaths cannot be erased. But both sides of the crime equation can work to ameliorate the new circumstances in which they find themselves and mitigate the pain surrounding them—past and present. The outcome can only be beneficial to both sides and to Society in general.

My point? I want to advocate for **something new**, to encourage a perhaps novel way of thinking. If a young man (or woman) has committed a murder as a teenager and has maintained an exemplary record within "the system" for at least 25 years, has earned the respect and admiration of those staffers inside (or counsellors outside) who have worked closely with these inmates and have recognized their positive attributes and transformation, ***serious consideration should be given for their release*** (perhaps under lifetime probation) to be able, **this time**, to make a positive mark and be given the chance to makes themselves better people and to make the world a better place.

There is good and goodness to be found in each of us— worthy of discovery, exploration, and manifestation. Perhaps, in the final analysis, we all deserve second chances.

Prisoners Can be Victimized Too

"Llegará el día en que dejará de huir de aquello que llevas dentro--siempre porque hay esperanza"

"The day will come when you will cease running away from what you have inside—because there is always hope."

[Paraphrasing the Spanish text which was tattooed on a man in prison.]

Too many people believe that if people are in prison, they are as guilty as hell, and, therefore, they deserve any kind of treatment that is dished out!

I can understand the lack of sympathy and empathy by so many even though I don't agree with that kind of mindset or for some, their total indifference. I have always believed that the purpose of incarceration is to punish fairly but also to rehabilitate. It flies in the face of reason that ugly, brutal, cruel mistreatment of inmates is what imprisonment is about. Such behavior under the color of law can lead not to rehabilitation but, instead, to the hardening of criminals, most of whom will eventually be released into a society for which they are not prepared.

It is absolutely a contradiction that we are working on such things as prison overcrowding and post-incarceration programs (which are meant for training and re-training and eventual jobs) when far too many of these former inmates have come back into society, into the community, as ruined human beings. They are relegated to ever-increasing difficulty at re-assimilating because of all the repressed anger and rage they harbor from their inmate experiences.

Let me give you some genuine examples that illustrate my

point. For quite some time now I have been working with prisoners, to many of whom I have become close. They often share their personal stories with me. I hear a litany of mounting complaints that often seem to be carbon copies of each other–in terms of the abuse they receive on the inside.

What about the young man who had been approached threateningly by a "friend"? When the problem started to escalate, both were handcuffed but the young man wound up with a broken wrist. When he filed a complaint, the system turned the tables on him and claimed that he had attacked the guard and then further retaliated by sending him to a different prison altogether—away from the classes and help groups in which he actively participated and from which he greatly benefitted and from the camaraderie he had established with his fellow inmates. Perhaps there was a time when such a story would have sounded incredible, but not today with the growing awareness of so many incidents of police battery.

And why did this happen? In part, because he is gay. "How repulsive!" is the common response as reflected by this statement by a guard, "You f—in' faggot! Why don't you just die!" And that quote is the least hateful of the ones that have been disclosed to me.

Homosexuality and mentally and physically disabled inmates are usually sectioned off and often are the brunt of continuously atrocious treatment by unsympathetic guards who believe that population to be nothing less than repulsive.

Homosexuality and mentally and physically disabled inmates are usually sectioned off and often are the brunt of continuously atrocious treatment by unsympathetic guards who believe that population to be nothing less than repulsive and thus treat them as the refuse of society, like animals—people who do not rate humane treatment (that would be afforded animals). These "masters" are degrading and humiliating in the way they interact with their "victims." It is hard to believe, but it has been repeatedly reported that many of these guards even encourage these incarcerated and bewildered souls to consider and even act on suicide.

Another seemingly universal complaint is the food: small, greasy, often watered-down portions—the result of which habitually leads to malnourishment or other serious ailments, like diabetes. Failing health is frequently ignored in the early stages by prison officials and often only recognized when major health issues ensue, thus costing the taxpayer thousands of dollars for any one individual, but, more critically, sometimes leading to the death of the inmates in question because of delayed or substandard treatment (remember, "justice delayed is justice denied").

Cell conditions are another story. It is not a rare anomaly that the heat is arbitrarily cut off to an entire cell block—for no apparent reason and without explanation. The resultant dampness and cold are another inexcusable, insupportable form of abuse.

What of solitary? Surely a punishment overused and abused! Many are forced to stay in tiny, dark cells for 23 hours a day (a fate Dzhokhar Tzarnaev may be facing). If you ever saw the Denzel Washington movie, The Hurricane (based on the life of the fighter, Rubin Carter), you were witness to the harsh reality of what transpires for people so incarcerated. It is common for them to lose their minds. And after all to which Carter was subjected, he was later found innocent of the crimes for which he was convicted—a result that can never undo the cruelty which he experienced.

If this is what we want for our prisoners, why not just execute them all? Rehabilitation, redemption, re-integration (just words) become virtually impossible outcomes for inmates who have received the severe and, generally, unthinkable treatment as described above.

If we like to think of ourselves as forgiving and compassionate people living in a humane society, we simply can no longer tolerate or accept such unholy practices. We must demand changes and we must do that now!

At the very least, retaliation of any kind for grievances must be absolutely prohibited and punished if found to take place. Programs must be accessible—system-wide—to rehabilitate, train and re-train, and to help re-integrate the formerly incarcerated into a society that can benefit from their newly productive participation.

The Case against Capital Punishment

There is a distinction between killing and murder. There are times when killing is justifiable—for self-defense, food, euthanasia, but the Scriptures are unambiguous when they

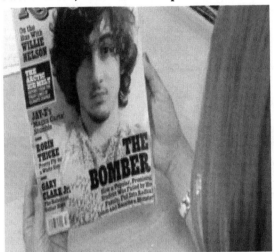

command "Thou shalt not murder" (and that must be interpreted as the premeditated, gratuitous taking of a life for no defensible reason).

Right now with the current Boston Massacre trial, the question is whether Dzhokhar Tsarnaev should be sentenced to death or placed in a maximum-security prison, where he would stay in his cell 23 hours a day) for the rest of his life. It is said that being assigned to the particular Colorado Supermax prison in question is thought to be worse than the death penalty.

But back to the point. . . For me, under no circumstances can I support capital punishment and thus, I must stand faithful to my principles and oppose it even if the crime is heinous and horrific.

I remember when Michael Dukakis—former Governor of Massachusetts—ran for President back in 1988. During one of the debates between Dukakis and George H. W. Bush, Bernard Shaw presented Dukakis with a hypothetical: "Governor, if Kitty Dukakis [his wife] were raped and murdered, would you favor an irrevocable death penalty for the killer?"

Dukakis—perhaps realizing he was jeopardizing his chances for election—answered honestly: "No, I don't, and I think you know that I've opposed the death penalty all of my life."

He should have been admired for his stance and his consistency, but the public was not ready for that kind of truthfulness. His polling numbers plummeted that night and his campaign never recovered from it.

Incredibly and perhaps paradoxically, after Bush won, he was comfortable rationalizing his support and encouragement of the Contra War in Nicaragua, which not only resulted in a multitude of needless murders but also devastated that nation's economy from which it is still trying to recover.

Chief Justice Rose Bird

Do you remember California Supreme Court Chief Justice Rose Bird? I do. Her autographed picture continues to hang above my desk. I had the opportunity to speak with her and still treasure the moment. She was a progressive and, among other beliefs, she clearly opposed the death penalty. Her Court found reason on legal grounds to return 64 death penalty appeals to the lower courts for reconsideration.

She was, however, constantly castigated for those decisions—ones she made to insure that before a person is put to death by the State, every right of the accused is taken into consideration. I know, people will ask, What about the rights of the victims and their families?

Keep in mind, she didn't come to those conclusions on her own. She had been joined by other justices in those determinations. She and her Court also "re-established" that the State Constitution mandates the State to provide free abortions for poor women. Her opponents, quite contradictorily, considered abortion a form of murder, but for those same opponents, the death penalty was okay. Her Court was also an early advocate of fair and just sentencing. Ultimately, she and two of her Court colleagues were turned out of office by a two-thirds vote of the California electorate.

Bird was just too liberal, too forward-thinking, and way ahead of her time for much of California society back then. It is ironic that polls show a dramatic shift in thinking by the general populace—between the 70s and 80s and now—that more closely reflect her beliefs during her time administering and managing the Court and, thus, no longer align with the views of her contemporary antagonists and critics.

What do we get from putting others to death? Is there some morbid satisfaction? Revenge? A distorted sense of justice?

After the first effort to remove her failed, she could have modified her position to pander to the growing opposition against her in order to retain her post, but she held to her principles. Stanley Mosk, a fellow California Justice, is quoted as saying,

"Rose Bird was pilloried because she generally voted to find some defect in death penalty convictions and to reverse them. . . . I think the death penalty is wrong, that a person has no right to kill, and the state has no right to kill [either]."

Perhaps because Mosk was less consistent in his death penalty rulings, he was saved from recall while three others that shared the bench with him were not so "lucky."

Only a few days ago, former Congressman Barney Frank from Massachusetts—where the Boston Marathon Massacre took place—affirmed his staunch anti-capital punishment beliefs. Though he stated in the interview that it wouldn't hurt his feelings if Tsarnaev died, he still could not support the State's role in putting him to death despite the cruelty and brutality of his crimes.

What do we get from putting others to death? Is there some morbid satisfaction? Revenge? A distorted sense of justice? Nothing we do can bring a murder victim back and assuage the pain of the victims' relatives and friends. There is no question that crime deserves punishment! But how do we determine what is a fair and just punishment for capital crimes? How do we take on the responsibility for putting another to death?

Those who are God-fearing might want to think twice about taking God's place in passing such judgements. Those who are agnostic or atheistic or believers in non-god worshipping faiths or have no faith at all must also consider the basis for their personal beliefs.

"Thou shalt not murder" is a universal tenet shared world-wide, a basic construct for all civilizations. It stands to reason, then, that it would behoove us to be clear about the moral and ethical justifications for asking the State to murder in our stead, on our behalf.

These are ideas worth pondering before we execute the next person. The death penalty makes it easier for us not to have to think about the convicted anymore. But these people are also our fellow human beings, sharing many of the same flaws and shortcomings, rage and resentments, weaknesses and frailties that are part of the human condition.

Can our consciences allow us to put to death those who were not born with the inner strength to resist the temptations to act on their feelings? Who are we to murder others in order to make ourselves feel better?!

CARING FOR THE MENTALLY ILL:
Whose Job Is It Anyway?

We see them all around us. Sometimes we stop to chat and maybe give them a few dollars or buy them a sandwich, but

have we ever thought about what happens to them after we go about our business? Do they become invisible to us, especially as night falls? Do they sleep during the day and stay up all night for their safety? Do they live in camps or a tent town along downtown sidewalks? Do they eat refuse out of garbage cans and wear throw-aways for garments?

Do we ever think about all that?

Well, earlier in December I attended a town hall meeting sponsored by the **Van Nuys Neighborhood Council** (co-sponsored by the **North Hollywood NC**) and featuring speakers from a variety of organizations. They had somewhat similar stories to tell, but all agreed on the *linkage* between **homelessness** and **mental illness**.

Mayor Garcetti certainly recognizes this problem and has committed his administration to ending veteran (about 6600 under the present count) and non-veteran homelessness in our City by 2016. Idealistically, the goal is to find permanent housing at the rate of 300 per month which should virtually eliminate veteran homelessness in the near future after which the other two categories of homelessness—the short-term and the chronic—would be addressed. There is a program called **Home for Good** (under the umbrella of the United Way) which is already trying to accomplish these goals.

One problem that we face is the proliferation of non-profit organizations (as well-intentioned as they are) which keep re-inventing the wheel and often working at cross-purposes. Thus, a **coordinated effort** must be designed. Such an endeavor, however, would require more resources than are available at the moment—something that poses another challenge. In addition, it is necessary that all stakeholders be involved in the decision-making: intake, diagnosis, treatment with follow-up, determination of and then application for assistance eligibility, provision of good nutrition and clothing, job training suitable to their abilities, and (in many ways, especially) **permanent housing**—each person being placed in an affordable apartment or licensed home (perhaps sharing SSI funds with others in their situation to help cover costs).

It is also important to get an accurate demographic count of who the target groups are, the age range and gender, where clients usually stay, what kind of income and/or assistance is available to them and for what benefits are they eligible, and so forth. These statistics will help the established programs know how to allocate offices, staff, and resources.

The **City Attorney's Office (Mike Feuer)** is deeply involved. It has established a program called **Operation Healthy Streets**. It works with the respective City Council districts as well as the **Department of Sanitation** (locked storage for personal items is available to the homeless—a situation which can minimize the robberies that too often victimize this very vulnerable group all over again).

Among the speakers were representatives from **Councilmembers Paul Krekorian** and **Nury Martinez** who shared information about programs like the **Valley Rescue Mission** and the **Homeless Connected Program**.

The Chief of Staff from the office of **Congressmember Tony Cárdenas** spoke knowledgeably and enthusiastically about the Congressmember's passion for addressing the twin issues of homelessness and the mentally ill. He stated that veterans' homelessness must be a shared responsibility from the local community all the way to Washington.

Since the Congressmember sits on the **Health, Energy, and Commerce Committee**, he wants to be a leader in finding ways to create more jobs and better job training. This, in itself, will contribute to mitigating some of the homeless and mental illness concerns. In addition, by maintaining, expanding, and improving upon the **Affordable Care Act**, all people will be better served in terms of physical and mental health.

Barbara Wilson, a prominent Mental Health Policy Specialist, spoke passionately about the connection between homelessness and the proliferating numbers of the mentally ill. She reminded us that in 1970 California was number one in the nation for providing for the mentally ill population. However, it was when **Reagan** was our governor some years later (1981) that many of those people were literally thrown out on the streets to make it pretty much on their own.

The reality is that those with mental disorders are still in great need of ongoing, in-patient care; follow-up by medical personal; provision of prescription drugs, etc. Currently, Los Angeles County has the **highest rate** of the mentally ill in the nation!! From first to nearly last (California now competes with Mississippi), California and Los Angeles, in particular, share the onus of offering the poorest mental health delivery system for these patients.

From certified mental hospitals back in the day (like the one that used to be located in Camarillo) *to* our **Twin Towers**, it appears that the **prison system** has been left to provide services for the mentally ill instead of their being furnished by more qualified mental health facilities. Our **LA County's jail system**, in fact, houses the greatest concentration of people that have been or should have been diagnosed as mentally ill. In considering our options, we must "go back to the future" and no longer leave the jail system as the arbiter of mental health care.

Philp Mangano, of the **American Roundtable to Abolish Homelessness**, stated, We must have the political will to see these issues through—from the beginning to wherever the needs take us. **Early intervention** is essential since severe, chronic, and often disabling mental illness onset takes place between the ages of 18 and 25. If not treated early on, such neglect can lead to criminal activity (really through no fault of their own—after all, if individuals are ill, they cannot possibly know they are ill, and therefore they will not know to seek help and treatment—a vicious tautological conundrum). We, at the local level, must do what no other entity can do for us. We must be the first in the health-care pyramid to mandate measures to mitigate and ameliorate these distressing exigencies.

Mangano is just one more professional who emphasized the need for *permanent housing.* Not only will this make a difference to the psyche and feeling of self-worth for these patients, but from a fiduciary point of view, such housing is cost-effective: what would normally cost the government from $35,000 to $150,000 per person per year for intervention services, would be dramatically reduced to between $12,000 and $25,000 per year. What a difference! Just think of how much more can be accomplished and for how many more as a result of this kind of help. Certainly a goodly part of taxpayer burden would be lifted when the health issues for the homeless and mentally ill are handled properly.

There seemed to be an endless list of expert speakers that night. The **Cornerstone Program** in Van Nuys (under the auspices of **Dr. Adrienne Sheff** and **LSCW Bonnie Roth**) is providing critical outreach to the neediest in the community. The program works in partnership with the **Van Nuys Police Division of LAPD** (many of whose officers were in attendance that evening).

LAPD Captain John McMahon shared just how much police time and energy is taken up with the homeless and the mentally ill, many of whom pose real or potential threats to members in the community. He added that there needs to be recognition among all people who work with or otherwise come into contact with these individuals that they are **human beings first**, people who are suffering from issues over which they have no control but whose needs must be met before it is too late. We need to ascertain suitable and practical ways to address these pressing issues.

Other groups include **Village Family Services** under which is the **TAY Program** (Transitional Age Youth) which provides a drop-in center for young people aged 14 through 24. Many come from foster care and are taught life skills and other kinds of training, in an effort to break the homeless cycle. There are also classes teaching parenting skills.

There is **PATH (People Assisting the Homeless)** with 22 locations statewide. It concentrates on building new *social networks* for the previously homeless so that they don't feel at a loss once they are removed from the previous milieu with which they were so familiar and where they had often interacted with unsavory characters. Helping them find a new family of friends who can also serve as good role models is so essential to their ultimate success, improved health, and outlook.

In addition, there is the long-standing **Midnight Mission**; the **LA Family Housing Program**; the **LA County Health Department**; the **San Fernando Valley Community Health Center**; the **Weingarten Center**; the **National Alliance on Mental Illness (NAMI)**; the **San Fernando Valley Rescue Mission**. These many alternatives necessitate *coordination*. In other words, they must work together in alliance instead of separately, thus avoiding inevitable confusion and redundancy by functioning independently of each other.

We must hold our leaders' feet to the fire. When we help the most needy, the poor, the abused, the elderly, the hungry and cold, the homeless, and the mentally ill—we all benefit.

We must never fall into the "Who cares?!" trap. We must act upon our concerns and help others to do the same. During this season when we are thinking about what we can do for others, consider getting involved in one of these organizations (or others), not just now but throughout the year.

CAN'T MISS THEM. THE HOMELESS ARE RIGHT THERE IN FRONT OF US!

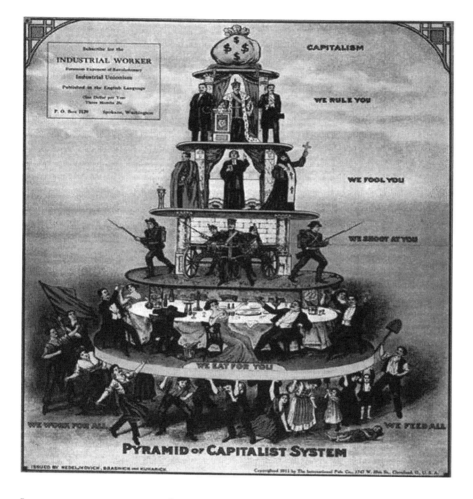

I once saw a poster of a metaphorical equilateral triangle, but it didn't illustrate a math problem or a pyramid or a financial scheme. In fact, it didn't represent equality at all!

Instead, it illustrates a top-down economic reality, a truth that reflects the unforgiving foundation of every single civilization since the beginning of time. At the very top—balancing precariously on that very narrow peak, that summit--stand the proverbial robber barons, the captains of industry, the politically powerful and well-connected. They're the people who know nothing of real labor (they consider their mental "exertions" more meaningful than actual physical drudgery); yet they stand on the shoulders of those who do, the people below them on the pyramid, the people who make it possible for that one percent to make all the money and to keep it. Those at the top are held up by the laborers below, crushing each level until the foundation of the entire structure is about to be crushed from their sheer weight.

And at the very bottom of the bottom—almost beneath the foundation—exist the invisibles, the homeless!

For some time, I have been an advocate for the homeless (as have many of you). I have been touched when I served meals to these special, grateful human beings. I have held their hands and embraced their trembling bodies as they cried out their stories. I have administered simple medications for people who needed so much more. I have observed the broken bodies of people incapable of working, barely able to walk. I have seen children whose only meals are provided by kitchens or by their schools—lucky if they get one warm meal a day. I have also listened to people who tell of trying to sleep while others walk about aimlessly or yell out inexplicably--the untreated mentally ill who wander around children and women who can barely sleep because they are afraid they will be accosted during the night.

Then there are the people who depend on buses to get them to work or a job interview but arrive too late due to impractical transportation schedules, and so they are fired or miss out on a potential position. What of the young people who are driven downtown only to be thrown out of the car by their own parents who no longer want them and tell them never to contact them again—children who have not finished school and are too young for work permits, so they turn to prostitution as the only way to survive? What of them?

And the shelters . . . people depend on shelters for a shower but may have to settle for a sponge bath because a shower is not available. And the shelters. . . if homeless individuals or families are lucky enough to be accepted into them, they can only stay so many days before they are turned out onto the streets once again.

I recount an incident from not all that long ago: I was on my way to an early Saturday morning conference on a cold winter's day when I approached a downtown off-ramp. There had been no traffic until I tried to get off the freeway. It took me a half hour just to get to the bottom but I still needed to make two quick lefts. What was the traffic jam? I am going to be late! I saw police cars and officers whom I thought were annoying homeless men and women who were just trying to sleep peacefully under the overpass. I began to roll down my window to scold the patrolmen, "Leave them alone! They are harmless!" Then I saw it. Oh, dear God. Two dead gentlemen, one covered already; the other, only up to his face. I have never forgotten that scene. I wanted to cry but I was also filled with helpless fury and a sense of powerlessness. I have shared that story countless times, hoping others would become equally outraged and would feel compelled to change a society that looks away when the less fortunate come toward us.

I share all this because there are so many misconceptions about the homeless, and the wretchedly shameful conditions they experience, about those who are but one small step from joining their ranks, from losing their homes only to sleep in cars or under a card board "roof" on the streets. Many people think they *choose* to live that way. I think, however, that people *choose* to believe the homeless want to live that way. They *choose* to believe this convenient untruth because so many people are unwilling to face what is really transpiring in their own communities. Accepting the veracities surrounding homelessness would force them to do something about it— their consciences would demand action, but it is so much easier to be in denial and blame the blameless. We talk about people "yearning to be free"—free from poverty, hunger, illness, abuse, abandonment, joblessness, homelessness. What would Emma Lazarus say about these unfortunates after all these years?

One of my former students, Joey Meyer, addressed this issue in his magnificent cinquain entitled "Cities":

Cities

are cold and dark

with quiet all around.

Some people are homeless in them.

Who cares?!

Whoa! I don't know about you, but I wasn't expecting that ending! That last line is filled with anger and disappointment. It demands, it insists, it challenges us to commit to do something real—not merely to give lip service to what is a travesty in the richest country in the world. We help everyone, everywhere when there is an emergency—as we should! We are lucky to be in that position. But at the same time we persist in looking away from the tragic circumstances that too many of our own people face every day.

Remember Edwin Markham's all-to-fitting poem, "The Man with a Hoe"? Over a hundred years ago he spoke so eloquently, so poignantly, so passionately about the evil his words reveal. How prescient he was! He warned us that this strong but battered protagonist has been "Bowed by the weight of centuries" with "the emptiness of ages in his face, And on his back, the burden of the world." This is the same man that the "masters, lords, and rulers" of the world have created to perform excruciating toil with little offered in return for his efforts. Markham ultimately asks how these lords of industry and power will answer to the rest of us (and to a higher power). How will they answer to those they have worked so mercilessly and taken for granted "after the silence of the centuries"?

I ask the same thing (though less eloquently). I speak not only on behalf of the homeless but for any of us who are down-and-out or about to be. We can no longer look away. There but for the grace of God go any of us. Yes, we should be our brothers' and sisters' keepers. I think it is a moral imperative. We really have no choice.

Intimidation through Bullying: Sixty Per Cent of Children Afraid To Go to School Because of Bullying:

Monica Harmon Speaks Out

Since **October is National Bullying Prevention Month**, how appropriate it is to take some time to address this issue.

Bullying is perpetrated by people, usually youngsters but frequently adults, whose aim is nothing less than malicious torment of their victims—targets often just a few years old.

I suppose bullying has been around since the beginning of time, but there are so many newer ways than ever before to victimize people—cyber-attacks through Tweets, Facebook, all kinds of social media.

Even the disabled are not off-limits, and it is not just people in a wheel chair but people who are mentally challenged or mentally ill—too many other categories to mention here. It is people whose religious practices (or non-practice) or whose skin color or hair texture is different. It is people who are overweight or underweight, who are fast or slow, who are good students or underachievers. The victims seem to be anyone who stands out from the crowd—for good or for bad.

The problem goes beyond the bully or even the victim—it is a pervasive issue we don't dare ignore!

Recently, I had the distinct pleasure of speaking with a very humble, self-effacing **Monica Harmon** (a Public Safety Advocate volunteer), who was just recognized by the Los Angeles City Council for her unwavering support of the victims of bullying.

Los Angeles Councilmembers Buscaino, Englander and LaBonge spoke in praise of her, but Felipe Fuentes (who, while an Asssemblymember in the State Legislature, worked on anti-bullying legislation) spent a little extra time in recognizing her as someone who leads by example, who is one tough advocate (for any of her many issues), who is creative and innovative in her pursuit of justice.

She founded the group, **Speak Out Against Bullying, Inc.**, which works with parents, teachers, students, community leaders to teach about this plague on our society. It holds townhalls and school assemblies to demonstrate what bullying really is--in all its manifestations. It also advises about how people can avoid being victims, how they can develop a stronger, more positive self-image, how by-standers can find the inner-strength to stand up *for* others, and how perpetrators and potential perpetrators can look at the potential consequences of their actions and choose alternate behavior beforehand.

It was Councilmember Mitch O'Farrell, himself an openly gay man who knows what it is like to be the object of senseless and unwarranted persecution, who initiated the award Harmon was given.

He provided alarming statistics pertinent to the bullying epidemic. One in seven children are harassed and intimidated every year (that is 7.2 million students per year), leading to feelings of low self-worth, isolation, self-mutilation, and suicide (some 4,400 deaths per year)—the third leading cause of death among young people.

And just last week there was another horrendous example of a suicidal response by a teenager-- this time in Florida [it seems "(t)here **is** something rotten in the state of -------"]. Twelve year old Rebecca Sedwick was so terrorized by cyber-attacks from two young perpetrators (12 and 14), that she took her young life. And just this week a young man in Nevada killed a teacher, wounded others, and then became a victim of gun violence himself.

For a child, there often seems to be no way out, no way to relieve that agonizing pain. Too many parents and teachers believe that bullying is no more than a rite (right) of passage and that targets should "man" up and learn how to take it and/or give it back. They don't intercede—they are often insensitive and indifferent--until it is too late. And when parents and teachers do report this kind of activity, they are frequently ignored. Is this the kind of society we want our children to experience?

Sixty per cent of children are afraid of going to school because they know they may be confronted by the threat of bullies (14 per cent of children are the predators or the prey). And LGBT youngsters are 7 times more likely to be victimized.

And what about the gun-toting youngsters who shoot up school mates and theaters and playgrounds and malls? There is evidence through studies of the diminished capacity of such perpetrators, people who themselves have been ignored and isolated and persecuted because of their differences from the rest, because of how they do not neatly fit in with others. Their minds are sick, sometimes because of untreated tumors, sometimes because of physical or mental abuse, sometimes for reasons unknown. They are also victims that need our sympathy, even when they do bad things.

Think of the two teens who slaughtered so many at Columbine High School in Colorado. There were clear signs they were troubled youth, but no one stepped in to help—no school administrators, counsellors, teachers, fellow students, parents. Full of angst, resentment, a sense of futility to their lives, they carried out their obscene plan.

Despite the horrors they committed, I felt a sense of sadness for them too. No crosses with their names on them to commemorate their miserable lives. They were ignored even in death. Perhaps they were victims as well. By not mourning their passing, Society is setting itself up for future assassinations.

Bullying has consequences. If we don't get to the cause, there will be further explosions from those mercurial souls who believe they have no other outlet than to quench their own pain through such unconscionable acts.

There are many viable alternatives to mere lip service regarding these matters. Monica shared with me what a superb partner the LAPD is—with its many youth programs and intervention networks. Harmon and her partners have been working relentlessly to suppress an adage that has too often been encouraged: Prove yourself! Be a bully! When good programs are introduced when children are very young and when those programs have the backing of parents and teachers, the effect is almost immediate—reduction of intimidating practices.

I'll never forget experiences with some of my students. One lovely, intelligent, personable ninth grader was so tormented by her "friends" that she transferred from our school a mere semester before her junior high graduation. I tried to do an intervention with her tormentors but to no avail. It seemed that when the group gained a new girl, the uneven number put my student as the odd "man" out. I think of her all the time too. I was heartsick over her leaving, but I hope the change worked out for her.

Another young man who was in my class just before the nutrition break, never wanted to leave. I came to realize that he was trying to think up things to ask me because he did not want to leave the room. I spoke with him about this and he opened up to me: Kids were always waiting for him outside the door to taunt and instill fear in him. We spoke with his parents, the counselors, reported the names of the students—nothing much happened.

Even though I continued to be supportive, I worry about him to this day. Whatever happened to him? Is he finally leading a happy life? I still fear for him. Children like him withdraw into themselves, never think they are good enough; they come to believe that there is something wrong with them instead of with the mean-spirited, children who probably have such a low self-image themselves that acting out is the only way they can feel superior to someone or something else.

Let us teach each other and particularly the young that being fair and compassionate and sticking up for others and being defenders, not aggressors, is not a sign of being weak. It shows the kind of strength that should be developed in each of us.

Let each of us spend some time considering what we can do to make a difference to the bullying nightmare.

Please also take some time to look up Monica's Website:

speakoutagainstbullying.org (something she designed all by herself—I am impressed). Feel free to contact Monica Harmon at monicaharmonla.aol.com.

TRANSGENDER EQUALITY: GET USED TO IT

It is only through the whimsical decision by Nature that we are not all hermaphrodites, let alone transgender (Am I shocking your sensibilities? Good). We all start out more or less the same *in utero* (with male *and* female hormones), but

the majority of people find they are more attracted to the opposite sex.

If we are true to ourselves, we have to admit that at some point in our lives, we have been drawn to someone of the same sex. Some are afraid of what they feel, others experiment; still others engage in what at the time was an honest homosexual relationship (think of Anne Heche).

Many, of course, are homosexual from the beginning, the majority of whom have to struggle to admit it to themselves (if Society were more open, there wouldn't be the inherent fear about coming out—an action, frankly, that is unnecessary). Some are attracted to both sexes (Marlon Brando), and others are transgender (consider the interesting introduction of DC Comic's Alysia Yeoh in *Batgirl*, albeit a fictional character but hopefully a good role model).

I always love it when people quote the Bible to me about how sinful such behavior is. It is obvious to me that such people have probably never read the Holy Scriptures nor understood them if they did.

How does one explain King David's love for Jonathan more than any woman? He loved no one better despite his many subsequent wives.

What about Jesus' love for that Beloved Disciple? Some scholars believe it is John; others, James—unless we consider the faithful Mary of Magdala. People insist on quoting Leviticus 18:22, a passage so massively misunderstood (no mention of a woman lying with another woman, by the way) that it is totally taken out of context (*abomination* in its original Hebrew meaning, for instance, indicates an act approaching evil and idolatrous worship because it mimics rituals of the polytheists, people from whom the early Hebrews were attempting to create a distinct separation).

At a time when the new monotheistic Judaism was under siege and temptation and surrounded by enemies who wanted to annihilate them, wasting a man's seed would have been sinful because procreation was needed to increase the tribe and its chances of survival and extend its viability (Judaism now being the most enduring organized religion in history).

As laws are being passed to overturn DOMA and reversing Don't Ask, Don't tell and more states are granting same-sex marriage (California, I remind you, was once again the leader), we are turning to another important issue, that of **transgender community members** and overturning roadblocks to their equal treatment before the law.

Governor Brown, in August and October of this year, signed two major bills. The first (AB 1266) allows transgender students the right to choose which restrooms and which locker rooms to use based upon the sex with which they identify themselves.

This law reminds me of the time only a few years ago when student applicants for the Magnet Program in the LAUSD had to select (for racial identification) the parent with whom they *most* closely identified! Can you imagine being forced to pick your Black father over your white mother just to get into a school of your choice?!

We fought hard to eliminate that question from the process, something soon followed by changes in the U.S. Census to allow people to identify in the way *most* suitable for them (Black *and* white; bi-racial, etc.). The new California laws similarly allow individuals to live as the people they truly are.

In October, Brown signed another bill, AB 1121, to make it easier for transgender individuals to amend their birth certificates and to change their names to reflect their "authentic selves." And they won't have to jump through a myriad of hoops to do so!

Surprising to no one, there are ferocious hounds already nipping at the heels of those laws in an effort to overturn them. The same organizations [the National Organization for Marriage (NOM) and the GOP] and the same leadership (such as Frank Schubert, a career hater who headed the fight to ban same-sex marriage through the 2008 Proposition 8—which, of course, was ultimately overturned) are spearheading another ballot measure initiative to overturn these most recent laws.

Says John O'Connor of Equality California, "Frank Schubert has built a political career on these anti-LGBT (Lesbian/Gay/Bi-Sexual/Transgender) measures that divide people. . . . We have turned the corner. The public is solidly in favor of LGBT equality now."

The Catholic and Mormon churches (under the veil of religious authority and interpretation) heavily funded the Prop. 8 campaigns and convinced millions of voters of the righteousness of their opposition to such marriages. It is likely that we can expect similar intrusions again. However, this time we will be ready for the tortured reasoning and onslaught of negative, scary, and distorted commercials to advance their twisted point of view. How some people and institutions continue to be motivated by pure hate and ignorance simply eludes me.

If there is a sin here, it is the millions of dollars repeatedly expended (and wasted) on promoting animus and defending hateful referenda, money that could be better spent, for instance, on the education of our children and healthcare for the public!

This transgender issue may be less palatable to some but so were mixed marriage and racial integration and religious oppression from not so long ago. None of those issues have been completely alleviated or accepted by all (and neither will this one), but as Gavin Newsom would say, Get used to it!

Equality was built into our Constitution—it is just taking a few hundred years to realize it for one and all.

Please join me and the many others in supporting this very significant issue promoting fairness, justice, and equality. For more information you may contact **Equality California at eqca.org** *or* **323-848-9801** *for more details.*

A Wedding Is Not Always Just a Wedding

For me, last Saturday was worthy of great celebration—my play daughter was getting married! Early twenties, beautiful, intelligent, compassionate. Why not expect that this day would be in the cards for her? She had met her spouse 6 years to the day before their nuptials. How romantic!

She had been a student of mine in middle school. I taught several of her sisters and a brother as well. The entire family had been to our home numerous times around the holidays. We had gone out to lunch together. My husband and I were guests at the older sister's wedding not more than a year ago—a big church wedding followed by a reception about which nearly every girl fantasizes.

This one, however, was to be small and intimate—family and close friends, an outdoor wedding in a lovely setting.

My husband and I were among the first there so it gave us the opportunity to watch as other guests took their seats, all waiting eagerly for the ceremony to begin. I just knew that her older sister and possibly her mother would be there. I was hoping her father would walk her down the aisle.

When the music commenced and the ceremony began, in marched the adorable flower girl, casting colorful blossoms on the white runner. Following her were the ladies and gentlemen in waiting. And after that, finally, was the father with tears in his eyes, walking in his beloved daughter, kissing her at the pulpit. Then, at last, appeared my student, all grown up, in a fitted, old-fashioned, beaded gown and matching veil. She was escorted, not by her father *or* her mother, but by a sister and brother. I could not hold back my own tears—my "little girl" was about to exchange vows and be truly happy— with a bright future ahead of her.

Yes, this was a same-sex wedding. As it was proceeding, the image of then-San Francisco Mayor Gavin Newsom (D) briefly crossed my mind: "This door's wide open now. It's going to happen, whether you like it or not"—he exclaimed before a wildly cheering crowd of California Prop. 8 supporters, way back in 2008. I thought of so many other friends and associates who could now join their lives—officially, lovingly, committedly—with the one they loved the most.

I had promised them this day would come—they were hesitant to believe me. *Now it is real.* Now a lot more than marriage is real. Hundreds of laws will protect these partners. They can have children together; they are entitled to healthcare benefits covered under each other's benefits packages. They can work at their chosen professions, and so much more.

I remember during my early days of teaching when gay teachers had to hide who they really were (and this was right after it was legally possible for my husband and me to marry—only since 1967). Black and white, gay and straight, Jew and gentile. This is another step higher on the civil rights ladder. These are the outcomes about which people like Martin Luther King, Jr. dreamed, spoke, sacrificed, and sometimes died.

But that Saturday was a day for celebration, jubilation, and happy tears. Though there may be the occasional backlash among those in the extreme right, let our enthusiastic cheers drown out their self-serving and selfish voices. To paraphrase a statement by Ohio Gov. John Kasich (R) and some lines from the historical fiction novel, *Catherine, Called Birdy*, When we die and arrive at the Pearly Gates, God is not going to ask us what our titles were or how much money we made. God is going to ask us what we did for the least of those among the multitudes.

That wedding marks a day of exaltation, of new beginnings and bright futures. And those who witnessed it will carry with them a new spirit to share with the doubters. Soon, I predict, such weddings will be as commonplace as having a bi-racial man or a woman or Latino or Muslim as President. Realistically though, such marriages are likely to become less extraordinary and more mundane before we ever witness other political miracles.

Juvenile Offenders: From Big Wheels to the Big House

Sex Trafficking: From Naive Innocence to Life on the Streets

I remember years ago when I was working with and for the homeless, I learned a lot about this neglected segment of our population.

Would it surprise you to know there are young people in far greater numbers than we might otherwise imagine, females who find themselves walking the streets of Los Angeles—hopeless, filled with fear, often brutalized by the pimps—the sex traffickers, "the quintessential predators with violent

backgrounds?" These men, so ironically, are the very people the victims thought they could depend on. We cannot escape the fact that there are literally thousands of these women who have become "strangers in a strange land," so it is imperative that the rest of us do something to change all that.

Some girls have been molested repeatedly at home, having been subjected to horrendous abuse—often from the mother's boyfriend. One anecdote tells of a mother's "companion" who tried to kill the girl until she managed to escape: He had attempted to drown her in a tub, put her in an oven until her mother intervened, raped her repeatedly—and she wasn't even a teenager.

As horrendous as these descriptions are, these children are often not even old enough to get a work permit, cannot finish school as they have no address to claim residence, often become too transient to be recipients of the little help that might be available. Officer Dawson of the LAPD has been clear that these are girls (not to be considered prostitutes but victims) who are legally too young to consent to sexual acts and, therefore, should not be punished for selling their bodies. And yet, look at the treatment we often sanction on behalf of enforcement to the detriment of these mere children.

Young people run away from home because of psychological, physical, or sexual abuse—or all three. Some have been abandoned by their parents—left with grandparents or placed in foster care—resulting in their feelings of alienation. There are those parents who drive to a god-forsaken neighborhood and simply drop their teens off at the curb, telling them emphatically they never want to hear from their own children again! Many young women escape from their "homes" because they feel they have no home, no welcoming schools or friends to trust.

Hungry, frightened, penniless—what do they do? Eventually, somehow, they look to the streets for salvation, for a sense of family. Instead, they find men who claim to love them but insist that the only way to demonstrate their love in return is by earning money for these monsters through soliciting more-than-willing johns.

Before these victims know it, these merciless, heartless, often brutal pimps take over—treating these once innocent girls like chattel.

Before these victims know it, these merciless, heartless, often brutal pimps take over—treating these once innocent girls like chattel. The girls are branded on their backs, faces, and necks to show other competing pimps just who "owns" them. To punish victim "transgressions," they are often gang-raped by a group of pimps, thrown into trunks, threatened with death (and some do die horrible deaths). And thus they are usually too afraid to seek help even when it is offered to them.

In some ways, perhaps worst of all are the foreign sex traffickers who, like false prophets, make false promises. They promise a family that their daughter will find a good job in America and enjoy the kind of life she has only dreamed about.

But there are also fathers who are willing to sell their daughters for a mere pair of boots! What are young daughters worth these days?!

Just last week I attended a symposium on this very subject. It was hosted by the Van Nuys Neighborhood Council with guest speakers representing a broad spectrum of law enforcement and other help organizations: the FBI, DEA, ICE, Homeland Security, the former Mary Magdalene Project (now Journey Out), LAPD (Van Nuys Vice Division), and staff from the offices of State Senator Robert Hertzberg, State Assemblymember Adrin Azarian, City Councilmember Nury Martinez (CD 6) (known for her ongoing concerns on this subject), and CARE 18 (dedicated to fighting human trafficking).

What was shared is not easy to summarize nor are the goals easy to accomplish, but a repeated theme was the need to change the current paradigm for addressing this pressing issue in our communities.

Arrests in themselves are counterproductive. They use up

significant time, money, and resources and, in the end, unfortunately, accomplish very little. In fact, we need a more victim-centered approach. In essence, the greater part of the work pertaining to this intolerable and unacceptable abuse must be centered on the girls, not to punish them (often for circumstances over which they have had little control) but to help them make the transition out of the life.

This issue can be analogized to the economic supply and demand economic theory: no johns—no pimps—no victims! Thus, traffickers and "clients" must be punished in a significant and severe manner, making them bear most of the responsibility for what is transpiring, making their lives as unlivable as those of the young women they have victimized.

If we dehumanize these females in our minds, that is how these girls will perceive themselves.

The girls [often 11 years of age, many 12-14, and some even younger (still others somehow making it into their 20s or 30s)] are used up like oranges before they are finally discarded as refuse ("You can't eat the orange and then throw the peel away" from Death of a Salesman). These young women were not born to this life and thus deserve to be helped to find a path out of it.

Our officers can no longer view these victims as dross—only good for the dust bin of society– but rather as human beings deserving of respect and dignity. Thankfully, law enforcement in our great City is beginning to understand that positive, constructive changes in policy must be made, will be efficacious, and many support doing just that.

Similarly, it is up to society to change its own attitude. It is simply counter-intuitive to punish essentially innocent people who for any number of reasons have lost their way and come under the power and control of vicious, heartless "masters." In many ways these women (and many men and boys) are indeed slaves!

It was stated at the conference that a three-pronged approach must be made to address the conundrum that has faced us (and countless other communities) since time immemorial:

- a new law enforcement approach
- the availability and access to victim services (with the creation and addition of effective diversion programs);
- improved and innovative community outreach which itself takes several forms:
  - o education for everyone on all aspects of the issue
  - o changing the psychological environment
  - o addressing the physical environment (with something as simple as increased street lighting on darker streets, thus making it less attractive and more difficult for johns and victims to engage in these nefarious practices).

It should not be overlooked that illicit drugs plays a part in all of this as well. The fact is that many of these victims, who are being transported from another country to our neighborhoods, are often made to carry the additional burden of being drug mules. The drug cartels represent an abhorrent, seemingly interminable sequence that is not the circle of life but of death—starting with drugs and prostitution and even money laundering and ending with huge profits—only to start all over again and again. "Merchandise" is created in one place and sold to a willing and eager market in another. Multi-millionaires are made at the circle's genesis—people who are willing to be cruel and murderous to advance their own avaricious purposes while victimizing the powerless.

Another aspect of the illegal practices referenced here includes child pornography and sex tourism. Certainly, our law enforcement agencies must seek out the purveyors of and participants in these kinds of pornography and then crack down mercilessly on the perpetrators with harsh, meaningful sentences (since, after all, they have "sentenced" their victims to lives forever scarred by their heartless, self-serving, horrifying schemes and tactics).

As hard as the DEA and AFT have for decades been struggling with this problem (often themselves being tortured or even killed while carrying out their duties), I am not alone when I believe not enough is being done by the higher echelons of our government. Many of us have come to view our government's dedication to eradicating these practices with suspicion and a jaundiced eye. Too often our current laws regarding these issues are repressive, oppressive, inadequate, and, for the most part, simply unreasonable. Too frequently the victims are coerced into plea bargains that actually work against their best interests.

The true goals of government with regard to the drug trade in our neighborhoods have become blurred. This reminds me of the recent movie, *Kill the Messenger*, based upon the true story of the highly acclaimed, award-winning journalist, Gary Webb, who was (during his lifetime that was cut short) ultimately thwarted in his efforts to reveal the truths about what is transpiring at every level in the drug/human trafficking trade.

As a result, the DEA/AFT are characterized within many communities as the enemy—even when they are trying to help. As a result, the officers of these agencies often become those persons from which one must run, with whom one must not cooperate. It should be obvious, then, that the neighborhoods must be re-educated about their own attitudes and perceptions. Cooperating with authorities must not carry the taboo that it has for far too long and cannot make pariahs (often with a "price" on their heads) for those trying to clean up their communities.

To quote Rabbi Hillel's famous exhortation: "If I am not for myself, who will be for me? If I am not for others, what am I? And if not now, when?"

From this I add, For those in our midst who are hopeless and tortured and feeling that there is nothing out there for them but to live out their empty, lonely, invisible lives until they die and vanish, who will help them if we do not?!

For more information and for ways to get involved, please check out the following:

- Children of the Night
- Saving Innocence
- Mary Magdalene Project (Journey Out)
- National Center for Missing and Exploited Children
- Your local representatives (City Councilmembers, County Supervisors, State Assembly and State Senate members

Cover Up: Was There Ever a Genuine War on Drugs?

I must begin with a huge apology to the many people who claimed that our own Federal government was behind injecting drugs into our inner-city communities! I was one of those incredulous people who maintained, despite ongoing outcries, that our government would never do such a thing!

I remember when Congresswoman Maxine Waters held a rally back in the '90s that accused the government of a conspiracy to destroy the Black community through creating a drug climate and drug dependency. It was asserted that 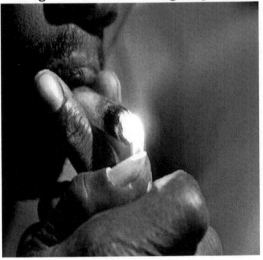 providing a young person with $5 worth of cocaine, for free, would lead to addictions almost impossible to overcome. Too often these young people were set on a life of crime in order to satiate their unrelenting drug cravings. The belief was that the government was trying to destroy the Black community from within (having not been able to accomplish this through centuries of slavery and the unimaginable syphilis experiments).

Then the leader of the Los Angeles Chapter of the NAACP was quoted as saying, "It is time for the government, the CIA, to come forward and accept responsibility for destroying human

228

lives."

For me and countless others, these "outrageous" claims seemed just too fantastic to which any credence could be given.

It was about this time, however, that Gary Webb, a journalist for the *San Jose Mercury News*, wrote a series called "Dark Alliance." The recent movie, *Kill the Messenger* (based upon his life and research), presents a dismal

picture of the "real" story behind the Iran-Contra, Drugs for Arms scenario.

According to his own writings and the film, he investigated (as thoroughly as he was allowed) the connection between the government's goal to free hostages held in Iran and its need to bring in bushels-full of covert money to arm the Contras against a Nicaraguan government which it did not support because of its Sandinista communist leanings.

In fact, I was in Nicaragua about this time with Habitat for Humanity and got, through our many interviews with government and NGO leaders, an entirely different picture of what was transpiring there. Under Daniel Ortega, the country's president, literacy had risen to 88% (higher than our own), college was offered for free to anyone who would dedicate four years (post-graduation) in helping to ameliorate a variety of conditions. Technology was enhanced and farmers could use state-of-the-art equipment to work their fields.

All this pertained until the American government began establishing a Contra resistance whose aim was to overthrow the successful Nicaraguan Ortega government. Thus, much of our money had to be re-allocated to support the Contras, diverting funding from more important citizen needs at home. Ultimately, because of embargos created by the Reagan administration, Nicaraguans could not obtain replacement parts for cars or tractors and other necessities. The land became littered with rusty, useless vehicles that were abandoned because operators were no longer able to keep them in working order.

And why? Because the college-educated Nicaraguan leadership adhered to a *pure* communist philosophy? Because its leaders supported education and healthcare for all (sound familiar)? Because they wanted to repair and rebuild their infrastructure, particularly after suffering the consequences of a horrendous earthquake?

I have in my possession a video produced decades ago which addresses these issues. The film was made available to very few people, but somehow (I forget how it happened) I was able to obtain one of them. It is called *Cover Up* (produced in 1988) and is absolutely remarkable for what it purports. If you can get one, you must see it for yourselves!

It seems that the National Security Agency, the NSA created a "shadow government" under the guise of advancing national security interests. In 1987 the Iran-Contra Hearings were held and produced a lengthy document of its findings. At first Reagan denied any knowledge of the arms-for-hostages accusation but a year later stepped back a little on that response.

The fact is that we sent arms (at marked-up prices) to Iran (to help them fight their then-enemy, Iraq). The profits were used by the CIA to arm the Contras against Nicaragua. Oliver North denied the allegations but it was later learned that the government shredded documents or altered them to keep the truth from coming out. On top of everything else, there were those who clearly wanted to eliminate the paper trail (the documents were compromising).

It was claimed that Reagan made a deal with Iran to free the hostages only after the election (the failure to rescue our hostages had been extremely damaging to Carter) and, thus, on the very day Reagan was inaugurated, the hostages were "miraculously" released.

The documentary goes on to state that such covert actions are simply not democratic. The fact is that our government over many years has been responsible, at least in part, for the overthrow of Iran, Guatemala, Brazil, and Ghana (generally for oil-related reasons—we wanted to have control over how we obtained our own oil resources).

This film further claims that, over a considerable span of time,

we also had a hand in the overthrow of other governments whose leadership aims did not align with our own and were not necessarily sympathetic with Western values: Greece, Egypt, Korea, Laos, Zaire, the Dominican Republic, Bolivia, Indonesia, Cambodia, Chile, Thailand, and Viet Nam (what we did there led to a war that took almost 60,000 soldiers from us and left countless warriors to fend for themselves after returning stateside—often resulting in interminable homelessness on the streets).

Abroad, threats were made and sometimes acted upon to force people to join rebel forces or be killed. Bombs were dropped in some areas which killed recalcitrant leaders who did not want to comply with the demands of these covert American forces. The documentary also asserts that the CIA worked with organized crime to form networks to support the CIA itself. For Reagan, the ends justified the means!

It is unbelievable that in 1984 the Readiness Exercise 1984 Act (Rex 84) under the Emergency Management Agency (which later became FEMA) actually considered suspending the U. S. Constitution under the guise of an emergency declaration. Why, you ask? To suppress political descent (think of the concurrent Civil Rights and Viet Nam protests of the '60s and '70s), to label opponents as terrorists, to make FEMA the anti-terrorism instrument!

There was actual consideration to create internment camps (the way we did with the Japanese-Americans during World War II) for people suspected of anti-American sentiment (think of McCarthyism). It even considered rounding up the half million undocumented that were in the country at the time.

Money was raised from off-shore accounts to be funneled into campaigns to defeat liberal candidates—people like George McGovern, Birch Bayh, and Frank Church who had been questioning what was transpiring under the CIA umbrella. Congress at the time was unwilling to investigate these issues for fear that such research would lead to culpability all the way up to the top—that meant the possibility of Reagan's involvement.

We waged dirty wars under approved covert actions. Many leaders were assassinated. I think of the socialist Salvador (the savior) Allende, President of Chile, who stood for raising up the common man over the demands of the industrial complex. And who did Chile get after Allende was assassinated? The thug, Augosto Pinochet! It seems (as an important part of these schemes) that these secret organizations pilfered arms out of Viet Nam to support those rebels who would work to overturn governments that did not support U. S. foreign policy.

What a circle of inconceivable horror. The corollary to all of this subversion taught these rebel groups how to destabilize governments by making their point through the use of torture, rape, and murder.

The list goes on and on: support for *Anastasio Somoza* of Nicaragua and *Muammar Gaddafi* (spelling varies) of Libya to name just two more. *Cover Up* further claims that former supporters of Somoza were trained in Honduras to overthrow the Sandinistas in Nicaragua. Some of the money that was covertly supplied to the rebels was supposed to feed and clothe the soldiers. The reality? Money was stolen for other questionable purposes which resulted in Contra soldiers often living on only one meal a day. A great way to make enemies of your friends!

What a circle of inconceivable horror. The corollary to all of this subversion taught these rebel groups how to destabilize governments by making their point through the use of torture, rape, and murder. The long-term consequences for us

U.S.-backed Contras on patrol.

and many other Western nations? We find ourselves today muddled and struggling in some capacity with Iran, Iraq, Pakistan, Afghanistan, Egypt, Libya, Syria, and more.

But what of the cocaine conspiracy? Despite government denial by such people as Oliver North, drug-trafficking became a reality with a perverse purpose. Arms were sent through Florida to Honduras and Costa Rica (where I once studied), the latter nation still very unhappy with the repeated, persistent, and generally unwanted interference by the U. S. Think also of the Banana Republics (not the clothing store chain) that were formed for U. S. commercial profit. Drugs were then sent into certain American communities, especially into San Francisco and Los Angeles. It seems (unbeknownst to most Americans and under the guise of preventing the Communist domino theory) that the war in Viet Nam was also prompted by a drug connection with opium growers in Cambodia and Laos.

It is ironic that so many of the very nations that we helped overthrow have become among the strongest economies in the world and our rivals!

The result of all those secretive machinations was that 4-5 million people back in the '80s (far more today) were hooked on cocaine here in our country. What is worse, even now, is that when the poorer inner-city addicts get arrested for possession of rock/crack cocaine, they are often given a sentence of at least 3 years in prison while the wealthier "consumer" who is caught with powder cocaine may get only 3 months.

Drug cartels which produced billionaires were often in cahoots with governments from a variety of nations to allow the creation and expansion of drug commerce (or look the other way). Years ago it was proven that millions of dollars from the drug industry had been secreted in Swiss bank accounts (under the auspices of shadow government leaders). Just consider the billions that have been made (since then) off the backs of naïve, often inner-city young people who were duped into taking that first hit and subsequently became mercilessly addicted.

Why do our government and others continue to underwrite the drug industry? For power over other nations or over our own communities? For oil (to perpetuate the myopic needs of dirty energy producers)? To force other countries to be refashioned in our own image? To control what information is disseminated to the public?

I know all this is mind-boggling—too baffling, too complicated, too overwhelming, too inconceivable to consider, let alone believe.

However, I lay out the facts as I see them, as I objectively researched this broad, all-encompassing issue. When I first heard many of these claims some years ago, I dismissed them as being too incredible. Statements made by people with an agenda, I thought. Blacks killing Blacks—a "natural" part of inner-city life. I am so embarrassed by my perceptions then. I hope to be forgiven by those whom I judged harshly and did not believe.

I see all this in a different light now. I pity and hurt for the many DEA officers who have been wounded or killed in an effort to make the War on Drugs succeed. I feel for the ones who survived their missions to live forever in a nightmare. I feel even worse for all the victims of the efforts by the "shadow government" to introduce hard drugs into communities for profit and control.

The fact is that we must deal with the consequences. For one, passing Proposition 47 would decriminalize many minor drug "crimes." We must insist that the "least of us" be given the same attention and concern as the rest of us take for granted. We must address the reality of what transpires within and/or near our own communities, regardless of the causes. The War on Drugs, as it is presently being waged, has not been fruitful. We must revamp our current laws and commit to working with people from cradle to grave to put and keep every person on a healthy path forward.

We cannot change history and whether you believe what I have stated here or not, it is still up to us to make the decisions that will reverse the harms perpetrated on too many unsuspecting people.

We must offer hope to the hopeless who often turn to drugs to dull the fears and anxieties they face every day. We must create safe and welcoming neighborhoods, offer alternatives for dysfunctional families, provide ways for people to feel useful, needed, wanted, and loved. Only in that way will we win the War on Drugs—but on our own terms!

CAN THE WORLD'S TIRED AND POOR EVER "BREATHE FREE" IN AMERICA? DACA/DAPA: The Unintentional Consequences of Not Addressing These Issues

President Obama's immigration strategies for the undocumented offered great promise for their futures in this country. After all, this is a nation known for its welcome,

prominently emblazoned on our Statue of Liberty (a gift from the French whose own motto is "Liberty, Equality, Fraternity"), so we *must* live up to this commitment—our word should be our bond:

"Give me your tired, your poor, Your huddled masses yearning to breathe free, The wretched refuse of your teeming shore. Send those, the homeless, temptest-tost to me, I lift my lamp beside the golden door." --Emma Lazarus

If this plaque is the first structure which many immigrants see when arriving at our land, why are so many so-called Americans unwilling to live up to its intentions and offer to others the opportunities they themselves have been given? When so many of our ancestors (or even ourselves) have left other countries ... in which they often found great injustices and oppression and few possibilities for anything but a grim future ... to find a new life, why is it, quite ironically, that once they become established here, so many forget their own pasts and turn their backs on other immigrants desiring the same opportunities of which they have been able to take advantage.

This attitude is simply confounding to me. Our centuries-long history has been spotted with law after law to keep "foreigners" out (remember the Alien and Sedition Laws?). And these strangers were not, for the most part, Latinos, but people from Europe, Africa, and Asia—people who largely built the country we have today, the one we take for granted.

And yet it always seems that the mantra so many (quietly or secretly) repeat is, "Now that I've got mine, you're not entitled to yours—you can't share a portion of the pot!"

Today, over the last few decades, we are witnessing an influx of large numbers of people crossing our borders (some legally, others as undocumented), 40% of whom are not Latinos. And regardless of background, they are also largely responsible for building our nation even now.

A critical issue facing us is that many of our young people (many of whom are excelling in our schools both academically and artistically) are being told that because their parents brought them here as young children without documentation, they are not welcome.

Great numbers have not only excelled in high school, but have also been so successful in colleges and universities that they have become our doctors, lawyers, scientists, and engineers who are making tremendous contributions in our communities.

At the same time, they are living under stressful conditions— always worrying about whether they will be forced to a land so unfamiliar to them that some have no fluency at all in the language of their "homeland." They live in constant fear that they will be separated (perhaps forever) from their families.

Many want to contribute in broader ways by voting or being a legislative staffer or even running for office themselves—considerations that do not apply to them now.

For all these reasons, President Obama has acted on this pressing issue (since the current Congress won't). He is not the first, however, who has tried unsuccessfully to enact fair and just legislation to resolve our immigration crisis. The then-Congressmember (now Senator) Jeff Flake (R) worked with current Congressmember Luis Gutiérrez (D) in a bi-partisan effort on a bill (2007) under the George W. Bush Administration. It was not a perfect law, and though Bush would likely have signed it, the measure failed to make it through Congress.

Under the present Administration, DACA (Deferred Action for Childhood Arrivals) went into effect in 2012. I remember helping to get very excited young people to sign up. These children had to have entered the country before the age of 16 and before 2007. They must be at least 15 and have proof that they are pursuing their education—high school, GED, college, and so forth. Their documents are good for 2 years on a renewable basis but do not provide a pathway to citizenship. It does, however, take the onus off the shoulders of these young people who can come out of the shadows without fear of deportation. As of 2014, one half million young people are living under DACA protection.

This year there is a new program, DAPA, (Deferred Action for Parental Responsibility) for the undocumented parents of DACA children or of their children born in America. Unfortunately, the measure is sadly being held up from implementation by a Texas court ruling (which is expected to be overturned in the near future). That ruling is also holding up the expansion of DACA which would grant 3-year renewals and also allow young people to apply who have entered the country before 2010.

In the meantime, applications for both programs are being accepted and kept on file (personal details will not be shared) until there is resolution to this pressing matter.

With that in mind, Congressmember Tony Cárdenas (California's 29th District) is sponsoring a forum this coming Saturday.

The opening ceremony will not only feature Congressmember Cárdenas but also the inspiring House Member Luis Gutiérrez. After that introduction, booths will have been set up to offer helpful literature. Trained "Family Defenders" will sit with prospective DACA/DAPA applicants and walk them through the process which is open to all. People do not need to live in Congressmember Cárdenas' District in order to attend and apply.

Furthermore, immigration attorneys will be available, for free, to answer questions that applicants might have about their background, and material will be distributed to answer a lot of the "How to/Where to" questions applicants might have.

This will be an outstanding program—well-organized and well-planned, and user-friendly. Spanish translators will be available and forms will be available in both English and Spanish.

If this information applies to you, please consider attending.

Even if it does not, please share the information that is listed below with others who could benefit.

DACA and DAPA have great potential. They offer promise to nearly all those who have been struggling with their status. These are programs that deserve being embraced.

For more information, please contact the following:
The office of Congressmember Cárdenas: 818-781-7407
   Department of Public Social Services: 866-613-3777
Background Check: 818-207-1612
Live Scan Fingerprinting: 818-892-6141
Obtain Forms: www.uscis.gov/childhoodarrivals
(**Never pay** for these forms!!!)
Beware of SCAM ARTISTS!!!

Comparative Prison Systems: America vs. Germany

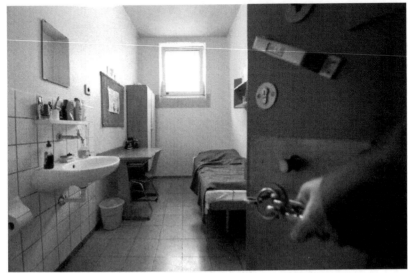

Credit: Joerg Koch/Anadolu Agency/Getty Images
A general view of the Landsberg Prison in Munich

Credit: AP Photo/Matthias Schrader
Inside view of one of the prison cells in Landsberg am Lech,
taken at a media event in the prison Landsberg am Lech,
southern Germany

Watching *60 Minutes* recent reprise of an earlier episode on how German prisons are run, inspired me to focus my attention on the broader issue of American criminal sentencing practices and prison conditions.

Let's be clear up front: Germany and The Netherlands and most of the European nations are largely homogeneous populations and generally do not face the kind of idiosyncratic problems that major American cities do. Nevertheless, there is no excuse for the sub-human treatment with which too many of our prisoners are confronted.

The fact is that American history is scarred with its inclinations toward violent, vindictive, and ruthless behavior. We have glorified novels and movies in which cowboys kill (often slaughter) Indians (Native Americans), in which Bonnie and Clyde-type gangsters viciously commit murder while audiences root for the bad guys; in which "Kill the Japs" was a rallying cry by many theater-goers during the post-World War II period; in which McCarthy hearing dupes betrayed innocent colleagues (based upon unfounded fears engendered by political hacks–think of people like Paul Robeson and Dalton Trumbo).

Yet, those same audiences are the first to push for law and order, harsh, heartless, oppressive punishments for even the most trivial of crimes. There is little compassion for the mentally ill who commit crimes as a direct consequence of their untreated disease. Many young people who have been caught up in the criminal world, have grown up in highly dysfunctional families and have resided in predatory neighborhoods where gang membership seemed the only way for many to receive protection from other predators. These are children who have experienced beatings and incest and other indescribable conditions and felt they had nowhere else to turn in order to survive.

Furthermore, America has a long history steeped in racist-based policy which especially pertains to our justice system. We cannot ignore the impact that slavery has had and continues to have on the political and socio-economic development of this nation. In more recent decades, starting in the 1970s, legislators with the full-throated backing of millions of voters, have promoted the "tough on crime" approach to punishment, one largely based on fear of the other and most often affecting minority communities.

As a result of our own history, there has been greater emphasis on mandatory minimums over which, based on extenuating circumstances, prosecutors and judges have little or no discretion or leeway (lately, in some places such sentencing is being addressed for mitigation). In addition, unreasonably long sentences have been part of our penal system, as issue that cannot rationally and reasonably be justified. Poorly trained prison and jail guards are often intimately involved in promoting violence (or look the other way) which occurs all too frequently among prisoners. In addition, guards often demonstrate through words and deeds their own belligerence and condescending behavior over those whom they have control (and this doesn't even include how frequently such guards allow gambling and drug use and distribution within the prison walls over which they have oversight).

It is not in their thinking to befriend and show compassion toward prisoners; they seem to prefer demeaning and demonstrating cringe-worthy behavior toward them. In American prisons, solitary confinement is used as a strategy to control every word and action of the prisoner–many remaining in the SHU for decades (the maximum time in German prisons generally does not exceed 8 hours!). Interestingly enough and perhaps ironically, countries such as Germany look at our solitary confinement policies as an abomination and a perversion of justice.

On top of this, there has been the for-profit aspect of our prison system. Because expanding the number of prisons is in direct proportion to the increasing number of convictions, private prisons have been proliferating. And to make such facilities even more profitable, their lobbyists have urged legislators to pass laws which lower the bar for criminalization and thus raise the numbers being incarcerated. That is why so many in prison today are there for drug-related issues–incarcerating them for relatively low-level, minor offenses and, consequently, ruining their lives post-incarceration because of their prison records. (This is one reason, by the way, to vote Yes on Proposition 64, one result of which will decriminalize simple personal use and sharing of marijuana.).

It is true that what works elsewhere may not work with an equal degree of success here in America. Our system seems to be all about crime and severe punishment whereas many other nations with low recidivism rates emphasize accountability and rehabilitation; they promote dignity and encourage prisoners to acquire skills for an easy and effective long-term and productive re-integration into society.

America has the highest (and most expensive–despite questionable results) rate of incarceration in the world with a concomitantly high rate of recidivism. As a result, in recent years American justice leaders from broad cross-sections of society have been visiting European prisons for the purpose of not only observing what transpires there but with the goal of modifying our own practices to create more promising results. Systems such as those in Pennsylvania are already making positive changes.

So what are places like Germany doing (a nation with a horrifying past but one that has become a legitimate leader in many progressive movements)? Sentencing practices are entirely different from what is found here in the U. S. Almost no sentences for any crime (excepting the most heinous and egregious committed by the most incorrigible perpetrators) exceeds 15 years (21 in The Netherlands). In Germany, the guards represent the cream of the crop of society. Among their ranks are committed lawyers, social workers, mental health experts (among other professionals) who are paid well–salaries commensurate with their qualifications and experiential backgrounds.

Emphasis is placed on humanizing the inmates. This differs greatly from America's prison strategies which allow denigrating prisoners–actions that push them further into a criminal abyss from which it is difficult for them to extricate themselves, a place in which no viable future is foreseen and a repetition of criminal acts is expected.

The German goal is to help prisoners understand the environment into which they were born, the consequent anger and resentments that grew out of those formidable years...

The German goal is to help prisoners understand the environment into which they were born, the consequent anger and resentments that grew out of those formidable years; how different life choices could have been made and how future choices can be positive, constructive ones; how training for occupations and professions (with degrees) is encouraged. Inmates are urged to pursue vocational jobs while in prison and must save a percentage of their earnings to help them make the post-incarceration transition.

Those inmates who have proven their trustworthiness and reliability are allowed to work outside the prison on a daily basis (all of whom voluntarily return after work). Many are periodically given permission to leave the facility for a few days a year to visit with family and friends.

Such treatment creates a positive mind-set for those incarcerated. Not only that, but as a direct result of such positive treatment and interactions, violence within the prison is virtually non-existent among prisoners and between staff and prisoners.

Contributing to engendering positive self-esteem is the fact that prisoners are trusted. They each have a private dormitory-like room with their own keys. Guards knock before entering. The rooms are spacious with natural sunlight (many inmates grow plants) and have a bathroom apart from the sleeping quarters. They sleep on real beds with real mattresses. Their linens can be purchased or brought from home. They dress with a sense of pride in the styles and fashions which they prefer (unlike the god-awful, pink, demeaning uniforms and underwear that Sheriff Joe Arpaio of Maricopa County, Arizona, makes them wear).

They have a phone to make calls to anyone (including family, friends, attorneys, media, etc.) and a television, radio, and computer (Internet access is not permitted). They can decorate their rooms as they please without fear that guards will raid their quarters and destroy items or take possessions away. Many have small libraries of books and magazines and study materials. They can cook their own meals (they also have access to a common kitchen where healthy, fresh foods are available). They earn reasonable pay for their work (unlike the 8¢ to 20¢ an hour "wage" that American prisoners make–from which a considerable amount of their earnings can be taken away for "restitution" and because of which the high cost of commissary items make needed purchases out of reach).

German prisoners are encouraged to maintain good health through exercise and eating nutritiously. Their medical needs are addressed immediately as a consequence of a ratio of one doctor per 127 prisoners (on average, the corresponding American numbers are 1 to 750).

Incidentally, Arpaio is now facing federal charges for contempt of court, an instruction which demanded that he refrain from racially profiling immigrants (which he has been doing, in part, to gain votes for his re-election campaigns). Despite the court decision, he has refused to comply with its requirements. Furthermore, he is also guilty of humiliating and degrading prisoners, many of whom, during periods of triple degree temperatures, he often "houses" in tents out in the scorching desert.

When American inmates are apprised of the dramatic differences in treatment, a sense of sadness, depression, and futility sets in. One interviewed American prisoner (who has been incarcerated since he was a teenager) stated that he felt that his life was over upon entering the prison and now that he knows how prison can and should be, the weight of prison life grows even heavier and more debilitating.

Based on the observations of the several delegations that travelled to Europe to visit its various prison systems, many have returned as enlightened leaders within the justice community and have become strong proponents in the subsequent struggle for fair play.

For example, Governor Malloy of Connecticut is an advocate for the "Second-Chance Society." Others from New Mexico and Wisconsin are seeking to address the cause behind the high propensity of incarcerating minority offenders at the same time that their white counterparts are often given rather lenient sentences for the same offenses (short terms or even probation or simple fines).

John Wetzel, head of Pennsylvania's prison program, has been a leader in reforming the state's prison system. He has tried to fashion many of the changes he has instituted based upon what he learned from the German prison system. Thus, guards are more highly trained (and, as a result, are adopting effective practices for working with those with mental health and other debilitating issues). Guards, he says, do better "when (they) understand the root cause of behavior." Pennsylvania is pursuing studies to comprehend what causes people to commit crimes in the first place and what can be done to prevent repetition of similar actions upon release. Such understanding can also help policing practitioners intercede to prevent commission of future crimes. Wetzel goes on to say "that public safety is a logical consequence of a good corrections system."

As one observer commented, "I think people can change. I think countries can change." With that in mind, we must encourage just, reasonable, merciful changes to our own system of justice–a system that must be more about rehabilitation and re-entry than retribution and revenge.

ABUSED CHILDREN: Who Else Should Be Mourned?

I see the crosses lining school yards and street lanes but one or two or three are always missing Who else deserves to be mourned?   Who else is being abandoned?   Who else is deemed a pariah in his or her respective community?

I think of the boys at Columbine Eric Harris and Dylan Klebold who murdered 12 students and one teacher and injured scores more I think of the Sandy Hook massacre Adam Lanza murdered his mother at their home and 20 children and 6 staff at the school I think of the Aurora Theatre where 24 were murdered and 140 others were severely injured by

Chernobyl Orphans

James Eagan Holmes Of course I think of the "actual" victims (our hearts genuinely and rightfully go out to them and their families), but why was and is there no compassion left for the perpetrators? No markers at all. Their existence needs to be honored too–in some way I feel sad.

What do all these boys or young men have in common? All were clearly disturbed individuals yet did not get the urgent help they desperately needed At Columbine, one of the shooters came from an early abusive childhood and then was adopted At Sandy Hook, the mother of the young man gave him a gun as a gift to offer him an opportunity to be responsible At Aurora, the shooter had been diagnosed with a number of psychoses, one of which was possibly *dysphoric mania*, a form of bipolar disorder.

There are so many other children among us (few of whom have committed crimes) who demonstrate anti-social and sociopathic behaviors Many are withdrawn or are manic or exhibit violent episodes Many times, children are diagnosed (often incorrectly) as having one or more of a variety of mental disorders Many suffer from severe emotional dysfunction What happens them when people in their lives don't look hard enough to seek answers for their problems? Too many simply fall through the cracks "Simply"? How outrageous!

Many of our children come from homes where parents are drug-addicted and/or alcoholics The mistreated experience uncontrolled and constant physical and mental abuse (often including sexual molestation) Many children are abandoned (voluntarily or not) by birth parents. As a consequence, some youngsters live with other relatives (but, regardless, feel abandoned by those who should have loved and protected them). They feel alienated despite how loving and caring the substitute home is. Others are sent from one foster home to another (a situation which never allows the child to feel a sense of stability and safety) where they often suffer from abuse in those homes as well.

Some dislocations are so extreme and stressful that the child, despite his or her desire to be loved and to belong, becomes a victim of *attachment disorder.* This is a diagnosis that has been recognized for a long time, yet far too few psychiatrists and therapists are familiar with the symptoms and, therefore, frequently misdiagnose children's mental and emotional issues What is worse, these professionals often prescribe strong medications which produce minimal positive results but, instead, often cause severe adverse side effects on their hopeful, innocent patients.

I remember when I was in college, I studied about an experiment with baby rhesus macaque monkeys (very similar in their early behavior patterns to human infants). Half were placed in cribs where they were lovingly and frequently handled and nurtured and fed by bottle while being held and cooed to. The other group was essentially left alone in their cribs—bottled formula propped up, no verbal communication, and a minimum of touch interaction (think of prisoners in the American system who lose their minds after months or even years in solitary confinement). The first group thrived and flourished The second group became very ill while many of these experimental victims even died (Is it any wonder that human prisoners, once released after draconian treatment, become recidivists–often perpetrating even worse crimes than the ones for which they were initially convicted?).

Later in my life, I was in the Soviet Union after Chernobyl. Many children there had lost both parents. They were placed in orphanages which were so understaffed that very little nurturing transpired. As these children grew so emerged mental and emotional pathologies. Ironically, many Americans, looking for an underprivileged child to bring into their families, chose to adopt a Russian child–only to realize later that these children began exhibiting symptoms of

Attachment Disorder once they returned to the United States.

This syndrome is characterized by an inability to form emotional relationships. Perceiving uncertain futures, it is not uncommon for them to steal and horde out of fear (at least subconsciously) that there would not be available to them food or other desired items which they knew they would need or might want. Constantly hanging over them is the thought that they might be abandoned and deprived again. Typical of these young people are anti-social, controlling, and often violent behaviors.

And for all such children, despite wanting to fit in and be "normal," there is something broken in them that they (and most caregivers) don't know how to fix Their symptoms, for the most part, can be traced directly to the various manifestations of early childhood of their victimization—not to overlook other factors such as being "drug babies" (passed on through their mothers).

We as a society can't simply throw up our hands nonchalantly and exclaim, "This is not my problem! They are not my children!" To say we are our brothers and sisters' keepers is perhaps too cliché The reality, however, is that what transpires in the minds and hearts of these young people does not affect them alone or only their family and friends Without question, what happens to them and what they do does affect the entire extended community—hence Columbine, Sandy Hook, Aurora, and countless more.

Thus, in a different but very real way, these children and young adults are victims too–though of a different sort. Their mental and emotional pain is so overwhelming that they have no idea how to find relief Many commit suicide or try to Many hope that through their actions, they will commit "suicide by cop." Many find themselves adrift in an endless nightmare of grays and blacks, of horrors unimaginable.

We must not and cannot forget or overlook the fact that these human beings are truly a part of each of us Undeniably, they are victims. Our schools need to make accommodations for the full spectrum of their mental and emotional illnesses that manifest themselves in so many different ways. Schools must be on the lookout for the scars (physical and psychological) of physical abuse Teachers need to be trained to recognize the signs.

Just as we have classes for the visually- and hearing-impaired, for physical disabilities, for the severely mentally disturbed (with teachers with specialized credentials), so must we have classes with a small teacher-student ratio with committed and highly trained teachers for children who would otherwise be "discarded"–children who are not only equally needy but, in many cases, even more needy than those in the other categories.

Without that recognition and special attention, these children become pigeon-holed as trouble- and mischief-makers with teachers who commonly believe that these "annoying" kids can behave if they really want to but disrupt, instead, for the sheer pleasure of disturbing others. We have to change that frame of mind which is so off the mark. We must if we want to help each of our children who attend our educational institutions.

Future parents must be educated, as well, in what to watch for in their children—born to them, fostered, or adopted. These guardians must be ready for early intervention. Pediatricians need a foundation on which they can make appropriate, informed diagnoses.

The child victims at Chernobyl became detached because they viewed their futures filled only with "repeated adversity with no forseeable end." Harry Frederick Harlow, the American psychologist who experimented with the macaque monkeys, early on hit upon the long-term effects of maternal separation, dependency needs, and social isolation. He observed glazed looks, self-mutilation, severe psychological psychoses, and even digestive disorders (such as continual diarrhea)–all symptoms which equally plague the monkeys and their human child counterparts. He also noted that even after a child is removed from such social and actual isolation, many (if not most) will never fully recover from their attachment disorder.

Now that we know the symptoms and most of the causes, what do we do?

There is hope that reversal of these symptoms is still possible if the root of the problem is recognized early enough and appropriate action is taken. These children need to understand and believe that there is hope for alleviating their pain and suffering in a meaningful and significant way Wrap-around services must include wrap-around love from every person who plays a role in their lives. No one should be told, unlike what Dr. Harlow predicted decades ago, that he or she is a lost soul. Perhaps what is most true is what the song so unpretentiously claims: "...all you need is love."

As Antwone Fisher wrote in one of his poems with words and sentiments that are so apt.

Who will cry for the little boy?
Lost and all alone.

Who will cry for the little boy?
Abandoned without his own?

Who will cry for the little boy?
He cried himself to sleep. Who
will cry for the little boy? He
never had for keeps.

Who will cry for the little boy?
He walked the burning sand.
Who will cry for the little boy?
The boy inside the man.

Who will cry for the little boy?
Who knows well hurt and pain.
Who will cry for the little boy?
He died again and again.

Who will cry for the little boy?
A good boy he tried to be. Who
will cry for the little boy? Who
cries inside of me.

Yes, I see (we see) the crosses (and other markers) lining
school yards and street lanes. No more, however, should they
include some names to the exclusion of others. We must
mourn all those who have left us too early but, for those still
living, promise to recognize and attend to their needs (*before*
it is too late)—each being who must be thought of in his or
her way as a gift from On High.

Juvenile Offenders: From Big Wheels to the Big House

Mental Health Self-Determination: Not Incarceration

by Rosemary Jenkins

For far too long, our jail and prison system has been utilized too often and largely for those suffering from mental health conditions and, thus, serves as a substitute for mental clinics and hospitals that can better provide a breadth of productive and effective therapies for those in need of such attention. Prisons were never intended to house the mentally ill!

Contrary to logic, many at the highest levels (such as Orange County, California, Sheriff Sandra Hutchens) who are involved in coordinating the incarceration system, literally purport that inmates *want* to stay in prison because their lives will be more fruitful while locked up! Such people claim that prison life is a pathway to stabilization and rehabilitation. How ludicrous!

Reality, however, purports just the opposite. While the *prison-industrial complex* continues to grow geometrically (including for-profit private prisons), those who are mentally ill and find themselves behind prison bars are victimized from mistreatment that can lead to further mental and physical deterioration. A plunge into such an abyss can be attributed, at least in part, to specific kinds of detention, such as solitary confinement in the SHU—the Solitary Housing Unit (perhaps the cruelest of punishments whose penalties are exacted for an indeterminate amount of time—often for years).

Lizzie Buchen (lizzie@curbprisonspending.org), an advocate and coordinator for Californians United for a Responsible Budget (CURB), has stated: "One of the most alarming features of these jail expansion projects is they are being promoted as ways to improve conditions for incarcerated people." In reality, the purpose seems to be to find new ways to make money and keep the prison population growing exponentially. There is little logic behind much of the sentencing process, especially for those involved in low-level crimes. Furthermore and most significantly, those who suffer from mental health problems need to be in out-patient treatment centers, not jails!

Studies have shown that incarceration for the mentally ill only exacerbates their health problems. Commonly, jailers and the medical staff are insufficient in numbers and are generally inadequately trained to handle the very distinct, unique, and discrete problems of this class of inmates.

Confronted with threats of violence, rape, and other traumas, even the sanest of prisoners can devolve into anxiety and/or paranoia because of these experiences or from fear of them. More than half of jailed prisoners suffer from some form of psychosis, mania, and/or major depression. A majority of inmates suffer from alcoholism and/or drug abuse and need the proper treatment to help them overcome this scourge. "Suicide is the number one cause of death in local jails and is [among] the top five for prisons"—an unbelievable statistic. Studies have shown that incarceration for the mentally ill only exacerbates their health problems. Commonly, jailers and the medical staff are insufficient in numbers and are generally inadequately trained to handle the very distinct, unique, and discrete problems of this class of inmates.

There are any number of individuals (like George Soros) and organizations such as CURB and the Family United Network (FUN) who have devoted themselves to reversing the outrageous scenarios that we see being repeated and perpetuated not only in California but throughout the nation Rosie Flores, from the California Partnership and the Riverside Alternatives to Jail Expansion, has stated, "It is clear the best treatment [for this category of people] and education cannot happen in jail."

The emphasis has to be on recognition implicit in the problems, preventative measures, and treatment rather than incarceration, the latter of which is financially costly for the taxpayer and has little return on investment for them Those in jail are suffering from varying degrees of mental illness and are more likely to decline and be ill-fitted to return to society as healthy and productive assets to their respective communities if appropriate remedies are not pursued.

Furthermore, the families and friends of those who find themselves behind prison walls also need to be educated so that they too can become advocates "to challenge mass incarceration and extreme punishment"—something the Eighth Amendment fundamentally forbids (you know the one that prohibits "cruel and unusual punishment"–a rule established from the start by our founding forebears for very legitimate and historical reasons).

CURB has determined that there are at least seven factors which should mandate alternatives to prison for the mentally ill:

- ▢ People with mental illness are disproportionately criminalized (at least 50% of the prison population has been identified as mentally ill whereas the general non-prison population with some degree of mental illness number only about 6%)

- ▢ Incarceration further damages mental health (such victims frequently face threats of violence, rape, racist acts, and other traumas; separation from loved ones is very debilitating; there is a loss of dignity and purpose and a feelings of hopelessness and futility which can leader people to untoward actions and even suicide

- ▢ Jails and prisons are generally ill-equipped to treat mental illness (as has been stated earlier, imprisonment of this segment of society is not cost-effective (compare clinic costs for a patient of $2200 a year to prison costs of $34,000)

- ▢ Jails are becoming de facto mental health providers—certainly not the intention of the prison system which has been created not only to exact punishment but to rehabilitate inmates for eventual return to society once the sentence has been served; people with mental conditions are far less likely to improve while incarcerated

⬚ We need to increase community programs, not incarceration (addressing methods to prevent social ills that lead to criminal activity and emphasize support and recovery pathways

⬚ There are alternatives to incarceration (San Francisco Behavioral Health Court is determined "to divert individuals with Mental illness from incarceration by connecting them to outside treatment and wraparound services"; the Integrated Recovery Network in Los Angeles works with the homeless population—which is largely made up of the mental ill—with the goal of helping with safe and clean housing, appropriate and adequate treatment, and dependable income)

⬚ People with mental illness deserve better: "Mental illness is not a choice. Its symptoms can lead people to engage in behaviors they otherwise would not do[Furthermore,] social workers should advocate for changes in policy and legislation to improve social conditions in order to meet basic human needs and promote social justice" of their clients.

Our jails and prisons are currently being utilized more to house the mentally ill than to house those who have been convicted of crimes for which mental illness was not a recognized but was a contributing factor. The mentally ill must be given the treatment that they need in order to function well in society, understanding that the crimes they may have committed are largely due to a lack of medical guidance which might have contained their anti-social symptoms (and this kind of attention needs to be done *before* they engage in any criminal activity)The jail system was never meant as a profit-making business whose only goal is to make money at the expense of the ultimate goal of helping prisoners to be rehabilitated and to be prepared for successful re- entry into society.

Of course, we cannot ignore that segment of the mentally ill population which may never be ready to succeed on their own or who may have committed such heinous crimes that their future actions might forever be a concern for the safety and security of the greater community.

In the end, sentencing must be proportionate to the crimes committed. Low-level and victimless crimes (in my view) should be addressed in separate courts with logical, compassionate, and ameliorative systems in place whose outcomes may not always include sentencing behind bars at all (think of the positive effects that instituting *California Proposition 47–2014* has produced).

Just some thoughts to be considered during this electoral year when we must choose leaders who will be charged with pursuing justice and mercy in their legislative and judicial capacities.

Juvenile Offenders: From Big Wheels to the Big House

Domestic Violence: Step Up! Speak Up!
By Rosemary Jenkins, LA Progressives, August 17, 2015

Domestic violence has many facets about which most people are unaware: It occurs not only when a man physically abuses his wife or partner but in other horrifying ways as well. It manifests itself through the psychological, emotional, sexual, and spiritual damage he inflicts on her. These victims are

subject to constant threats, in part, because the offenders have the power to take advantage of their positions in the family hierarchy. And beyond that, too often these aggressive men (and sometimes women) do similar, if not worse, damage to their own children.

I was fortunate last week to attend a wonderful forum, open to all, and sponsored by Congressmember Tony Cárdenas, whose purpose was to define, inform, and educate about domestic violence, offering (among other aspects of the discussion) instruction in how to recognize such cruel behavior and what to do about it.

It emphasized that it is truly within the realm of reality for a victim to be able to start a new life outside the confines of a destructive home if the target or anyone else has the nerve to report it. Consequently, the forum placed the responsibility on all of us to disclose such possibilities to the proper authorities. That means we have a moral obligation to step up if we are aware of or even suspect there is the remotest likelihood of such behavior going on in a home—whether your own or your neighbors' (without any negative repercussions if the accusation is incorrect). Better to report a case which turns out to be innocent than allow an adult or the children to become or continue to be victims in an outrageous, intolerable, and unacceptable environment.

For many, the sad reality is that too often the police are not called in to intervene until it is too late—until someone has been brutalized or murdered, leaving the children to bear life-long scars.

It was suggested over and over the importance of people "to step up and speak up" not only on behalf of themselves but for all those who were not there and yet urgently need the help that was offered at that site. For many, the sad reality is that too often the police are not called in to intervene until it is too late—until someone has been brutalized or murdered, leaving the children to bear life-long scars.

The effort in advance to reach out to the public was tremendous. Distributing flyers, knocking on doors, sending e-mails, making presentations from the pulpit at many religious institutions were all part of the outreach for this forum. Translation services by an intern, who incidentally did an outstanding job, were available for both English-only and Spanish-only speaking listeners.

Children who accompanied their parents were treated to a movie and refreshments in a separate room so that they were not exposed to the details exposed at the conference and would not have to relive their own experiences or listen to those of others. Thus, this process also insured the privacy of the adults from children who might otherwise overhear their stories.

There were between 40 and 50 people of all ages who came to listen. It became readily apparent to me and the organizers that, had it not been for the fear of coming out in the open, attendance would have been greater. We need to do a better job at assuaging those apprehensions.

It is ironic that too frequently mothers don't believe their daughters (or sons) who claim that someone in the family is sexually molesting them. They take the side of the abuser instead of the child. And then when these children gather up the nerve to flee such an unhealthy environment, they find themselves being abused again by pimps offering false promises.

I have spoken in the past about how too many of our young people are so destroyed by what they have observed transpiring in their own homes (where their mother is being continuously beaten, screamed at, cursed at, and sometimes even killed) that they run away to find a "real" home among local gang members who make them feel important and wanted.

Many of those who wind up in the gang life, as a way to support themselves, somehow are sucked into the sex trafficking business—either as the pimps or the prostitutes.

Numerous young women are unwittingly lured into such practices with promises of a safe and secure home and then find that when they are forced into prostitution, they cannot get out for fear of being beaten or killed.

We cannot ignore the existence of such trafficking in our own neighborhoods. It is there and until we choose to intervene, it will continue to be a bane on all our lives.

In other instances, these children find themselves abandoned by their guardians. They are dropped off somewhere in the middle of nowhere to fend for themselves, having been disowned by one or both of their parents. And even if the child is left with a loving grandparent, the youngster is overwhelmed by the sense of abandonment and, eventually, often winds up perpetrating the same damage on others because that is the only role-modelling to which this young victim has been exposed.

Too often, children observe and then repress the memories of what they have experienced—only to have them resurface later in life when it manifests itself through violent acts on others. It is a vicious cycle that must be broken now—not sometime in the future.

It was noted at the conference that the culture in which so much of this violence is found has become a "normal, expected, nearly acceptable" way of life. It is "your cross to bear" and nothing can be done to change that. This chronic behavior is generally rationalized and justified within the Latino community in particular.

These brutal behaviors, however, *do* cross socio-economic lines. Nevertheless, victims are often stigmatized by other family members, neighbors, friends, and so forth if victims do speak up. And the stigma goes beyond the mother/wife to the children, and the entire family. They find themselves caught up in a spider's net and come to believe there is no way out, no alternative to their lives of pain and suffering.

Much too frequently, children are afraid to speak up. They attend school (where they may find themselves victims again but this time from peer or staff violence). School is too often a place where they don't feel safe and thus cannot concentrate and, as a result, often cause trouble because of all the pent-up anger and fear they harbor and because of the belief that no one is on their side. They also worry that if they share their experiences with authorities, their mothers will suffer at the hands of the man in the house who is perpetrating the crimes. These children often do not report what is happening because sometimes they have seen for themselves or heard of other situations in which the victim-mother takes the side of her abuser out of fear of retribution by him at a later time. The fact remains that without reporting, the savagery is then allowed to be sustained relentlessly.

It was repeatedly stated at the meeting (and quite emphatically at that) that because Los Angeles is a sanctuary city (thank goodness), victims can report these crimes (without fear of legal reprisals, even for people who are undocumented) and will receive the assistance that is so badly needed. Victims, regardless of status, must not fear deportation from our City for reporting these sadistic and brutish actions—despite the frightening stories they might otherwise hear that goes on elsewhere.

Furthermore, many Spanish-only victims are fearful of sharing their stories with English-only officers and/or representatives from other agencies. It is because of that that there is a new focus on training and providing expert staff who can speak the language and who might have, themselves, been victims of similar experiences. Officers are contemporaneously being trained specifically on how to interact with those who have been part of domestic violence incidents. Being aware of this should allay some of the apprehension that victims possess.

Too many women (often the pregnant ones that are most vulnerable) do not know their rights, regardless of documentation status. In fact, all people who reside in America are protected by our justice system. Congressmember Cárdenas pointed out that women can seek asylum for themselves and their children when they are victims of domestic violence. No one needs to suffer the malicious and evil behavior that is a constant in their lives.

There is the additional fear that if such abuse is reported that the children will be taken away from the mother on the basis that the home is unsafe for them. These issues are being addressed so that mothers will no longer have to worry that they will lose their children by reporting the hostile behaviors of their partners.

In fact, it is understood that both the mother and her children need to be removed immediately from the hostile atmosphere found within the home and that both mother and children must be allowed to stay together in a safe place. Efforts are, therefore, made on their behalf to find suitable and safe housing for them—without fear of retaliation by their husbands or from legal authorities.

Domestic violence touches everyone. Thus, it is the responsibility of all of us to act on what we know or have experienced. Many communities deny that such behavior exists: "Not here in our neighborhood! Our men would not do those kinds of things!" Such crimes that do go unreported can also affect the rest of us directly when children who find themselves on their own wind up committing crimes against their neighbors or local businesses—often in an effort just to survive.

And what of those who claim they do not want help? That stance is usually taken out of fear, but if what is known is reported to the police, they will investigate and try to convince the victims that they can be protected, along with their children, and can be rescued from the nightmare in which they find themselves.

Similarly, if the brutality is so bad that medical attention is sought, the attending physicians and staff are obligated to report it with absolutely no repercussions to the victims or their families.

Finally, after the presentation by a panel of experts (including the Congressmember and his wife, Norma), there was the opportunity for attendees to ask questions and then to meet at tables with legal aid attorneys (and other people representing a number of agencies and organizations) whose goal is to share (with specifics) just how these counsellors can help change the circumstances for those experiencing so many domestic horrors—offering them positive options which will lead to a freedom they have not felt for most of their lives.

It is important to note that any *abogados* who charge thousands of dollars for these same services are **not** legitimate but exist to take advantage of vulnerable clients. Seek help only from those attorneys who are recommended by your local officials.

In the near future, you will find an article written by a woman whose own experiences reflect what has been cited here. In the meantime, see something; say something! Indeed!

Below, you will find a number of references for such counsel which is *free* for those seeking help.

1. **Expediente Rojo Project**: expedienterojo.org
2. Independent registered **psychologists/therapists** specializing in domestic violence cases (various; obtain references); Rosa Maria Villalpando spoke at the conference: Call: 213-309-5016
3. **LAFLA** (Legal Aid Foundation of Los Angeles): Call: 888-373-7888
4. **DCFS** (Department of Children and Family Services— Los Angeles): 24/7 services available. Call 800-540-4000
5. *Consulado de México*: Call: 213-351-6800 (Patricia Pérez G.)
6. **LAPD**—any station within the City of Los Angeles; Mission: Call: 818-838-9800; Foothills: 818-756-8861
7. **Strength United**, a CSUN agency: 24/7. Call 818-886-0453; 661-253-0258
8. **El Nido [the nest] Family Center**: Call 818-896-7776
9. **New Directions for Youth**: Call 818-375-1000
10. **Communities in Schools**: Call 818-891-9399
11. **Neighborhood Legal Services of Los Angeles County** (free assistance); Call: 800-433-6251 (Monday, Wednesday, Friday from 9 a.m. to 1 p.m.)
12. **South Asian helpline**: Call 562-402-4132
13. **Chrysalis** (Changing Lives through Jobs): Call: 818-794-4200 (Monday through Thursday with 8 a.m. orientation meetings)
14. **Office of Congressmember Tony Cárdenas (CD 29)**; Call: 818-504-0090/781-7407

Juvenile Offenders: From Big Wheels to the Big House

The Mentally Ill Do Not Belong in Jail

by Rosemary Jenkins

[researched from several pieces by Rina Palta and Frank Stoltze for KPCC]

An important goal for Los Angeles District Attorney, Jacky Lacey, is to ascertain the right place for housing the mentally ill, many of whom have committed minor crimes and, thus, do not belong in a jail setting which can only exacerbates their problems. She wants to make appropriate treatment of this sector of our society a priority.

The critical issue is to create places for them from the beginning where their issues can be addressed on a short- and long-term basis. Jails for most are simply not acceptable. Lacey's recommendations, though, should not be interpreted to mean that those who do pose an extreme danger will not be placed in a jail setting that can accommodate their special needs.

In addition, she (like officials in many other cities, such as Memphis, Tennessee) is determined to require special training for all law enforcement officers in how to interact with the mentally ill, many of whom are lower-level offenders and ought *not* to be treated like vicious criminals.

She has recognized that in Los Angeles about 20% of its jail population suffers from extreme mental illness (recycling about 3500 mentally ill people each day) but not of the nature that should label them criminals that need to be behind bars.

Statistics show that when police officers have received suitable training for handling the mentally ill, officer-involved use of force and even shootings are greatly reduced. Instead, positive alternatives to incarceration are offered that can successfully reduce recidivism and improve the mental health outlook for the ill.

The Los Angeles Board of Supervisors has set aside 40 million dollars to help implement her recommendations. California's *SB 82* contains a commitment to fund mental health emergency rooms and "options for inpatient treatment, from clinics to permanent housing with on-site services."

It is fitting, then, that the Los Angeles Sheriff's Department has also chosen to mandate training for its officers with regard to their interactions with the mentally ill who do find themselves within its jail system.

It should be noted that the LA County jail system is currently being sued by a number of civil rights attorneys to end the "Skid Row to jail cycle." Too often, when the mentally ill are released from the County jail, they are not offered the post-incarceration care they require and wind up where they started—homeless on the streets with no way to care for themselves. What they need as they are being released is a referral to social workers who can handle their cases and transportation to get to their offices—all of which would be of no cost to them.

Said one victim of the system, "When I was released, I was given a 30-day prescription for Risperdal, which I couldn't fill because I had no money and didn't know there were free pharmacies." This gentleman has "been homeless for 20 years and suffers from bipolar disorder, schizophrenia and depression." His story is a perfect example of what is wrong with the current system whose job it is to mitigate the issues surrounding the lives of these people but which has not followed through in a way that can truly help them.

The fact is that most of the mentally ill in question "often lack the capacity to navigate a complicated web of county mental health facilities and services," among them the psychiatric and medical assistance that they so desperately need. District Attorney Lacey has said that we must create a network for lower-level offenders who don't belong in jail but do need help to navigate the obstacles in life they so often encounter but do not know how to handle.

For those who complain so vociferously about the homeless whom they claim are so unsightly and ruin the neighborhood, perhaps instead they should use their voices to insist that our leaders address the needs of those who are suffering--actions that can improve conditions and benefit everyone.

Let's Finally Say "Yes" to Bail Reform
by Rosemary Jenkins, LA Progressive

As is my way of doing things, I like to take a balanced approach before I make a decision on anything—research

both sides of an issue and listen objectively to proponents and opponents who have a stake in the outcome—most with valid, salient points which justify their positions. Thus, determining my personal stand on SB 10 Bail Reform (authored by State Senator Bob Hertzberg) has been no different.

Bail Reform (which affects all Californians) has followed a long, winding path. The bill, working its way through the State Legislature (now continued into 2018), addresses this challenging, multi-faceted issue as strong feelings have been expressed on both sides. On the one hand, the bail industry, skeptical policing departments (particularly those in rural areas), and even portions of the prison-industrial complex are strong in their opposition. Many police officers are wary as a result of Propositions 47 and 57, sincerely believing that dangerous criminals could be unleashed upon an unwitting public, making the work of law enforcement officers that much harder and more frustrating.

Though these concerns are very real for those opposing this

bill, the truth, as I have learned, is quite different. Those in our jails, who would directly benefit from implementation of this bill, are not those who were arrested for a major crime such as murder, attempted murder, rape, armed robbery, or other forms of violence. Quite to the contrary, many of those incarcerated for far lesser crimes have been waiting an interminable length of time just to be officially charged or scheduled for their preliminary hearings.

During the long wait, many have given up hope and are filled with a sense of hopelessness and futility and, as a result, a very large percentage of such inmates (many of whom have been isolated from family and friends) agree to a plea bargain by which they agree to go to prison (often for something they did not commit). They do this in order to avoid the possibility of being sentenced to potentially even longer terms once up-charges are added. The threat of such indictments are far-and-above what should be imposed for the relatively minor crimes for which they were initially arrested. This is a coercive tactic often employed by the prosecutor's office in order to avoid the time and cost of trials.

Countless people, languishing in county jails for relatively minor crimes such as unpaid traffic tickets or expired driver's licenses or possession of a small amount of marijuana, are there because they cannot pay their bail or even the 10% non-refundable charge imposed by the bail bonds industry.

Looking deeper, the fact is there is great profitability in the prison system as a whole–with California being no exception. In actuality, countless people, languishing in county jails for relatively minor crimes such as unpaid traffic tickets or expired driver's licenses or possession of a small amount of marijuana, are there because they cannot pay their bail or even the 10% non-refundable charge imposed by the bail bonds industry.

Thus, we have a bail system and private prisons making inordinate profits off people who frequently should not have been in jail in the first place, bail practices which justify the existence and growth of for-profit facilities and businesses. An additional reality is that the preponderance of those adversely affected by current bail structures are the poor and minorities, victims of biases of which the general public is generally unaware.

Under the Hertzberg plan, we can eliminate what can now be called a debtors' prison system—something the U. S. Constitution prohibits. Should this bill become law, a Judicial Council would be created which would establish (as much as is realistically possible) fair, color-blind criteria which would utilize risk-assessment tools for determining who should benefit from pre-trial release. These would be people without a felonious past, who are not a flight risk, who engaged in victimless crimes or crimes of minimal impact. These are not people accused of (or have a history of) violence and uncontrollable mental illness.

As to funding, yes, there will be additional taxpayer costs incurred by having to create and maintain the panel as referenced above. In truth though, many of the incarcerated who are affected by the lack of bail availability (which was never meant to keep a person locked up for a long period of time) will find they have lost their jobs while they were detained and, subsequently, their homes (when you don't earn money, you can't pay your bills). Many lose their families because of the stress and financial burden heaped upon them by current practices. There are further consequences: When the formerly incarcerated lose employment, they cannot pay local, state, or federal taxes (such as sales tax on cars, computers, cell phones, or college text books)–a situation that affects the greater community which generally depends on the benefits from taxes for services the government normally renders.

Inaction on this bill will adversely affect the taxpayer who always picks up the shortfall for a broad spectrum of welfare entitlements when human needs are not otherwise met (housing, food, health services, to name the most consequent), especially for those who were unreasonably held behind bars for far too long and for their families. An unnecessary taxpayer burden will grow exponentially if something practical and pragmatic is not done. Certainly, SB 10 is part of the answer to this pressing problem.

Additionally, those released from jails, who for whatever reasons are not beneficiaries of the benefits mentioned, will most likely (as many studies indicate) wind up on the streets among the homeless—another pressing issue. However, under SB 10, such a burden upon the taxpayer would be mitigated and more than offset in the long run by the lesser costs derived through the benefits from fairer bail rulings by the Judicial Council.

The bail system as it is currently set up is antithetical to what our Founding Forebears had in mind. The program as it stands is inefficient, unfair, and convoluted. No more can we sanction debtors' prisons (described so vividly by Charles Dickens when not only the debtors but their families shared the humiliation of living behind bars for low-level infractions).

We can neither go back to those days nor retain the kind of unfair, unequal system we have today. It is, therefore, for all these reasons that I am unequivocal in my support of SB 10, this thoroughly vetted and outstanding piece of legislation on Bail Reform. I urge our state legislators, the governor, and the public in general to support this bill as well!

CHAPTER THREE

OTHER COMMENTARIES

These Articles Are Pertinent to Juvenile and Restorative Justice—from Early Patterns of Life to Current Situations, Many of Which Demonstrate Causative Factors Which Can Lead to a Criminal Lifestyle.

Surviving Domestic Violence

by Sheryl C.

Please allow me to share with all the women out there (and the men who interact with us) about the impact of domestic violence. I am talking to the women who are in the midst of or have gone through such abuse. I am also addressing my comments to those women who have not experienced these terrors but need to recognize the signs before they themselves become future victims. My goal is to save at least one of you from a lifetime of hell or worse.

I was born in Roswell, New Mexico. My father had taken off to California for several weeks without my mother's knowledge of where he was. She was pregnant with me during this time and gave birth to me—all along without a husband at her side but with three other very frightened children—two sisters and a brother.

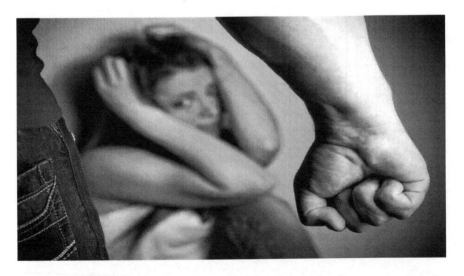

My father finally resurfaced and sent for us to start a new life in California. Of course, as an infant, I was completely oblivious of what was going on.

Once we settled down, I believed we had a normal home life. My father always worked two jobs to take care of the family. However, when my father was not working, he was always away, drinking with his friends. He was what you would call a functioning alcoholic. Unfortunately and because of that, I never had a relationship with my father though I still wanted to love him because he was my father.

My mom was very hard-working, cleaning houses and then taking care of her family, which had grown in number by then. She was a very good mother, a very loving mother–always there for us when we needed her.

I have lots of great memories with my brothers and sisters, lots of fun with our cousins too. We have a large family so there was always something to do. Lots of memories. I grew up very sheltered and so was very naïve. My older brother was always very protective and watched over me. He warned me about boys and, in particular, to stay away from his friends.

But I was 14 and very naïve! I developed a crush on one of his friends and the feeling was mutual. We dated secretly. I didn't pay attention to the fact that he was always drinking and smoking weed.

I had never really had an example of how a man should treat a woman. At home I witnessed my father mistreating my mother, showing no respect and never treating her in a loving manner. When my family learned of our dating, all hell broke loose but we continued seeing each other anyway.

I should have listened to the warnings because by the time

I was 16, he slapped me for the first time, busting my lip, and having to lie to my family to explain how that happened.

I should have listened to their warnings because by the time I was 16, he slapped me for the first time, busting my lip, and having to lie to my family to explain how that happened.

The next time it was another slap—each one much harder than the one before. Sooner than I realized, his abuse was getting out of hand. Soon he hit me so hard that I wound up in the hospital and needed 100 stitches to repair both split lips. He offered my mother a "plausible" excuse which she somehow accepted, but I was not able to eat for a month—drinking only out of a straw.

Despite all this, he gave himself permission to be even more abusive—it became easier for him. I know you're thinking, What in the world made me stay with someone like that?! But I was in love. I knew his behavior was wrong and yet did not know how to stop it.

During our five years of dating, we broke up many times. During one down time, I met a really nice young man. I got pregnant and the father was elated, but I was devastated because I still loved my ex. My new man offered to marry me, but when my ex heard about this, he begged me to return to him with the promise he would never hurt me again. I fell for his words. I had an abortion for which I have never forgiven myself (I have begged God to forgive me for killing my baby but the pain will *never* go away). I told both men that I had a miscarriage—a lie they were willing to accept.

Incredibly, on September 13, 1981, I married "the monster." Immediately I knew things just didn't seem right. I knew this marriage should never have taken place because not long after the wedding, the bruises began to appear. There were welts on my head and black eyes that I tried to hide. I was afraid to lose my husband despite all the violence. I know my decisions seem incredible to you and certainly to me now—but not then.

Like my own father, he was rarely home, especially over the weekends. He was always with other women and his friends. Arguments would ensue. One time we got into such a bad fight that he hit me repeatedly and banged my head several times against the door jams.

Six months into this so called marriage I realized that I had had enough—it was an unhealthy marriage. I knew I had to leave, so I moved out. Ironically, I found that I was pregnant again and felt I had to return to the man who was guilty of so many abusive acts against me.

Despite all this, I have to admit that I had a good pregnancy. It was a happy time for me. My husband was not physically abusive during that time although he did lash out at me verbally (but not physically). When my son was born, that was one of the greatest moments in my life. He was just beautiful.

Yet not too long after the birth of my son, the cycle began again. It started with verbal, mental, and, yes, finally physical abuse. It seems that all that goes hand in hand. Two weeks after I delivered my son, he kicked me so hard that my tail bone was fractured. I screamed so loud from the pain it caused me, but no one seemed to care. I could not sit or walk properly after what seemed like forever.

I know what I am about to say makes absolutely no sense, but I wanted another child so desperately. We planned on it because we wanted the two to be close in age. This time, however, when I got pregnant, the physical abuse did not stop.

We would argue so much, especially over his controlling and meddling mother. She had become a thorn in our lives. During one such argument, even though I was pregnant and holding our young son at the time, he hit me so hard that my left eye burst open–the blood just sprayed out everywhere. I could not see out of my eye. My eye lid just hung down.

It gets worse. He called his mother to take me to the hospital. She picked me up and drove me there and then just yelled, "Get out!" I was on my own. The injury was so bad that I thought I was going to lose my eye or at least my eyesight.

The police were called to file a report and my sister was contacted. When she arrived at my room, she didn't recognize me. I can still hear her screams of outrage and pain. It is still hard to grasp the magnitude of the ugliness this man had put me through during all that time. And yet I was still there to receive his punishment.

I lived with my sister for many months and when my old boyfriend heard of this, he wanted to come to my rescue. He even offered to take me back and raise my children. Incredible as it sounds, I decided to return to my husband. This cycle of constant pain and torture seems to be the definition of what domestic abuse is, and part of that pattern is the return of the abused to the abuser. For me, I wanted to do anything that could keep my family together.

In the meantime, my children were growing up, witnesses to abuse. The pattern was not only repeated but came to seem normal. There were not any good role models—neither the father nor the mother. Years later, my own son became an abuser and is serving time for that. We women must break this awful cycle, if not for us alone, then certainly for our children. lives.

A week after my daughter turned one, I told my husband that I wanted a divorce. At first, he agreed but then proceeded to beat me so brutally that neighbors called the police. When they showed up, my children and I were hysterical. The police removed us from that house of horrors.

This event occurred before the current laws were on the books, so (believe it or not) they did not arrest him (and quite stupidly, I never filed a police report on him on any of those occasions—except when the police came to my hospital bedside). Somehow, through all this, I had always thought my husband would and should be there to protect me, yet all along he was the one I needed to be protected from. All I can do now is shake my head in disbelief over my foolish ignorance.

My family tried to convince me that I was a human, a person of value, and needed to demand that kind of respect. They also reminded me that my decisions needed to be the best for my children as well. I was finally convinced that I needed to file for a divorce. Needless to say, that didn't go over well. In the middle of the night, he had come over to where I was staying with my parents and took my car. How would I take my children to school or go to work?

Finally, the hearing for our divorce approached. But one night as I was getting out of my car after work, he came up from behind me and covered my mouth so I couldn't scream. He whispered in my ear to give him my son in the divorce or he would kill me. I believed he would act on his words—I was so terrified.

On that dreadful court day, I was alone while he had his

entourage with him. Of course, his family was there in great number. I relinquished my rights to my son on that day. I felt such hate for him and for the family that was laughing at me and my suffering. I just wanted to die from the pain of having to give away my son. I realized that if I had made the reports that I rightfully should have, the court would never have allowed this to happen. On the other hand, I truly believe I would not be alive today to share my story.

Over time, my ex-husband would ask me to come back home. My first and continued reaction was to reject this awful offer. But at length I could not take being separated from my son. The family was in distress, so, yes, I chose to return to him for my children's sake.

It soon became apparent to him that I no longer had any love for him and that I would cringe at his attempts at intimacy. Not surprisingly then, the abuse started again. I tried to hide the abuse form my family (who worried so much) and from my co-workers. Yet, there was the occasional black eye and dislocated arm and broken knee which required surgery (when that incident happened, it sounded like a pencil breaking).

The worst part of all of this is that my children suffered from the time they were in the womb and continuing through the violence they heard and witnessed as they were growing up. It can be no surprise that our children, filled with emotional and psychological pain, grew up to be angry adults. My son, as a teenager, literally had to pull his father, his paternal grandmother, and his aunt off of his mother when they were trying to hurt me.

No son or daughter should ever be put into that kind of repeated predicament. My son is now serving time in prison for domestic violence, and my daughter is the hostile and aggressive one in her relationships. My poor babies. As children, they were always so scared. He would not hit until they got older. Our son got into fist fights with his father and that same father threw my daughter out of the house when she was only 16. Our house was literally not a home, and yet what did I do to help?

One time, he tried to hit my grandchild whom I was holding. As I tried to protect the baby, he began hitting me. Once again my left side was under attack. My eye was so damaged, I could not see and to this day, I see white flashes and black floaters in that eye.

Finally, my daughter talked some sense into me to leave him. It was 2011. That was when I finally got up the courage to do so.

We left. I found a job. I was scared but committed to making a permanent change in our lives.. It was the best decision I could have ever made. Now we are so happy in our new apartment, our sanctuary, where there is such peacefulness each morning when we wake up. This is the happiest I have been since I was a young teenager before all my joy and happiness were stripped from me.

I am now enjoying life to the fullest. I actually have friends. I am enrolled in a Community College in order to get a better job. I am doing all the things I was not able to do over the past 40 years.

Interestingly enough, my former husband still doesn't understand what he did that was wrong—the thought process shared by so many abusers. It is mind-boggling how they blind themselves to reality and refuse to take any responsibility. My ex-husband had stripped me of all my dignity as a woman. He made me always feel no better than a child—not worthy of the respect any adult (or any person) deserves. He would say I could do nothing right, that I was a stupid moron, that I was stupid, fat, ugly, disgusting–among other disgusting words. He convinced me that no one would ever want me. He made me feel worthless and unable to control my life.

I am so grateful for my faith which is what ultimately saved my life. I survived a 35-year "prison term." I had become a broken woman. I had allowed myself to be the victim for so many years. But not anymore!

During all that time of abuse, I thought I felt a sense of security because I had the house, the cars, the successful business that my husband had started–all the material things that one could want and that money could buy and it was at my fingertips. Ask me, Would I change my life to get all that back? Absolutely not!

The fact is, I have a man now that loves me with all his heart and soul. God has blessed me with such a beautiful man (someone who has also had his 35 years of hell), but someone with whom we have so much in common. He is a tender, sensitive soul. If you have ever read a fairy tale love story, here is another one to add to your list.

There is hope for all of you out there. I never said it would be easy because it won't be. However the peace you and your children will come to know will supersede all the struggles you will experience while finding your way to freedom.

Some of us do have the good fortune to be able to escape. However, there are far too many of us women who never make it out alive. That's the reality and the tragedy that is just too prevalent throughout our nation.

That is why all women (and men) must fight to educate about domestic abuse, to prevent it, and to penalize it when it does transpire. My heart goes out to all the women and children that are going through any form of abuse. I pray that sharing my story opens the eyes of all who read this column and move them to do something about it.

Incidental information about SAN QUENTIN NEWS

San Quentin News is the only prisoner-operated newspaper in the California prison system. Its reporters have a unique access to, and knowledge of, the workings of the state prison system that set them apart from any other journalists in the field. The newspaper focuses on providing an accurate view of prison life to its readers and on the analysis of criminal justice policy.

Currently 11,000 Newspapers are Distributed Monthly. Private individual funders and foundations make the printing and distribution of San Quentin News possible:

- Columbia Foundation, $68,000.00 (2013)
- Annenberg Foundation, $2,000.00 (2012)
- RESIST, $2,000.00 (2012)
- Marin Community Foundation, $5,000.00 (2011)

Individual donors provided San Quentin News with more than $9,000 in 2014. The cost of printing and distribution for 13,000 SQ Newspapers is approximately $23,000.00 annually. Our immediate goals by end of 2016 is to circulate between 20-30 thousand newspapers to the 17 prisons currently receiving the newspaper, have more prisons and other institutions added to our circulation list, and to add part-time external support to aid with distribution and website maintenance. Our long-term goal is to provide all prisoners housed in California Department of Corrections and Rehabilitation facilities (roughly 120,000) with access to a San Quentin Newspaper.

We thank you for your continued support by which we can reach our goals and achieve our mission of providing incarcerated women and men, criminal justice leaders and community advocates with the information and inspiration they need to better their lives, their communities and the lives of those affected by crime and violence.

■■■

"Managing *San Quentin News* includes overseeing its content while listening to ideas, writing, co-writing, and re-writing stories with a level of compassion that fairly expose matters behind prison walls previously unknown to the public. A central part of the newspaper is to humanize incarcerated people while giving readers an honest take on the consequences of breaking the law. However, managing a prisoner-run newspaper where its published is the Department of Corrections as well as adhering to the tenets of journalism has an implicit conflict that must be acknowledged. . . . [Nevertheless], there are stories that address harsh living conditions behind bars—The Hole, Death Row, medical care, and so forth. [This periodical] would not be a legitimate news agency if these types of stories were ignored."

-- Juan Moreno Haines
Managing Editor for the *San Quentin News*

Reprinted with permission

A Review of *SB 260*

SB 260 holds young people responsible for the crimes they committed, but it recognizes that youth are different from adults and gives them a chance to demonstrate remorse and rehabilitation.

This bill would hold young people accountable by requiring a lengthy minimum prison sentence, but provide people who were under the age of 18 at the time of their crime an opportunity to work toward rehabilitation and the possibility of a lower sentence. It establishes a judicial review process to evaluate their cases after serving 10 years in prison.

PROBLEM & NEED FOR THE BILL:

Over 6,500 people currently in California prisons were under the age of 18 at the time of their crime. They were juveniles, but tried as adults and sentenced to adult prison terms. Many are transferred to the adult system without consideration of their ability to change. Tremendous growth and maturity often occurs in the late teens through the mid-20s. The current system provides no viable mechanism for reviewing a case after a young person has grown up and matured. California law should motivate young people to focus on rehabilitation, and provide opportunities for judicial review and a modified sentence for individuals who can prove they merit a second chance.

Existing sentencing laws ignore recent scientific evidence on adolescent development and neuro-science. Research has shown that certain areas of the brain, particularly those that affect judgment and decision-making, do not fully develop until the early 20's. The US Supreme Court stated in its *2005 Roper v. Simmons* decision, "[t]he reality that juveniles still struggle to define their identity means it is less supportable to conclude that even a heinous crime committed by a juvenile is evidence of irretrievably depraved character." Moreover, the fact that young adults are still developing means that they are uniquely situated for personal growth and rehabilitation.

1. The US Supreme Court recently held unconstitutional mandatory life without parole sentences for people under the age of 18, and required courts to consider the youthfulness of defendants facing that sentence.

The California Supreme Court recently ruled that a sentence exceeding the life expectancy of a juvenile is the equivalent of life without parole, and unconstitutional in non-homicide cases.

2. These decisions recognize that it is wrong to deny someone who commits a crime under the age of 18 the opportunity to demonstrate rehabilitation.

Piecemeal changes to California law since the 1990s have removed many safeguards and points for review that once existed for youth charged with crimes. California transfers without careful consideration of amenability to rehabilitation many youth under the age of 18 years old to the adult criminal justice system where they face adult prison terms.

For example, laws now mandate the automatic transfer of youth as young as 14 years old to adult court for certain crimes, or permit a direct file in adult court without any review of the youth's circumstances in other cases.

The role of judges and a careful, considered process before transferring youth to the adult criminal justice system has been severely limited.

EXISTING LAW:

Existing law sentences youth to adult terms with no opportunity for judicial review of the sentences outside of ordinary appeals. Existing law provides that the secretary of the Department of Corrections and Rehabilitation or the Board of Parole Hearings may recommend to the court an inmate's sentence be recalled, and that a court may recall an inmate's sentence. However, current law fails to take into account factors of rehabilitation and remorse as well as the youthfulness of the offender, or what the US Supreme Court describes in *Miller v. Alabama*, as the "hallmarks of youth."

WHAT THIS BILL WOULD DO:

SB 260 would establish a judicial review process for cases where an individual was under 18 years of age at the time of the offense and prosecuted as an adult.

1. *Miller v. Alabama (2012)*

2. *People v. Caballero (2012)*

FACTSHEET for SB 260 (Hancock):

Review for Juveniles Sentenced to Adult Prison Terms as amended on 4/4/2013:

Specifically, a young person who was under the age of 18 at the time of the crime and tried in the adult criminal justice system would be able to return to the sentencing court to review the case after serving 10 years in prison. In making a determination about whether to resentence an individual, the judge would consider the input of prosecutors and victims, the individual's prison disciplinary record, and weigh factors indicating whether the individual is rehabilitated or on a path to rehabilitation, including, but not limited to, whether the person is availing himself or herself of rehabilitative, educational, or vocational programs, and whether the person has remorse for their criminal behavior.

The judge may consider any other relevant evidence. If a judge finds that a different sentence is merited, the judge may reduce, suspend or stay all or a portion of the existing sentence. There is no mandate to do so.

Individuals could petition the sentencing court for an additional review if there are substantial changes of circumstances proven by the individual.

SUPPORT:

As of 4/10/13 Human Rights Watch (sponsor), Youth Law Center (co-sponsor), The Friends Committee (co-sponsor), USC School of Law Post-Conviction Clinic (co-sponsor), A Place Called Home, American Civil Liberties Union, American Friends Service Committee, American Probation and Parole Association, Amnesty International Advancement Project, Bar Association of San Francisco, Berkeley Organizing Congregations for Action, Black Organizing Project, Boys and Girls Club of San Gabriel Valley, California Catholic Conference, California Church.

Note:

California SB 260 was passed in 2014: applies to those tried but were under the age of 18 at the time the crime was committed.

California SB 260 was passed in 2015: applies to those tried but were under the age of 23 at the time the crime was committed.

California SB 260 was passed in 2017: applies to those tried but were under the age of 25 at the time the crime was committed.

SB 261, Hancock. YOUTH OFFENDER PAROLE HEARINGS

An act to amend Sections 3051 and 4801 of the Penal Code, relating to parole.

Approved by Governor & Filed with Secretary of State

October 03, 2015

LEGISLATIVE COUNSEL'S DIGEST

Existing law generally requires the Board of Parole Hearings to conduct youth offender parole hearings to consider the release of offenders who committed specified crimes when they were under 18 years of age and who were sentenced to state prison.

This bill would instead require the Board of Parole Hearings to conduct a youth offender parole hearing for offenders sentenced to state prison who committed those specified crimes when they were under 23 years of age. The bill would require the board to complete, by July 1, 2017, all youth offender parole hearings for individuals who were sentenced to indeterminate life terms who become entitled to have their parole suitability considered at a youth offender parole hearing on the effective date of the bill. The bill would require the board to complete all youth offender parole hearings for individuals who were sentenced to determinate terms who become entitled to have their parole suitability considered at a youth offender parole hearing on the effective date of the bill by July 1, 2021, and would require the board, for these individuals, to conduct a specified consultation before July 1, 2017.

Bill Text:

THE PEOPLE OF THE STATE OF CALIFORNIA DO ENACT AS FOLLOWS:

Juvenile Offenders: From Big Wheels to the Big House

SECTION 1:

Section 3051 of the Penal Code is amended to read:

(a) (1) A youth offender parole hearing is a hearing by the Board of Parole Hearings for the purpose of reviewing the parole suitability of any prisoner who was under 23 years of age at the time of his or her controlling offense.

(2) For the purposes of this section, the following definitions shall apply:

(A) "Incarceration" means detention in a city or county jail, a local juvenile facility, a mental health facility, a Division of Juvenile Justice facility, or a Department of Corrections and Rehabilitation facility.

(B) "Controlling offense" means the offense or enhancement for which any sentencing court imposed the longest term of imprisonment.

(b) (1) A person who was convicted of a controlling offense that was committed before the person had attained 23 years of age and for which the sentence is a determinate sentence shall be eligible for release on parole at a youth offender parole hearing by the board during his or her 15th year of incarceration, unless previously released pursuant to other statutory provisions.

(2) A person who was convicted of a controlling offense that was committed before the person had attained 23 years of age and for which the sentence is a life term of less than 25 years to life shall be eligible for release on parole by the board during his or her 20th year of incarceration at a youth offender parole hearing, unless previously released or entitled to an earlier parole consideration hearing pursuant to other statutory provisions.

(3) A person who was convicted of a controlling offense that was committed before the person had attained 23 years of age and for which the sentence is a life term of 25 years to life shall be eligible for release on parole by the board during his or her 25th year of incarceration at a youth offender parole hearing, unless previously released or entitled to an earlier parole consideration hearing pursuant to other statutory provisions.

(c) An individual subject to this section shall meet with the board pursuant to subdivision (a) of Section 3041.

(d) The board shall conduct a youth offender parole hearing to consider release. At the youth offender parole hearing, the board shall release the individual on parole as provided in Section 3041, except that the board shall act in accordance with subdivision (c) of Section 4801.

(e) The youth offender parole hearing to consider release shall provide for a meaningful opportunity to obtain release. The board shall review and, as necessary, revise existing regulations and adopt new regulations regarding determinations of suitability made pursuant to this section, subdivision (c) of Section 4801, and other related topics, consistent with relevant case law, in order to provide that meaningful opportunity for release.

(f) (1) In assessing growth and maturity, psychological evaluations and risk assessment instruments, if used by the board, shall be administered by licensed psychologists employed by the board and shall take into consideration the diminished culpability of juveniles as compared to that of adults, the hallmark features of youth, and any subsequent growth and increased maturity of the individual.

(2) Family members, friends, school personnel, faith leaders, and representatives from community-based organizations

with knowledge about the individual before the crime or his or her growth and maturity since the time of the crime may submit statements for review by the board.

(3) Nothing in this section is intended to alter the rights of victims at parole hearings.

(g) If parole is not granted, the board shall set the time for a subsequent youth offender parole hearing in accordance with paragraph (3) of subdivision (b) of Section 3041.5. In exercising its discretion pursuant to paragraph (4) of subdivision (b) and subdivision (d) of Section 3041.5, the board shall consider the factors in subdivision (c) of Section 4801. No subsequent youth offender parole hearing shall be necessary if the offender is released pursuant to other statutory provisions prior to the date of the subsequent hearing.

(h) This section shall not apply to cases in which sentencing occurs pursuant to Section 1170.12, subdivisions (b) to (i), inclusive, of Section 667, or Section 667.61, or in which an individual was sentenced to life in prison without the possibility of parole. This section shall not apply to an individual to whom this section would otherwise apply, but who, subsequent to attaining 23 years of age, commits an additional crime for which malice aforethought is a necessary element of the crime or for which the individual is sentenced to life in prison.

(i) (1) The board shall complete all youth offender parole hearings for individuals who became entitled to have their parole suitability considered at a youth offender parole hearing prior to the effective date of the act that added paragraph (2) by July 1, 2015.

(2) (A) The board shall complete all youth offender parole hearings for individuals who were sentenced to

indeterminate life terms and who become entitled to have their parole suitability considered at a youth offender parole hearing on the effective date of the act that added this paragraph by July 1, 2017.

(B) The board shall complete all youth offender parole hearings for individuals who were sentenced to determinate terms and who become entitled to have their parole suitability considered at a youth offender parole hearing on the effective date of the act that added this paragraph by July 1, 2021. The board shall, for all individuals described in this subparagraph, conduct the consultation described in subdivision (a) of Section 3041 before July 1, 2017.

SECTION 2:

Section 4801 of the Penal Code is amended to read:

(a) The Board of Parole Hearings may report to the Governor, from time to time, the names of any and all persons imprisoned in any state prison who, in its judgment, ought to have a commutation of sentence or be pardoned and set at liberty on account of good conduct, or unusual term of sentence, or any other cause, including evidence of intimate partner battering and its effects. For purposes of this section, "intimate partner battering and its effects" may include evidence of the nature and effects of physical, emotional, or mental abuse upon the beliefs, perceptions, or behavior of victims of domestic violence if it appears the criminal behavior was the result of that victimization.

(b) (1) The board, in reviewing a prisoner's suitability for parole pursuant to Section 3041.5, shall give great weight to any information or evidence that, at the time of the commission of the crime, the prisoner had experienced intimate partner battering, but was convicted of an offense that occurred prior to August 29, 1996. The board shall state on the record the information or evidence that it considered pursuant to this subdivision, and the reasons for the parole decision. The board shall annually report to the Legislature and the Governor on the cases the board considered pursuant to this subdivision during the previous year, including the board's decisions and the specific and detailed findings of its investigations of these cases.

(2) The report for the Legislature to be submitted pursuant to paragraph (1) shall be submitted pursuant to Section 9795 of the Government Code.

(3) The fact that a prisoner has presented evidence of intimate partner battering cannot be used to support a finding that the prisoner lacks insight into his or her crime and its causes.

(c) When a prisoner committed his or her controlling offense, as defined in subdivision (a) of Section 3051, prior to attaining 23 years of age, the board, in reviewing a prisoner's suitability for parole pursuant to Section 3041.5, shall give great weight to the diminished culpability of juveniles as compared to adults, the hallmark features of youth, and any subsequent growth and increased maturity of the prisoner in accordance with relevant case law.

****

Recent Court Cases on Extreme Sentences for Youth Which Pertain to Both *SB 260* and *SB 261*

Graham v. Florida (2010); *People v. Caballero* (2012); *Miller v. Alabama* (2012); *People v. Gutierrez & People v. Moffett* (2014); *Alatriste on H.C. & Bonilla on H.C* (2014 and 2015)

A Disconnect Between Law and Neuroscience: Modern Brain Science, Media Influences, and Juvenile Justice

By Kevin W. Saunders
Michigan State University College of Law

Utah Law Review, Vol. 2005, pp. 695-741, 2005
MSU Legal Studies Research Paper No. 03-12

Abstract:

Modern brain science has discovered a second period of physical development of the brain in the adolescent years. Paralleling the cognitive development of infancy and early childhood, the judgmental and inhibitory regions of the brain go through a process of synaptic overblooming and later paring in this later period of life. Just as environment affects cognitive development, it appears it also has an effect on judgment and inhibition. This has consequences that should influence the development of the law. First, if environment affects which synapses remain in the developed brain and later influence judgment, there is greater reason to be concerned about the media environment children face. Second, if children are unable to make adult judgments and inhibit their actions, rather than simply being unwilling to do so, that should speak in favor of a juvenile justice system that recognizes that juvenile offenders may be more amendable to rehabilitation than adults.

Norway Prisons Taking Rehabilitation to Another Level
by Anouthinh Pangthong, Journalism Guild Writer,
San Quentin News

[reprinted with permission]

The United States and Norwegian penal systems could not be more opposite from one another, according to American journalist Jessica Benko.

In Norway, the practice of capital punishment was banned in 1902 and life sentences were abolished in 1981; the maximum sentence for any crime is 21 years. In addition, unlike its American counterpart, the Norwegian correctional system is based heavily on rehabilitation.

An example is the construction of Halden Fengsel prison. Its perimeter is devoid of electric fences topped by razor wires. Nonexistent are the armed towers like those across prisons throughout the U.S.

Halden Fengsel houses some 251 of Norway's 3,800 inmates and uses non-conventional approaches in a non-conventional setting.

Benko visited Halden Fengsel and describes the prison as "the physical expression of an entire national philosophy about the relative merits of punishment and forgiveness.

"Better out than in" is an unofficial Norwegian Correctional Service motto. In 1998, Norway's Ministry of Justice recalculated the goals and methodology of the Correctional Service, putting forth a new approach to rehabilitation and incarceration. It included education, job training, skills development and therapy.

Norway's criminal justice system emphasizes rehabilitation and reintegration and assisting inmates with housing and job placement before they are released from prison.

Benko says of Halden, "Every aspect of the facility was designed to ease psychological pressures, mitigate conflict and minimize interpersonal friction."

In 2011, Anders Behring Breivik attacked a government building in the capitol city, which resulted in hundreds of injuries, followed by a bloody massacre at a summer camp where 77 students died.

Due to magnitude of this crime, Breivik was sentenced to "preventive detention," which means that after 21 years his sentence can be extended by five-years. These extensions can go on indefinitely if he is determined to be a danger to public safety.

Breivik is not at Halden Fengsel; he is in a high-security wing at Ila Prison (by himself in three rooms, according to his recent biography).

There are approximately 2.2 million people incarcerated in America's prisons. The U.S. makes up 5 percent of the world's population, and has 25 percent of the world's incarcerated.

In a 1967 report, The Challenge of Crime in a Free Society, concerns were raised about correctional facilities. "Life in many institutions is at best barren and futile, at worst unspeakably brutal and degrading...The conditions in which they live are the poorest possible preparation for their successful re-entry into society and often merely reinforce in them a pattern of manipulation and destructiveness."

Robert Martinson, a sociology researcher at the City University of New York, authored a 1974 article in which he argues the rehabilitative effects of programs. He writes, "With few and isolated exceptions, the rehabilitative efforts that have been reported so far have had no appreciable effect on recidivism.

As a result of that report, several media organizations used Martinson's claims to discredit rehabilitation in America's prisons. California Gov. Jerry Brown, in 1975, said of rehabilitative programs, "They don't rehabilitate; they don't deter; they don't punish, and they don't protect."

Critics quickly challenged Martinson's "choice to overlook the successful programs and their characteristics in favor of a broad conclusion devoid of context." Martinson published a new report in 1979 from new analyses that adamantly retracted his earlier summation.

He states in this report, "Contrary to my previous position, some treatment programs do have an appreciable effect on recidivism." A 1984 Senate report demanding tougher sentencing guidelines cited Martinson's 1974 report; however, Martinson's retraction did not appear in the Senate report.

Norway's Halden Fengsel, with its non-imposing architectural design and rehabilitative setting, represents a stark alternative to the retributive component in America's criminal justice system.

Ragnar Kristoffersen, an anthropologist, quotes a verse

thought to be by Dostoyevsky, "The degree of a civilization in a society can be judged by entering its prisons."

[Note by Mark E. Vigil]: "A reality check for people who still live under the misinformed notion that America is still the best place to live. It is good to see countries providing their prisoners new, modernized placed to do their time rather than the waste of time we do here [Mule Creek State Prison]."

Juvenile Offenders: From Big Wheels to the Big House

Class Action Lawsuit Filed to End Isolation
by Juan Moreno Haines
Managing Editor, *San Quentin News*

"On a regular basis, prisoners can be heard screaming and yelling in fits," while "security gates and cell doors constantly slam open and close," according to court papers filed in a federal District Court in Northern California by six men on Death Row.

The class action lawsuit was filed on behalf of all prisoners housed inside the Adjustment Center at San Quentin State Prison, who spend 21 to 24 hours per day behind the solid steel doors of cells that measure approximately six feet wide and nine feet long.

No inmates are held in cells for hours a day, because they're entitled to 10 hours a week in the prison exercise yard, the CDCR press office reports.

"Some days ... all you can hear all day long is screaming, hollering, and banging from prisoners who can no longer endure the isolation," according to the June 17 law-suit. "High ceilings and the enclosed steel cells in the unit amplify this noise. The cacophony continues throughout the day and night."

The lawsuit claims prisoners remain in the Adjustment Center with no exposure to natural light, no access to religious services, and devoid of recreational, vocational and educational programming. They are denied contact visits and regular telephone calls.

Prisoners subjected to extreme isolation suffer from a host of psychological disorders, including anxiety and nervousness, headaches, lethargy and chronic tiredness, trouble sleeping, obsessive ruminations and oversensitivity to stimuli as a result of isolation, the lawsuit claims.

The lawsuit further alleges that prison officials persistently and intentionally deny these men the normal human contact and socialization necessary for a person's mental and physical well-being.

All men sentenced to death in California must begin their incarceration in the Adjustment Center. A few remain there indefinitely; some return for lengthy and indefinite stays.

The plaintiffs are:

Bobby Lopez is a 50-year-old prisoner. He has been housed in the Adjustment Center for 17 years. Lopez has been on Death Row since November 1997.

Marco Topete is a 42-year-old prisoner. He has been housed in the Adjustment Center for three years. Topete has been on Death Row since February 2012.

John Myles is a 43-year-old prisoner. He has been housed in the Adjustment Center for 11 years. Myles has been on Death Row since May 2001.

Ricardo Roldan is a 44-year-old prisoner. He has been housed in the Adjustment Center for eight years. Roldan has been on Death Row since January 1993.

John Gonzales is a 38-year-old prisoner. He has been housed in the Adjustment Center for four years. Gonzales has been on Death Row since December 1998.

Ronaldo Medrano Ayala is a 65-year-old prisoner. He has been housed in the Adjustment Center for 26 years. Ayala has been on Death Row since February 1989.

A new security check system, Guard One, adds to the noise in the Adjustment Center. It is designed to account for correctional officers' suicide checks. The system uses a hand-held wand and a sensor affixed to cell doors that must connect to register that a suicide check was conducted.

Every 30 minutes, correctional officers must visually check each prisoner in the Adjustment Center and then touch the end of the wand to the sensor as confirmation of a suicide check. In practice, the lawsuit claims, guards slam the wand against the sensor creating a loud bang against the cell door.

Some plaintiffs say they wake up whenever the Guard One check is conducted, resulting in sleep for 30-minute increments at best.

Topete says he is awakened every time the Guard One check is performed and experiences exhaustion daily as a result of constant sleep interruption.

Ayala says the sleep deprivation makes him agitated and immediately angry at any little thing.

Lopez says he feels drained of energy all the time.

With the exception of men in special health care or mental health care management programs, the men of Death Row are housed in one of three units at San Quentin: Northern Segregation, East Block and the Adjustment Center.

Condemned prisoners are classified as Grade A or Grade B, based on the vague standard of whether they present a "high risk" of violence or escape or are "difficult management cases," according to the lawsuit.

Grade A classified prisoners can work, get an advanced education, call their families every day, touch their loved ones during 2 ½-hour visits, receive quarterly packages and special purchase orders, order additional food and recreation items from the commissary, create art, recreate with equipment, access the vast San Quentin Library and worship in group settings while on Death Row.

Prisoners classified as Grade B are denied all possibilities for work, enrichment and socialization. They receive only minimal recreation; limited, non-contact visiting; access to a book cart; and only an annual package and special order, the means by which they can receive new clothes, a radio or a television.

All the prisoners in the Adjustment Center are Grade B. The lawsuit alleges that there is no meaningful review of plaintiffs' Grade B classification and there is no reasonable means of earning their way into Grade A.

Plaintiffs live with the constant knowledge that, despite their compliance with rules, prison officials have almost complete and unchecked control over their release from the Adjustment Center, the lawsuit states.

As of April, there were 93 condemned men housed in the Adjustment Center. Nearly 78 percent of the condemned population has been on Death Row for a decade or more.

Between 1976, when the national death penalty moratorium was lifted, and 2006 when it was put back in place, California executed 13 men. California has not executed a condemned prisoner since 2006. The average time they spent on Death Row was 17.5 years.

It takes approximately 25 years to exhaust death penalty appeals.

REFERENCING ARTICLES ON THE SUBJECT OF MENTAL HEALTH AND THE JUSTICE SYSTEM
summarized and edited by Rosemary Jenkins
(researched from bi-weekly *Pacific Standard* from 2015)

1. MENTAL HEALTH COURTS CAN WORK
"(A) growing body of mental health court research [2015] indicates that it is plausible that these courts have the ability to . . . reduce criminal recidivism rates of persons with mental illness.'"

—"Does the Evidence Support the Case for Mental Health Courts? A Review of the Literature," Honegger, L.N., Law and Human Behavior, 2015.

2. AND THE RESULTS HAVE STAYING POWER FOR GRADUATES
While certain research suggests "that people who complete mental health court are more motivated to change their behavior, it also shows that, at a minimum, the courts do not hinder the process of recovery—and might well improve it."

—"Long-Term Recidivism of Mental Health Court Defendants," Ray, B., International Journal of Law and Psychiatry, 2014.

3. DROPOUTS DON'T SEEM TO BE HARMED—UNLESS THEY ARE SEVERELY PUNISHED

"(A)ccording to one study, mental health courts are less likely to foster recidivism than regular courts." In the case of those who did not finish court-mandated programs, recidivism seemed to be in direct proportion to the magnitude of the punishment—as much as five times greater than those who were placed in jails. Some have concluded that for many mentally ill defendants, their cases should have been dismissed rather than go through the court system with consequent sentencing.

—"What Happens to Mental Health Court Non-Completers?" Ray, B., *et al.*, Behavioral Science and the Law, 2015.

4. MENTAL ILLNESS DOESN'T CAUSE CRIME—BUT IT HAMPERS REHABILITATION

Too many mentally ill defendants find themselves in jails that "have become, essentially, the biggest psychiatric hospitals in the country." Thus, to provide productive results, mental health courts must provide the mentally ill with the tools they need to modify their behavior in order to function well in society.

—"When Research Challenges Policy and Practice: Toward a New Understanding of Mental Health Courts," Fisler, C., Judges' Journal, 2015.

In this manner, balance was restored and the potential for the colony could once again be realized.

Juvenile Offenders: From Big Wheels to the Big House

Study: Children of Incarcerated Parents Show Signs of Mental Health Problems

by Micheal Cooke, Journalism Guild Writer, *San Quentin News*

Children of incarcerated parents exhibit mental health and behavior problems, a university study concludes.

"These kids are saddled with disadvantages," said Kristin Turney, study author and assistant professor of sociology at the University of California at Irvine. "They're not only dealing with parental incarceration, but also mental health issues. It might make finding a job more difficult, or they may be forced to grow up faster than peers."

The study was presented at the 109th annual meeting of the American Sociological Association. It was published in the September Journal of Health and Social Behavior.

Having a parent in prison is "associated with children's behavior problems and conditions such as attention deficit hyperactivity disorder, learning disabilities, speech or language problems and developmental delays." Printed by the American Sociological Review and reported in *USA Today* on Aug. 25, [2015] the review described how the emotional and physical trauma of being in prison not only impacts the incarcerated, but also those who are connected to them.

The study paints a complex picture that suggests the consequences of incarceration can socialize men to respond to conflict rapidly and with extreme violence. It also can dramatically increase the risk of separation and divorce in marital or intimate relationships and causes severe depression and mental health problems for women left behind by a romantic partner.

Children of incarcerated fathers likely experience less favorable parenting overall. Social selective processes, such as race and social class, are predictive of incarceration rather than a causal effect, with minority and poorly educated men more likely than others to experience confinement, the study reports.

However, Glen Elliott, a medical director and chief psychiatrist at the Children's Health Council, disagreed with the conclusions. He stated that diseases such as ADHD are generally inherited behavioral conditions. "You can't assume that these are causal relationships," Elliott said.

Susan Brown, a professor of sociology at Bowling Green State University, noted the study gave "compelling evidence." Brown said, "I think that it raises a number of important issues."

The study concluded incarceration represents a substantial barrier to involvement in parenting after release, and family member contact is a vital deterrent to recidivism. It said increased visiting opportunities, and reduced barriers, such as access to affordable transportation to prisons, may benefit parents and their family members.

PRESIDENT OBAMA WANTS TO OFFER GRANTS FOR COLLEGE AID TO PRISON INMATES
summarized by Rosemary Jenkins

[researched from a 2015 article by Jennifer C. Kerr and Josh Lederman for AP]

President Obama was the first sitting President to visit a Federal prison and see and hear for himself from first-hand interaction what is actually transpiring in such institutions. The experience was eye-opening for him and for all of us.

What is observed in the television show, *Lock Up*, and from other similar broadcasts underlines the travesty we call our American system of incarceration. These episodes have been compelling, offering great insight and a new sensitivity about the men and women who, often as mere children, have been sent away for lengthy periods of time under unimaginable conditions. Their excessive terms often result not in rehabilitation but in hardening those people who, in their youth, hadn't figured out productive ways to survive their own abominable conditions and instead followed a tragic path.

Despite what many may think, many educators and others working in the justice system have found that there are viable alternatives that can turn around the lives these offenders. To these experts, then, providing a means to achieve a higher education, certifications, and career training is the key to the change that both the system and the inmates need.

The President, in part as a consequence of these revelations, instructed Attorney General Loretta Lynch and then-Secretary of Education, Arne Duncan, to create a Second Chance Pell Pilot Program.

Duncan has been quoted as saying, "America is a nation of second chances. Giving people who have made mistakes in their lives a chance to get back on track and become contributing members of society is fundamental to who we are."

Back in 1994, Congress prevented inmates from receiving student aid. The fact is, that decree (perhaps inadvertently) has created a different type of class system. Those with relatives and friends who can afford to subsidize their education will generally do so, but those who come from poverty or whose families have abandoned them are really not, for the most part, in a position to obtain the skills that can be used successfully as they go through the process of re-integrating into society--post-incarceration.

The right-wing in Congress claims that overturning the inmate exclusion for Pell Grants would be unfair to taxpayers, let alone to other potential students who have never committed a crime. Actually, Secretary Duncan has stated that the new prison-grant program "can also be a cost-saver for taxpayers." Furthermore, Education Undersecretary Ted Mitchell has asserted that the program will "not compromise or displace any Pell Grant eligibility for any other populations" [consider similar policy for Affirmative Action].

The reality is that if we ignore this very large segment of our population, we are inviting greater recidivism often due to committing even more violent crimes. Of course, to be somewhat cynical, administrators of private prisons might well want to discourage the creation of such programs if creating it would mean fewer inmates from whom they can make a profit.

The fact is that Pell Grants, which do not have to be repaid, are intended for people of low income and little means (and that includes inmates who have come from poverty). The

Higher Education Act of 1995 allows, despite opposition by many conservatives, experimental pilot programs such as what the Obama Administration is currently introducing.

We know from recent studies that 43% of prison participants, on average, are less likely to engage in criminal activity again. There are already some colleges and universities which have partnered with some prisons and have witnessed outstanding outcomes from inmate participants, many of whom have received college degrees and certifications in various professions. Upon release, these men and women have become invaluable assets to their respective communities. Many such beneficiaries are now working with at-risk youth and other vulnerable groups to help them find alternate ways to succeed in life, other than taking a path of crime.

What is needed here is a Hurrah! for President Obama. His insight and leadership on this issue is unparalleled by predecessors holding his position. Not only is he promoting student aid for qualified prisoners but he is calling for reviews of how solitary confinement has been used and abused, how "long mandatory minimum sentences now in place [should] be reduced or discarded entirely," and how voting rights ought to be restored to those who have served their time (after all, voting gives people an opportunity to be genuine stakeholders in their communities.)

Indeed, America has been and must continue to be a nation of second chances.

Ban the Box Campaign
By Kokayi Kwa Jitihidi at LAANE [now at LA County Fed] and
Saun Hough at The Jericho Training Center

Our **Ban the Box** campaign calls for removing the question and check box, "Have you been convicted by a court?" from applications for employment, housing, public benefits, insurance, loans and other services. These questions mean lifelong discrimination and exclusion because of a past arrest or conviction record.

All of Us or None is recognized nationwide as the core of a Ban the Box movement that is sweeping the country. As of May 2013, 50 cities or counties, and 9 states have removed questions about conviction history from their public employment applications. Several of these cities or counties also require that their vendors adopt the same hiring practices as for public employment, which increases job opportunities even more.

Campaigns to Ban the Box around the U.S. have been started by a wide variety of people: formerly-incarcerated people, neighborhood legal services agencies, City Council members, Mayors, other elected officials. For any of our campaigns to win, it's crucial that we build broad coalitions that recognize the grassroots voice of people who have been directly affected by this discrimination.

To start a campaign in your area, check out our **Ban the Box Campaign Tools**.

Contact Jesse Stout, jesse@prisonerswithchildren.org or banthebox@prisonerswithchildren.org for a hard copy of our Ban the Box Organizers' Toolkit and more information.

In San Francisco, we are currently drafting legislation that will expand access to housing and jobs for people with conviction records. This legislation will set standards for how and when employers **and** housing providers may consider conviction records.

Nationally, we are promoting the **Fair Chance Pledge**: banning the box at nonprofits and foundations.

Rosemary Jenkins-meredithetc.com/juvenile-offenders/

Ban the Box: U.S. Cities, Counties, and States Adopt Fair Hiring Policies
by Michelle Natividad Rodriguez and Navantara Mehta
both with Criminal Records and Employment Expertise

September 25, 2015 National Employment Law Project

Nationwide, over 100 cities and counties have adopted what is widely known as "ban the box" so that employers consider a job candidate's qualifications first, without the stigma of a conviction record. These initiatives provide applicants a fair chance by removing the conviction history question on the job application and delaying the background check inquiry until later in the hiring.

Momentum for the policy has grown exponentially, particularly in recent years. There are a total of 19 states representing nearly every region of the country that have adopted the policies —California (2013, 2010), Colorado (2012), Connecticut (2010), Delaware (2014), Georgia (2015), Hawaii (1998), Illinois (2014, 2013), Maryland (2013), Massachusetts (2010), Minnesota (2013, 2009), Nebraska (2014), New Jersey (2014), New Mexico (2010), New York (2015), Ohio (2015), Oregon (2015), Rhode Island (2013), Vermont (2015), and Virginia (2015). Seven states— Hawaii, Illinois, Massachusetts, Minnesota, New Jersey, Oregon and Rhode Island—have removed the conviction history question on job applications for private employers, which advocates embrace as the next step in the evolution of these policies.

Federally, the U.S. Equal Employment Opportunity Commission (EEOC) endorsed removing the conviction question from the job application as a best practice in its 2012 guidance making clear that federal civil rights laws regulate employment decisions based on arrests and convictions. The Obama Administration's My Brother's Keeper Task Force also gave the movement a boost when it endorsed hiring practices "which give applicants a fair chance and allows employers the opportunity to judge individual job candidates on their merits."

Fair-chance policies benefit everyone because they're good for families and the local community. At a recent event in Oakland for employers to discuss reentry issues, one business owner spoke to the personal benefit he finds from hiring people with records. "I've seen how a job makes all the difference," says Derreck B. Johnson, founder and president of Home of Chicken and Waffles in Oakland. "When I give someone a chance and he becomes my best employee, I know that I'm doing right by my community."

This resource guide documents the states, Washington D.C., and the over 100 cities and counties—that have taken steps to remove barriers to employment for qualified workers with records. Seven states, Washington D.C., and 26 cities and counties now extend the fair-chance policy to government contractors or private employers. Of the localities, Baltimore, Buffalo, Chicago, Columbia (MO), Montgomery County (MD), New York City, Newark, Philadelphia, Prince George's County (MD), Rochester, San Francisco, Seattle, and Washington D.C. extend their fair-chance laws to private employers in the area. A chart summarizing all the policies is at the end of this guide.

To support your state and local efforts to enact a fair-chance policy, check out NELP's Fair Chance – Ban the Box Toolkit, which provides a step-by-step guide for advocates on how to launch a "ban the box" campaign. Embedded in the Toolkit is a range of resources to draft a law, to build your network, to support your outreach, and even to develop your media outreach. Here, are just a few of the resources:

- A one-page factsheet, explains the basics of the policy.
- A Voices in Support factsheet highlights voices around the nation in support.
- A Best Practices and Model Policies guide provides model laws.
- The Research Summary is a compilation of supportive research.
- The Compilation of Media provides links to notable articles, examples of op-eds, and e-campaign materials.

For additional information, contact Senior Staff Attorney Michelle Natividad Rodriguez at mrodriguez@nelp.org

Juvenile Offenders: From Big Wheels to the Big House

Prison - - From a Different Perspective
by Karen Heil

From the point-of-view of a staff member at one of our California state prisons, I want to share some of my experiences regarding prison life from a different perspective–from that of a free person working on behalf of the inmates in a prison.

Before doing so, however, let me tell you a little about myself so you'll have some understanding of why I feel so passionate about the work I do and the men I serve.

I grew up in a small town in northern Texas during the 50's. There were quite a few prominent rich people who lived there but most came from the lower-income working poor. This was also during the time of segregation. Attending elementary and junior high schools there, I was always pretty popular but not for the reasons you might think. There were always some popular kids in class like those who played football, did cheerleading, or came from prominent, affluent families in our town. I think what made me popular in the classroom is that I was involved in none of those activities, yet I was always kind to kids that everyone else didn't like. Even at such a young age, I reached out with empathy to the kids who were not liked, who were poor, or who had physical or mental developmental issues, so how I interacted with all these schoolmates made me popular for my compassion.

Maybe it was a way of making up for the emptiness in my own life or maybe it was a reaction to the way things were at home. Regardless of the reasons, I felt drawn to kids that seemed helpless --as if no one else in the world could love them. Since there was always quite a population of that group of kids, it seems that whenever it was time to elect the homecoming princess, the class president, or someone to represent the class in the county spelling bee, they would vote for me. The really popular kids could never figure out why I would always win and I didn't understand it either until way into my adulthood. I came to understand later in life that it was a gift given to me from God--to actually know the worth of EVERY soul.

So why did I choose to work at a prison? Good question. Have I ever regretted it? Not for one moment. I have a favorite song (that seems to explain my choice) entitled "The Least of These" and the last verse goes like this:

HIS LIFE IS SAD FOR HE IS HELD,

IN A GRAY AND LONELY PRISON CELL

YEAR AFTER YEAR, BEHIND DARK WALLS

DON'T KNOW HIS CRIME BUT I KNOW THIS MUCH

IT'S REALLY NOT FOR ME TO JUDGE

THAT'S GOD'S DOMAIN AS I RECALL

AND THE ONLY THING THAT HE EXPECTS OF ME

IS TO WILLINGLY FORGIVE AS HE'S FORGIVEN ME

AND BLESS MY BROTHER IN HIS NEED.

LORD HELP ME LOVE THE LEAST OF THESE

HELP ME TO GO – WHERE THY LIFE LEADS ME

GIVE ME A HEART THAT SEES ANOTHER'S NEED

AND LOVES TO SHARE WITH THE LEAST OF THESE.

Despite my own decisions and the reasons for them, it is understandable that many people would have difficulty recognizing the worth of these often neglected and abandoned souls, but working at Mule Creek State Prison has truly changed my life.

I started work at there about 11 years ago, first working in the clinics and for the last 3 years in what's called Receiving and Release. It's in this area that the inmates are bused in and out of the prison. When coming to prison, an inmate loses two things right away: your name (because now you are known only by your CDC number) and your dignity. The reason is that any time you go anywhere, whether it be to or from work, or out to medical or to court, it's the same routine: strip out, lift up your nuts, bend over, spread your cheeks, cough. Enough said about loss of dignity.

I have been sponsoring self-help groups with the inmates for the last 10 years-- my true passion for continuing to work at the prison. I have been able to see on a personal basis how it is possible for men who really want to change, can do so. One of the groups I sponsor is called the Juvenile Diversion Program, or JDP. I work closely with 21 men in this particular group whom I would consider "The Best of the Best" inside of prison. Once a month they work closely with at- risk youth from Stockton, Lodi, and San Joaquin County–trying to show them a way to make better choices and decisions in their lives so that they don't end up in prison, or worse, dead.

The oldest man in the group, Mark, was 51. He had been down since he was 16 for a gang related murder. He paroled this year after 35 years. The youngest two in the group are 23 and 25. The younger one received a life sentence of 129 years to life; the latter, 124 to life. Both for gang-related murders. Yet here they are, doing all they can to give back to their communities by trying to keep these youth from making the same mistakes they had made. Of the 21 men, 16 of them are in for a murder they committed at a very young age.

As we receive continued updates and hear the news that some of the student visitors have dropped out of gangs and are going back to school or are learning trades or heading to college, our hearts are filled with gratitude. And yet, at least 5 of these young boys didn't make it-- killed in drive-by shootings before they had a chance to prove themselves. When this kind of news comes, it's devastating for these men--these dedicated inmates who have worked so closely and have grown genuine attachments with them. Tears are shed, guilt is felt, and training intensifies.

These men have changed many of these young boys' lives for the better, and they have changed mine. I have grown to love and respect (yes, I use the words love and respect) these men over the years as if they were my own sons. In return, they have expressed gratitude to me numerous times for making them feel human again and that they have worth and for being the mom most of them never had. I know there is a special place for them in heaven, and in my heart they will remain with me for the rest of my life. I try to remind them daily that they are NOT defined by the worst thing they have ever done.

I once read a talk by a spiritual leader that said this: to effectively serve others we must see them through a parent's eyes. Only then can we begin to comprehend the true worth of a soul. Only then can we sense the love that Heavenly Father has for all of His children. Only then can we assume the mantle of being our brother's keeper.

Many people who may read this will be of the mindset that we should just put them all on an island away from the outside world and let them die. It's easy for many to believe this way because they have never personally been confronted with senseless tragedy. But I have and yet still feel the compassion I believe I am meant to demonstrate.

At the age of 14, a special young boy came into my family's life. His heart was pure and he never had a bad day. He served his country in the military for 8 years. His whole life was spent in the service of others. And yet on New Year's Eve in 2013, he was gunned down by gang members while trying to help a young father of 3 children who was being attacked. A gun was pulled and seconds later this son of mine was gone. He was only 36 years old.

The hardest thing for me was to go back to work and face the very men I was working with, knowing most of them were in prison for the same kind of action. Yet, something unexpected and so welcome transpired. They wept with me, encouraged me, mourned with me. They helped my heart to heal quickly as I realized that here they sat, next to me, changed men, not criminals--not animals. They convinced me that someday, that young man who committed this heinious crime, would have the opportunity to change as they had done--if given the opportunity. I had to forgive because holding on to resentments is like drinking poison and waiting for the other person to die!

Are there many staffers at the prison who feel the way I do? No. Maybe a hand full. I know that I have been tainted in my own feelings towards many individuals, mostly correctional officers who do not believe in rehabilitation. They do not believe these men will ever change. Once a dog, always a dog.

Most of my self-help work has been done on a level 4 yard which is the highest security level in a prison. The mindset on that yard by staff makes me sick and angry. I often hear officers refer to the inmates as scum of the earth, filthy animals, and other names I can't print. And that's to their faces. I've been called an inmate lover, told to go hug a thug, and other names so horrid, I do not choose to repeat. But it doesn't change how I feel toward "my" men. The men on that yard refer to me as "Mama bear" and "Care Bear." They know I will go the distance <u>with</u> them and <u>for</u> them, to help them when I know they are in the right. Therefore, I too have made a lot of enemies on that yard.

Despite everything, I look back on my eleven years here at Mule Creek with pride. And yet sometimes I ask myself, did I do the right thing? I gave up promotions along the way in order to continue working with these men. I have been blessed to see some of the fruits of my love though. There are so many names (I don't name them because I want to preserve their privacy), so many success stories--men I have worked with, seen their amazing transformations, and watched as they paroled, and are now successful in every way.

To end on a spiritual note, the words (paraphrased) from the *25th Chapter of Matthew* come to mind:

Come, ye blessed of my Father, inherit the kingdom prepared for you from the foundation of the world: What you were willing to do for Me, you must be willing to do for the stranger--whether he (or she) is sick, hungry, unclothed, or even **in prison.** Verily I say unto you, Inasmuch as ye have done it unto one of the **least of these my brethren, ye have done it unto me.**

Other have shared the following with me:

The *Qu'ran 2:186* offers this message: "And when My servants question thee concerning Me, then surely I am nigh. I answer the prayer of the suppliant when he crieth unto Me. So let them hear My call and let them trust in Me, in order that they may be led aright."

I was told that Jewish philosophy coincides when it states emphatically, "If none will speak up for one of us, then who will stand for me?" It is, therefore, our mission, without any preconditions, to help those in most need. We must seek justice, love mercy, and walk humbly with one's God. . . .

And so it is up to each of us to answer the call to help and nourish and show compassion to the least of us (and that includes those who have fallen and chosen divergent paths but are worthy of redemption and second chances).

When I retire next year, it won't be easy making ends meet. But by far, I will be the richest woman on earth! I hope I will have made my mark not only on the prisoners with whom I have come into contact over the years but with the others with whom I share my story.

CHAPTER FOUR

Vignettes, Poems, and Artwork by Inmates –
Writings Meant To Inspire

Pieces appearing in *LA Progressive* and *Hollywood Progressive*

CITIES

Cities

Are cold and dark

With quiet all around.

Some people are homeless in them.

Who cares?!

[a cinquain written by Joey Meyer, a former student of Ms. Jenkins]

From Big Wheels to the Big House
by A. Wilson

Thinking of You
by Mark E. Vigil

From Innocent Childhood to Parenthood to the Confines of Jail
by Mark E. Vigil

Hanging Out
by Anonymous

Inside my Cell
by Mark E. Vigil

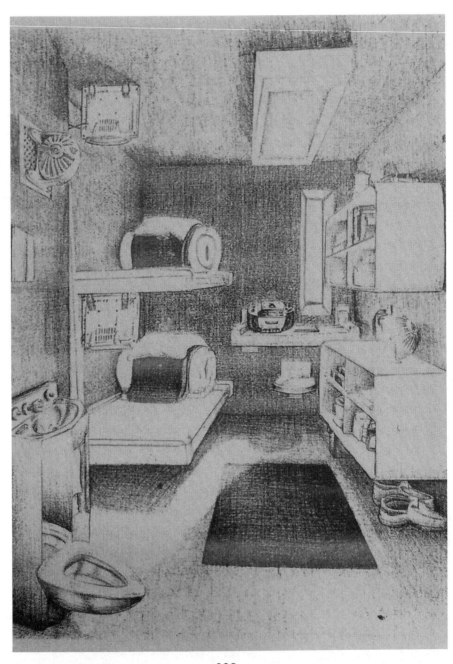

PRISON HORROR—Sleeping into Darkness
by Mark E. Vigil

Alone but Ready
by Hector "Sleepy" Romero

Juvenile Offenders: From Big Wheels to the Big House

Chess, Anyone?
by Hector "Sleepy" Romero

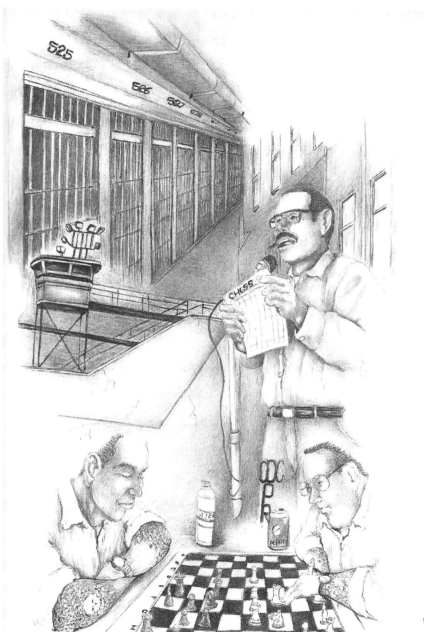

The Long Road to Nowhere
by Hector "Sleepy" Romer

In My Victim's shoes
by Louie Gomez
[excerpt from above article entitled seeking Redemption"]

It's a Tuesday. I'm walking home after a long day's work. I'm tired and hungry. I'm almost home. I wonder what my brother's doing right now.

Who's in that car driving by real slow? They're looking at me. Do I know them? I don't think so. They look like *cholos* (Hispanic street-gang members). I hope they don't mess with me–I'm almost home. My heart is starting to beat really fast. I try to keep up with the beats by walking faster. I'm almost home–I'll be alright. Oh no! The car is stopping by the curb in front of me.

Three *cholos* are getting out. They're walking my way. What do I do? What do they want? I hope they are just looking for someone else. Wait! One has something in his hands. It looks like a rifle, a gun. I think they are going to try to rob me. Many of my friends have been robbed by *cholos*. They almost got me one time, but I ran and got away. That was a long time before.

I'm starting to panic–my adrenalin is running. Should I run? I have a little money, but I can't afford to lose what I have. I worked very hard for my money. I need to pay bills, and I need to send some home to Mexico for my family who depends on me. Without me, they can't make it.

The *cholos* block my path. The one with the gun points it at me and starts yelling.

"Give me your *feria* (money)!"

"I don't have any," I say.

I keep moving forward. I'm almost home. I can make it. They are just little punks, but there are three of them. I don't think I can take them all at the same time, and one has a gun pointed at me, demanding money, yelling profanities. I turn to the right, but another *cholo* starts blocking my way and also starts yelling.

"Give up the money, *baboso* (slimy one)!" And he pushes me.

"I have no money," I say to him.

He begins to throw punches at my face, but I block them all. I have to keep moving before they shoot me or all jump on me. I'm more scared now. I have to keep moving. Should I run? Yes! I can run into that apartment building. People will come out. They know me there and will help me.

It's dark in the building. I can barely see anything. I hear a bang like a fire-cracker. I instantly feel a kinda funny, forceful impact just as a sharp pain hit my side. I don't know if I'm shot or just grazed. I just don't know–I really don't want to know. I can still stand and move though.

I turn and see the *cholo* with the gun; he's at the door. He is pointing the gun at my face, coming towards me, and demanding money. I grab the gun hard with both hands. If I can take it away, I can defend myself. Why doesn't anyone hear us?! Why doesn't anyone come out of the apartments?!

There is something wrong with me. It hurts inside. Here comes another one of those *cholos* through the door. I have to get the gun or they are going to kill me. The other *cholo* starts yelling.

"Let go, *pendejo* (stupid)!"

I ignore him and struggle harder to get the gun. I then feel two hard blows and a stinging sensation to my stomach. I pull even harder. I need the gun. The gun will scare them away.

Where is everybody? Why doesn't anyone come out to help or call the cops? I feel two more hard blows to my back–they hurt worse than the first two. They knock the air out of me. I feel like I'm suffocating. I immediately drop to the ground. I can't run or fight anymore. I'm terrified now. I have to give them my money before they hurt me some more. I pull out my wallet and hold it as high as I can and then yell.

"Here! Take my money! Here!"

One of them takes my wallet. Finally, all of the *cholos* run away.

Finally, it's over. They leave me alone but I can't breathe right. There is something seriously wrong with me. My lung is making a weird noise. I try to command my body to get up. They're gone now, so it's alright.

"Come on, breathe," but it does no good.

My heart is beating faster than ever now. I feel all wet. Is that my blood flooding the hard floor beneath me? I feel saturated. What is that wet, warm slush? But I don't really want to know. I can't breathe no matter how hard I try.

Oh, God! Don't let me die. It hurts so bad. I've never felt this much pain before. Please God, help me. I'm only 27. My family in Mexico needs me. They depend on the money I send. I worked so hard to come to this country to try and make a better life for my family. I have so many hopes, plans, and dreams. I want to see my children grow up and be happy. It can't end like this. This isn't fair!

Where's my brother? I hope the *cholos* don't get him too.

It's almost impossible to breathe now. I'm getting nauseous. I think I just threw up clots of blood. I'm getting very cold. Oh, God! Please forgive me for all the wrong I've done. Please bless and protect all my family. I love them so very much. I'm so cold. I can't feel my body any more. Now I just want to let go. . . .

Dangerous Minds
by Ronald Patterson

The same energy
that is used to destroy
can be used to build.

It's a simple matter
of the application of knowledge.

The same energy
that is used to build a prison
can be used to build a palace.

It's a simple matter
of the vision of the architect.

The same energy
that causes one to hate
can be utilized to show love.

It's a simple matter
of understanding one's self
and appreciating one another.

The same energy
that is used to commit murder
can save someone's life.

It's a simple matter
of correcting one's values.

The same energy
that is used
can be used for good.

Rosemary Jenkins-<u>meredithetc.com/juvenile-offenders/</u>

It's a simple matter
of options
that you choose for yourself.

You can become a dangerous mind
or you can choose simply
to be a powerful mind.

It's simply a matter
of the dangers
of not minding.

Life on a desperate road—
a manacle maze with no outlet-
with nothing to show but our empty hands.

A spoken plan
that I have yet to see manifest.

As episodes mimic each other,
I can't help but to find myself
as part of the loop-
standing on a pile of expended shells-
raising hell.

As I aim for this star
for which I was told to shoot,
they want a scoop
on a man with no feet
that can't run away from his reality. . . .

Handcuffed to tragedy,
tenacious as a toddler
a translucent man—
a token of traversity
that has touched it all

348

but still has empty hands.

Still swimmin' laps in quick sand
with only weed, alcohol, nicotine, and caffeine
to show him love.

Takin' a shit and being quiet—
his only relief.

Spreading realism from hug to hug,
Blood to Blood—
we are forever young
as solid soldiers'souls
on a weary road
back to God.

Empty Hands
by Ronald Patterson

Our bodies grow old
as we dance
on the threshold of Supreme Oneness—
battered and bruised,
taking a tally of our losses
and wondering how much more we will lose.

Understanding that what we carry
is too heavy for the average, simple man.

So, thus-thus,
we look close and see
the Power that is instilled
in our empty hands.

The Butterfly Complex
by Mark E. Vigil

Imagine a butterfly that stubbornly refused to fly south for the winter. This stubborn creature thought, Why fly somewhere else when I can stay in a place more familiar to me? After all, the journey south would require work and no doubt would be filled with countless dangers. Why bother?

The butterfly watched in smug silence as all the rest of his butterfly colony prepared for their long journey to the new world.

Ignoring the warnings to get ready, the little butterfly flapped its wings and defied the advice of his elders. Instead, he criticized the others for being stuck on ancient customs that seemed foolish and had no meaning in his life.

The more they urged him to prepare, the more stubborn he became. He had never been to the mountains of Chapultepec in Mexico, but he was sure the Canadian winter would not be so bad. He could deal with it.

The skies were clear overhead, the wind still warm. They are fools, he thought. Why leave when I could stay and have fun?

When the last of the butterfly colony had flown away, the trees surrounding the woods where he grew up began to grow cold and dark.

As the leaves in the trees began to fall and the warmth of his kind vanished, only then did the reality of his choice to stay begin to set in.

He noticed the sound of the wind become stronger. He also observed how the remaining creatures became less friendly than before.

As the leaves in the trees began to fall and the warmth of his kind vanished, only then did the reality of his choice to stay begin to set in. How could he have been so wrong in thinking he could defy years of butterfly migrations?

With each day that passed, his resolve diminished. His once-defiant spirit was dashed by the harsh realities of his choice not to fly south. With little strength left to fly, he began to ponder what his life might have been like had he just listened to those who understood the consequences of staying behind in such a harsh place for the winter.

It was then that he realized the fatal error in his thinking. After all, he was a butterfly—colorful and bright—meant to soar through the skies as if floating on the wind. This miraculous gift from Nature was made possible only if the butterfly cycle were complete. Yet, because he broke from it, he altered the pattern of life, affecting all those others who had depended on him to do his part in upholding the integrity of the butterfly cycle.

When the little butterfly fell to earth, his body was cold and weary. He thought of all the things he had never done and all the beautiful places he would never see. He flapped his wings for the last time—wings that would never reach their full potential. But just before the little butterfly was about to gasp his last breath, a small sparrow who had been watching from a distance swooped down and carried him to safety, to the safe comfort of his kind.

In this manner, balance was restored and the potential for the colony could once again be realized.

Pieces of My Dream
by Mark E. Vigil

Once upon a time, there existed a boy whose heart and mind yearned to understand the things he could not even define.

All the world was a huge mystery–one filled with so many wonders and contradictions that fueled his ever-growing imagination and curiosity with all the elements of life and its multitude of splendors.

The boy's deep brown eyes, the size of marbles, shined as they took in all of God's creations, that filled his budding soul with the many textures and flavors that would come to comprise the boy's childhood.

The world seemed a beautiful place back then–though not of the story-book kind. Rather, it was of the love and human connections that sustained him in the safe comforts–big and small–of innocence and joy for life.

In those days, the boy was capable of such human traits. The tattered rags he wore did not matter then, nor did the times when he had no shoes to wear. Those were the moments the boy felt closer to the earth, beneath his scarred, dirt-stained brown feet that could run for miles and never tire. Despite all these things, his restless spirit still ran wild.

He felt connected to the world around him, free to roam the fields and places he recognized as his home. The boy made playgrounds of the junk-yards and city dumps that surrounded the vistas around his neighborhood on every side. The extreme poverty of his youth was his motivation to make something of himself.

To create something from the almost nothing that was his world. Maybe he would not become a doctor or a lawyer, but perhaps some kind of bright star amidst that ball of mud the boy called home—something that would validate his existence!

This was the stage from which he rose to become who he was to be. He greeted each morning with a smile, as if it were his last–knowing only the moment, not caring about the possibilities of tomorrow. Tomorrow—that was a currency the boy could not bank on.

The boy loved the adventures he experienced beyond the safe confines of his home. The streets of his barrio were his theater where he saw the fourth world unfold before him. He digested and devoured every aspect of this gray, lively world filled with all the inequities and tragedies that were a constant part of his daily life.

The boy's parents tried in vain to shield and protect him each time he strayed too far from home, but before long, the boy left home and never returned.

The boy's parents tried in vain to shield and protect him each time he strayed too far from home, but before long, the boy left home and never returned.

What became of this boy?

Lost and led astray, the boy began to drift from all the good things within his life, and he submerged himself in things that hindered and poisoned his heart and mind.

Where blue skies once existed, dark clouds now formed over him. He tried to find his way back home, but the path back was somehow blocked by the very things that had pulled him away from all the goodness he had ever known. He felt conflicted and torn inside.

The boy had bitten from the apple of all the bad elements of this world and before he realized how far he had fallen, he made a fatal mistake that cost another man his life!

The boy was devastated and lost by this tragic turn of events. He knew he had done wrong. He knew this because he finally understood God's word—Thou shalt not kill! But he could not take back his sin—the deed was done and a man's life was forever gone.

When the boy's crime was discovered, he was punished and condemned for the life he had destroyed. Life in prison would be his penance.

Locked away, the boy's spirit grew dark and grim. He was sent miles from home to places barely suitable for human existence, where he would continue his societal descent into the bowels of a prison system he did not understand, a system that had complete control over him.

Numbed by his internal pain and the collective self-destructive demons of prison life, the boy's soul was smashed to pieces like the shell of Humpty-Dumpty's great fall.

Through the years that stretched into decades, the boy emerged a man, though still scared and deeply affected by the things he had experienced on his journey through distance and time.

And so it was that the man who was a boy came to realize that for all the wrongs he had ever done, he could now begin to make things right by choosing to transform himself into a better person. Prison may have made him worse in the beginning but it also rendered him whole again.

In this chaotic fashion, the seeds of human compassion grew within him, and the boy's humanity was restored.

This I know because I was that boy!!

Live Your Life Today
by Keith L. White

Little homie, live your life today.
I mean, you don't have to live your life *this way*.
I know that this road
May get cold
But, little homie, live your life today.

"It takes a village to raise a child" and a woman to give him birth
But yet a village can bring him down, and a woman can get him hurt.
So he's heartless, no emotions, he put his feelings aside.
Dodey's gettin' him high? Fiendin' and schemin'—all that's in his eyes.
Ain't fixin' to cry 'cause he was born to live yet livin' to die.
'Cause if this is the truth, he'd rather be livin' a lie.

And I feel his pain too, but I took a Tylenol and Dayquil
'Cause I gotta "keep on pushin'" like Marvin Gaye and Curtis Mayfield.
See, Momma told me 'bout the good times, and I'm wonderin' how them days feel
'Cause nowadays it's brothas (yo' color) that can't wait to see you lay still.
But you gotta stay real, and keep it a hundred with YOU—
Even if that's what these so-called "brothas" don't really want you to do.
See, I love the blackness but I'm searchin' for the light
'Cause while you're livin' for tomorrow, I'm hopin' for tonight.
And you don't want to feel the same thang, so just maintain!
Do yo' thang, thang.
Kick back, have patience, and watch and see how many thangs

358

change.

Little homie, live your life today.
I mean, you don't have to live your life this way.
I know that this road
May get cold
But, little homie, live your life today.

The Other Half Is a Blessing
by Keith L. White

by Keith L. White

Used and abused left me confused and trippin'.
Abandoned by family, so I turned to dudes sportin' blue and
crippin'.
Got into the gang lifestyle and was used to chillin'.
Even adopted all the contaminated rules to livin'.
All of my friends was liars, thieves, and addicts.
They'd do anything to get high and support their habits.
Never listened to the preacher's warnin' when he said, "The
Lord dun had it. . . ."
And it was too late when that morgue took that body, covered
it with sheets and tagged it.

Committed crimes one too many times, now I'm chained in
prison.
I blamed the world for my flaws, so I never changed my
vision.
Everything I heard, said, and done all come with tension
In this hole in a rock, daydreamin' 'bout things I ain't even did
yet.
They say a man ain't to cry, so I'm pretendin' that it's sweat.
But you ain't even gotta look into my eyes to see that they is
wet.

Yeah, my younger dayz is gone. Consumed by the streets
And they say that better dayz is comin'
Yet it's pursued by defeat.
"Was gang-bangin' worth it?" asked the dudes that I meet.
Visualize a life sentence in a tomb of concrete.

Mothers cry as bullets fly, sons die due to self-oppression.
Look into that mirror in your cell. Do that answer your question?
Nine-tenths of reality is only half of the lesson.
Once you understand it, praise God,
'Cause the other half is a blessin'.

A Piece of the Truth
by Keith L. White

Many folks paved the way, but the streets got closed.
It wasn't a two-way street, but a dead-end road.
Everybody turned back, but me, I stayed
'Cause I knew it was a different path to the road they'd paved.

I went through back streets and even alleys at night.
It was dark the whole way, but I made it back to a light.
Folks tried to stop me along the way.
Yeah. man, it never failed.
I lost focus of my mission and I landed in jail.

I was mad for a while, but I came back to my senses
When a voice spoke in my head and I stopped to listen.
Wisdom was its name. "Son, listen," he told me.
"I'm from the place you're tryin' to get to!"
I said, "Really?! Then show me."

I felt a chill through my body, and my soul was all shook
When *Wisdom* led me to the Hallelujah book.

I've since found Peace and Wisdom together—
All my days been better
Amid the truth that I sought no matter the whether.

Juvenile Offenders: From Big Wheels to the Big House

One Slip—A Rap Song
by Ronald Patterson

My loyalty was given up cheap.
I was a friend
till the end
or so I thought
–cause we fought our battles together.
I was wrong.
It seems all loyalty is gone
when da' trouble comes.

Like bread crumbz—left to find my own way
back to da' light–
eaten by greedy homies
now lost in da' night.

My right-hand man
who shook hands with da' left
took triple 6 steps
to kill me off with one breath.

A death by fabricated wordz.
Verbs like a spear,
they threw at da' jury
that stuck me wit deze years—
that stuck me with deze tears
(that are not outwardly exposed).

My mind steady runnin' scenarios.
Like a dog's nose, I smell trouble
way before it's near—
spawned by my own hatred
which comes from being here.

Switched to being enemies

what the homies did.
If I would have only seen it
when we was li'l kidz.

You would have been did,
with the same love
you falsely propagated—
initiated wit envy
within your soul.

Betrayed and lost a Homie,
soldier wit a heart of gold.
Left to grow old
like stories over bonfires—
losing all desire,
my visions runnin' higher.

So I'm burning in
cause I stay surrounded by non-thinkers
that're bound to crash.

Like a plane grounded,
I'm steady hounded
by the want to stop breathing air.

And tho' I can't blame God,
my life wasn't fair!

"I don't care!"
But if I utter that,
I'd be lyin'.

"I don't fear!" nothing physical
and I don't fear dyin'.

I'm steady tryin' to forget the fact

that I'm forgotten—
left lost in forever
in dis' realm of rotten.

Everybody seems to be plottin'
for a bigger plan.
Bodies belong to gangs,
but eyes reveal a lonely man.

What's in my head is nothin'!
Same thing I was born wit—
no longer trippin' off da' menial
that I was torn wit,
scorned wit.

Wanting money
as a po' kid.
Now I got life in prison
and I just want to live.

One slip,
One trip,
One fall,
One crude mistake
and you can lose it all.

Cause I lost it all.

Finger Waves
by Juan Moreno Haines

Several people I knew walked past me while I was getting

a haircut to be styled. It would be the first time in my life doing something like this. The thought of getting my hair styled made me feel awkward, as I'm instinctively self-conscious. I have this relentless scorn coming from inside my head saying, "You're not good enough - there are too many flaws. People don't care about you as a person." These negative thoughts make me avoid looking at myself. However, I have developed ways to navigate through daily life by making the interest of others my own, which gives me a sense that I'm needed and worthy. But, even as I'm sitting in the barber's chair, the deceptions are hard at work.

In the back of the housing unit, a three-foot wall blocks off the barbershop, giving it its own space. A latched iron gate plays as a door for people to enter and exit the establishment. It's a well-lit and clean place where inmates cut each other's hair in one of three metal chairs. The whole area smells of the perfume barbers use to make the place appear disinfected. A look of normality comes from two barber poles painted on the back wall. As I'm sitting in the middle chair, Cowboy's clippers glide over my head. Tiny bits of curlyhair fall onto my t-shirt, I wipe a few off.

Cowboy is an eccentric who dresses quite differently than the typical inmate. His self-styled hair makes many wonder how he gets that picture-perfect look all by himself. The tapered sides of his haircut is even. The parts are narrow and straight. The brushed in waves shine.

He wears a pocket watch and a tool belt that holds all kinds of things, combs and pens and chains and other knick-knacks. He wears two wristwatches at times. He walks the five tiers in the housing units every day buying and selling. Cowboy is what's called "A Hustle-Man." I know people who talk to him and say he's a compassionate person. But, those who don't know him come away with the prejudices and misconceptions that are expected from ignorance.

"I got a jar of coffee for a book of stamps."

"Snack bar! I got candy, cookies, sodas."

You want it, and Cowboy will supply them.

"I buy used or new photo albums."

"Hey, Juan you ought to let me do something with that," he said while pointing at my head. I was sitting on the top bunk; looking at him through steel bars. I smiled and gave him thumbs up.

Some question his limitations. No one has found it.

A couple days earlier, while Cowboy was making his rounds, he stopped by my cell.

"Hey, Juan you ought to let me do something with that," he said while pointing at my head. I was sitting on the top bunk; looking at him through steel bars. I smiled and gave him humbs up.

Yeah, I thought, maybe one day I would get a decent haircut. I've never taken too much interest in fixing my appearance, especially my hair. Coming from a military family, it has been crew cuts with tapered sides. However, the past few years I kept my head bald - easy maintenance. But, deep down, I didn't like the look. So, recently I let my hair grow out only to reveal a receding hairline and a bald spot on the crown of my head. I couldn't see the bald spot unless I angled a mirror in the face of another mirror.

Prison ages people in very different ways. I'm used to getting comments that I don't look my age and I'm constantly complimented about my athletic ability - how I run with the youngsters in basketball. My body shape is frequently compared to Bruce Lee's. These things make me feel good. Maybe people are just being kind. Nevertheless, the "hair" dung is a reminder that I am getting up in age.

Cowboy came by my cell a couple times more, telling me that he's not a barber. "I'm a hair specialist." He told me that he had ways to hide my bald spot. That got my attention. "Okay," I said, "Do it."

So, three days before my 60th birthday, there I was, sitting in that middle chair, Cowboy doing his thing, with me wondering what the hell I was doing. All I knew, loneliness was clawing at me and doing this was going to draw attention.

"Hey, Juan you gettin a perm?" one of the other barbers, Zo asked.

My nervous smile said it all.

"Cowboy's fixing me up."

I felt like Cowboy was doing something special. I quietly sat there, arms folded in front, as inmates walked past, some slowed with eyes shifting to me. I had a sense of being gawked upon.

"Lettin' Cowboy do something with that mess, huh?" one guy said.

"Gotta do somethin' for my 60th birthday," I shot back, feeling less self-conscious in those hurtful ways.

It was early morning. I'd been in
the chair for about a half-hour.

Cowboy had finish cutting. Now he lined my scalp
with something cold, slick and greasy.

"Let me know, if it begins to burn," Cowboy said.

He began parting my hair and applying something that smelled chemical-like. It made my head tingle.

"Is there a difference between

tingling and burning?" I asked.

He continued to work, saying, "It's
okay to tingle."

This being something completely new for me, there were
questions I wanted to ask but didn't
because I didn't want to appear too stupid about things that
Black men did to their hair. I would ask my cellie about these
things later.

Cowboy worked the comb, parting my hair and applying the
perm.

More people walked past, now stopping.

"Getting that finger wave, huh?"

I'd heard of a finger wave, but I
didn't know exactly what it was.

"You must be gettin' a visit, Juan.
Who's the lucky lady?"

"Bring back the 70s, Juan. You're
doin' it right."

"You pirnpin' boy."

I began feeling good about myself. I didn't know a simple
haircut and styling could attract so much good-natured
kindness. I'm not used to my *person* being the center of
attention. It's always been my *work.*

Cowboy finished.

"Whenever you need a touch up, just come by," he said. "I wanted to do this for you, because you are one of the only people who never changed up. You always treated me right."

When I rose out of the chair and walked past people their eyes went to my head and there were lots of smiles and friendly remarks.

"That really fits you, Juan."

Raheem, who always teases me about my bald spot stopped and peered over me.

"I can't even see the bald spot. Is this Cowboy's work?"

"Yeah," I said anxiously wanting to see for myself.

When I got to my cell, I grabbed my mirror and angled myself to see it.

My hair gleamed in 13 wavy rows across my head and there was a distinguished part on the left. My smile widened, seeing that the bald spot was gone.

The parade of people complimenting my hair continued the whole day. The next morning, it was the same, all over the yard. Several people told me that they were going to grow their hair out and have Cowboy hook them up, too.

I asked my cellie what to do to keep them in longer. He gave me a wave cap to wear at night and told me that even after I brush them out they'd come back with a little gel.

Another friend told me that he had some extra gel and he'd

give it to me. I didn't know what gel was, but I was going to do some fast learning.

On the morning of my birthday, I took extra time, fixing my hair. I'm used to rubbing a little lotion or hair grease on a baldhead and mat's that, Adding the Murray's, brushing, and slicking my hair back pulled me out of depression. That day, I worked hard at getting that satisfying look people give when I help them. It's priceless. But, finding satisfaction in who I am feels strange. It makes me feel selfish, and brings back those times when I, cheated, robbed and stole from everyone I met. I'm working .on these conflicting feelings.

Having been in prison just over 21 years along with knowing that I'm finding my way back to the streets, here's what I'm telling myself:

"There's no way I should be depressed. I look good, feel good and am doing good things for everybody, including myself."

The next day, the feel-good momentum carried as I walked around, chest sticking out a little more than usual and sporting a *real* smile.

When I Think of Haiti
By Ronald Patterson

When I think of Haiti, I think of Refugees—
Refugees and Brothers and Sisters From the Hoods like you
and me.
Yet not Crips and Bloods,
Though some are thugs, But also good people. And
Revolutionaries Living in huts of mud.
I think of my best friend. Houses with roofs of tin, U.S.—13-
year gun ban. Well, we'll lift that,
Now that Gérard Latortue, Our man has stepped in.
I think of what I would do, If it were me.

Of a country that fought
And won the right to be free.
Toussaint L'Ouverture
Running Napoleon out of there, Beautiful women, proud Black
men, Grateful to say, "We from there." Hip-Hop, Reggae, R & B,
Black folks beating steel drums
And still fighting to be free.

When I think of Haiti,
I think of green things, And slave republics, Sugar cane—
grown with blood, Little nappy-head kids,
Too pure to know hate,
Born Black so they show love.

Yeah, I think of a place
I would like to go.
Like most from Africa,
Maybe that place is where I'm from?
Like Stephanie Mills once said,

"A place like Home.
A resting place of peace
Where some of my friends are from
Where love is overflowing." Not blood, guns, and unrest. Rain
drops on green grass
And Black women with so much ass!

I think of Wyclef
Going back to shine some light
And asking our ancestors for direction. Ask Allah, Jesus,
Buddha, and Jehovah for blessings.
Black angels coming down for me, Giving me their courage,
Their strength.

When I think of Haiti.

Juvenile Offenders: From Big Wheels to the Big House

Afterward: Stepping into Tomorrow
by Mark Edward Vigil

It feels strangely weird knowing that any day now the Governor of California will potentially sign the paperwork that will effectively terminate my life sentence after serving some 35 plus years of perpetual incarceration inside the state prison system.

Having been found suitable for parole, the prospects for my future life as a free man have become very real--no longer some far-off pipe dream or a solitary convict's fantasy (as it has been for me ever since I came to prison in 1980).

Thus, I say "strangely weird" because I will finally emerge from these heavily fortified walls and gates and *step into tomorrow*—alas, embracing the ever-elusive wings of freedom that I once believed I would never see.

The sheer force of everything I experienced and absorbed along my way helped to shape and mold me into the man I am today. It is these experiences that I will take with me as I go back into the free world.

Just what that world will look like remains a huge mystery to me. Will it be enough to sustain me out there?! Probably not. A lot has changed during my Rip Van Winkle slumber.

I entered the prison system just as President Jimmy Carter was trading places with President Ronald Reagan to take his own place in the White House.

The Cold War was about to come to an end and the American hostages held captive in Iran were about to be freed while a team of young men (Steve Jobs and Steve Wozniak) were about to revolutionize the world by making computers more practical for use in our daily lives.

All these events would shape the world in a multitude of ways. Yet, since that by-gone era, I have remained side-lined through each change and technological leap forward in time.

Trapped literally inside my own mind, I watched the wheels of time go round and round--the way the late John Lennon described in his song, "Watching the Wheels," that debuted around that same time. And now I am on the verge of finally going home!

Because I am a level-4 inmate, I have been excluded from receiving any real job skills and technical training. There exist no computer literacy classes and absolutely no opportunity for me to participate in a re-entry program before I hit the streets. What puzzles me the most, then, in all this re-entry process is that there is little or no effort by the State to really help me prepare for the inevitable changes to come in my post-incarceration life.

As grateful as I am, I am also mindful of the fact that my analog way of thinking needs to be updated in order to be able to handle the many changes in society that have occurred in my absence.

Instead, I sit and wait in yet another state of limbo--something the CDCR (California Department of Corrections and Rehabilitation) is notorious for. Having not been prepared for the challenges of tomorrow, I remain here--filled with apprehensions.

It scares me! I don't want to fall between the cracks. I don't want to be part of the recidivism statistics. But I do want to be numbered among the success stories—no matter how long it takes. The dreams that were interrupted so many years ago will now have a chance of being fulfilled. God willing, all the tools I lack now will eventually be obtainable as I step into tomorrow.

> Tethered to the stone of
> time for what seems forever,
> the incarcerated man emerges--
> skin (so pale) and bones from the
> shadows of his prison.
>
> He steps into tomorrow--not
> really knowing, not the least
> bit certain of the road ahead.
>
> Is this a dream. . .is this reality?
> Has he died a revenant's death
> and come back again?
>
> His freedom and rebirth would
> seem so.
>
> --Pino (Mark Edward Vigil)

FOLLOW UP: Home from Prison after 36 Years
by Mark Vigil

When I walked out of prison for the first time in 36 years, I had no clue at what I would encounter on the other side of those electrical fences.

Would I be able to compete and survive at 52 years of age in the modern world? That thought on its own caused me much consternation and was coupled with the notion of how my family would embrace the aging man who was finally returning home to them after so many years of absence.

There were a plethora of questions ruminating within my mind as to how I would fare. One thing I knew within my heart was I had to go forth with God's blessing and figure out how to begin the process of my return.

The minute I stepped out of prison on April 21, 2016, I was greeted by my uncle David who drove me to a nearby IHOP to eat my first meal in society since 1980. I couldn't believe I was consuming pancakes, sausage, bacon, eggs, orange juice, and coffee and not prison food.

He brought me my dress-outs (the clothes they give you once you are paroled), all of which were provided by my beautiful fiancée Denise (someone I had known as a teenager) who spared no expense to make sure the initial phase of my transition went smoothly. I eagerly went into the restroom to change into my new duds—clothes. I had not worn for all the years of my imprisonment Clothes with color (not the drab, prison-stamped blues that I had worn for all those years).

She made sure I had everything I needed from a cell phone (which I had never even seen before, let alone known how to work) to clothing and, of course, her companionship which remains the wind in my sails each day I continue on this journey like most post-incarcerated individuals aren't nearly as lucky as I have been, having such a strong support system to prop me up.

My family greeted me that evening when I made my way back to Southern California. It was an odd day for many of us because the day I went home, my older brother was having open-heart surgery. We made our way to the hospital where my family (led by our matriarch, Aunt Sally) had gathered to support my brother and await my arrival--there were mixed feelings of joy for me and concern for my brother.

Later, we all met up at a nearby restaurant where we all shared a meal together, something which had my head spinning in all directions. People whose voices I hadn't heard since my childhood were present that evening.

From that night, my life changed. I went to do the transitional phase of my parole in Vista, California, at a place called Amity (friendship). There, my path to freedom took root. Every day at "The Ranch," they allowed me the time to get all the necessary things I required in order to establish myself in society and be treated once again like a human being.

I must admit that there were days I thought I would fall short and felt totally lost. But each time those negative thoughts came to the surface of my mind, the advisors kept guiding me to the next phase--something I'll forever be grateful for.

They made sure I did not fail in my journey by helping me get my birth certificate, Social Security Card, identification card, and driver's license and also allowed me to find my way around the free world on my own. I was offered the opportunity to find a job while I was there and took advantage of that. For a long time, I had to ride my bicycle for miles each day to and from a job that really taught me a lot of important things. By saving from my paycheck, I was even able to buy an older car (1999 Ford Explorer) from a neighbor of Amity and began fixing it up with the help and advice of others. It is my first car ever! So now I am really on my way, having the freedom that my own transportation gives me.

By the time I left that caring little nest of Amity, I was fully ready to go out on my own to make a life for myself.

At the moment, I am about to begin a job that could very well become a career for me. I have hopes that it will afford me the means to provide for my family and keep me moving in the right direction.

I plan to get an additional license for truck driving I also want the chance to be part of anti- recidivism programs in order to help mentor at-risk youth in need of guidance and encouragement, actions that may keep them from the broken path that I had taken in my youth. I do not think that any human being deserves to endure such a path. So I long to be the example which is not easy.

The point is to keep learning to improve my essence so that I may become the man God always intended I should be. Only God knows that.

To my aunt Sally and uncle Johnny and to my brothers and sisters as well as to my family and friends--all of whom enabled me to find my way home again--I can never thank you enough.

EPILOGUE

by Mark E. Vigil--A Free Man

On November 19, 2015, I was found suitable for parole by the California Board of Prison Terms--an accomplishment I never imagined I would one day realize. It was the fourth time in 35 years, that I had sought to demonstrate to its members my growth and maturity but understanding, at the same time, that in the eyes of the Justice System there are no promises or guarantees.

I once described going before the Board like Sisyphus (the legendary ruler of Corinth) who was punished by being made to roll a stone up a hill that would inevitably roll back down again.

It seemed whenever I was close to my own top, the stone of incarceration would roll back down upon me. Thus freedom would elude me every time I went before the Board For many years I had given up the struggle to get out. There was a time I even resigned myself to dying in prison After all, I just knew the Board would never let me out, so why even try?

As a result of this defeatist attitude, I accepted my fate and immersed myself in what I can only describe as a counter-productive attitude of further criminality and anti-social behavior within those prison walls (what could have become the signature of my entire 35-year journey through the California prison system) had I not eventually decided to make a change.

I have often thought of this journey through the bowels of the California Prison System as a passage on a huge ship slowly sailing through time. Each different prison of my sojourn behind bars became an island unto itself--replete with a million perilous dangers and experiences that we, as Juvenile Offenders, were cast—like characters in a tragic play that somehow became the bane of our collective reality and that we were meant to act out.

Yet I and others came to this life as *juvenile* offenders--the great irony being that we were deemed mature enough to serve life sentences for the crimes for which we were convicted, but not quite old enough to purchase a pack of cigarettes or possess a *Playboy* magazine?

On treacherous seas and waters, we became instant captains and navigators We were barely able to see over the bow of our ship, a vessel that sailed on a journey that delivered us far away from the safe and familiar shores we once inhabited and thought of as home and from the people and places that meant the most to us.

Homer's epic poem may have been created to serve some greater meaning about which I was unaware, but for us prisoners, it is that journey that resonates most. I recall having the privilege of reading the *Odyssey* when I was housed in the SHU at San Quentin circa 1983And although I could not fully comprehend each word or line in the story, I still managed to relate to Homer's magnificent tome.

Odysseus was fighting to get back to all that he loved—his wife Penelope (who encountered her own trials during his absence); his son, Telemachus, his valued friends, and his beloved Ithaca In my mind, I wanted that too—that perilous but ultimately rewarding journey--but I was trapped within my ship and could not find my way back home. It seemed the more I tried, the further I was cast adrift at sea.

For many Juvenile Offenders who had lacked the psychological and emotional wherewithal to control their lives and make healthy and rational decisions while they were young, the consequences for their lives were often devastating Their impulsiveness led to poor decision- making which ultimately led to incarceration.

As a result of our trespasses, we were jailed, clothed, and fed prison gruel for life without ever being made aware of why what we had done while still "free" young men was so wrong It is a struggle for everyone inside to get a grip on the forces that put them there For me, I knew it was morally and ethically wrong to take the life of another human being but somehow I didn't understand what my responsibility for my actions was nor did I understand what I needed to do to feel contrition and to change my life's focus and become a reformed human being.

For most of us Juvenile Offenders, we had been taught better by our parents and family, yet we had rejected their teachings. The lure of the streets was more attractive to us

It occurs to me now that the problem for us was that we simply lacked the emotional intelligence to comprehend the bigger picture and what our actions could mean in the short- and long-run. Though I enjoyed reading the *Odyssey*, I somehow lacked the ability to grasp its overall meaning until much later.

Such understanding would not occur until I had cultivated my intellectual capacity and a literal desire to apply these lessons to my daily life, so as to think beyond the superficial boundaries of my *barrio* mentality and the constrictions of prison life.

This does not in any way exonerate me from the many wrongs I have committed during my lifetime, but it does, however, demonstrate something about myself that I really had known all along but had refused to acknowledge. What I understand about myself now is what others in my situation need to recognize and address as well.

I was an immature kid at the age of 16 when I committed the cowardly act that brought me to prison. I was vastly ignorant of what made me not the least bit capable of dealing with the internal conflicts that were raging inside of me which rendered me a danger to not only myself but to everyone around me.

This book, therefore, is the culmination of the collective journey through time of those whose articles are included in it. Each writer has run the gamut of the prison system and has come to realize that there is more to life than wasting what remains of it—lost in the grips of drugs, gangs, and criminality.

Come April 19, 2016, I will finally be able to return to the Ithaca of my past--no longer a boy but a gray-haired man who fully understands what a gift life is. I realize now that our lives are not meant to be spent so many, many years in places like this

Life, after all, is to be lived and expressed in positive ways— not to squander the many promises of our lives. Many have nearly drowned in a sea of gang life and drug use. When given the chance, then, we must lead lives far removed from the dysfunctional communities where potential opportunities for good are never realized but lost and thrown away to the bloody and lifeless trenches of filthy prison yards with all their concomitant horrors.

Fortunately for me, by the grace of God, I have been granted a second chance to rise from the dead, and build my life anew-- far away from the horrors and trenches of those filthy prison yards that only serve as warehouses and cesspools for those who remain imprisoned because of their flawed way of thinking

All this is to say, Make *your* journey meaningful. Allow yourself time to grow and mature before taking actions that you will at some future date undoubtedly regret. See the world and by all means experience life on your own terms rather than allowing others to dictate the unsavory path they try to convince you to take. Don't listen to the voices of evil from outside but respond to those inner voices that are begging you to stay on the path that many knowing and wiser people in your formative years were imploring you to take.

Your life matters. We are not meant to live our lives inside these cages! May you listen to the voices in your life that urge you to do the right thing for yourself and for your community rather than to abide what corrupt fools say, misfits who seek to drag you into their vast hole of perpetual misery.

Do something good with the lives you have been given, my friends. Make your journey as you would your dreams--not a nightmare but a living, colorful experience of all sorts of wonderful things that only you can make possible.

I hope my words will speak volumes about the process, the stages, the pitfalls, and the evolution of one's soul as it emerges from the shadows. The culmination for putting together these dissonant parts has produced the person that I am today.

ACKNOWLEDGEMENTS

First, and perhaps foremost, I must thank Dick Price and Sharon Kyle, founders and publishers of the outstanding *LA Progressive* and *Hollywood Progressive* (among other platforms), who offered their sites as platforms for the majority of these articles which, otherwise, might never have seen the light of day. These pieces have, in large part, been written by offenders who, as juveniles, committed their crimes, yet their works offer the reader great insight into their world—past, present, and hopefully, future.

I am also appreciative of the part Ken Draper played in publishing some of my other articles on issues pertinent to this subject. Those posts were printed in his *City Watch LA*. George Thomas of the *Van Nuys News Press* must be thanked as well for all his support and willingness to publish a number of my articles.

Next, recognition is due in large part to the two gentlemen, Mark E. Vigil and Anthony Andrew Ferguson, who conceived the idea for this project and tirelessly worked together and with others to see it through. In the early stages, they came to me, seeking my assistance (which I enthusiastically gave) in putting the material together for publication, and here we are.

As you have read this book, undoubtedly you have come across some of their articles and poetry (that have been so earnestly and passionately written) and have, thus, seen for yourselves how their own growth and development have been and can be an inspiration to others who might find themselves in their place.

It is also incumbent upon us to thank all those who contributed their well-researched articles on the subject. I must say I am particularly taken by the autobiographical column by Sheryl C. on the oft-neglected subject of domestic abuse.

It is through my corresponding with inmate, Ronald Patterson, that I was given the opportunity to contact his cousin, Meredith Coleman McGee, who was kind enough to offer us this opportunity to publish the contents of this book under her guidance and has played such a pivotal role in advising and editing the manuscript.

Quite coincidentally and serendipitously, it turns out that Ronald is a first cousin of James Meredith who played a pivotal role in the Civil Rights Movement. Mr. Meredith was courageously able to stand firm and become the first Black student to attend and thus integrate the University of Mississippi—Ole Miss—back in the day when such action was so daunting and even dangerous. Ronald is also cousin to the publisher of this book, Meredith McGee, who is the niece of Mr. Meredith. What a small world!

I am so touched and even somewhat incredulous that Congressmember Barbara Lee was willing to write the Introduction for this book despite her heavy schedule. She has played an ongoing role in introducing and supporting a variety of progressive positions, including the need for prison and justice reform—a situation so vital to the welfare and well-being of our respective communities.

I must thank my husband, as well, because he encouraged me to do this project when there were so many obstacles that would be encountered before bringing it to fruition. He was unselfish in giving me the time and space to accomplish this. Not many partners are willing to do this!

And finally, I would be remiss if I did not mention the following: For the last several years, an annual ceremony is held at Mule Creek State Prison which honors several of the at-risk young men from Lodi and Stockton in California who have been involved in its Juvenile Diversion Program. The occasion recognizes individual achievements in turning their lives around. At the same time, the program also acknowledges the many inmates (who are an integral part of the JDP) whose devotion and dedication helped to make the many accomplishments of their charges possible, and in so doing, their involvement has been instrumental in changing their own lives—making them ready for well-deserved second chances.

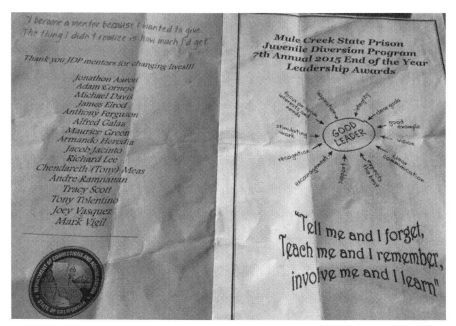

"Too bad there wasn't something like this for us. . . ."

Surrender Your Life to the Madness
by Mark E. Vigil

1.

INDEX

ABOUT THE AUTHOR

Rosemary Jenkins is the author of *The Southern Phoenix*; *Leticia in Her Wedding Dress and Other Poems*; *A Quick-and-Easy Reference to Correct Grammar and Composition*; and *Vignettes for Understanding Literary and Related Concepts* as well as articles for *citywatchla.com* and *laprogressive.com*. Mrs. Jenkins is a wife, mother, grandmother, a journalist, and social justice advocate. She was a long-time educator in the Los Angeles Unified School District, teaching middle and high school literature, grammar, composition, the humanities, and American and European history.

NOTES

Made in the USA
Lexington, KY
29 September 2018